Hillary is the Best Choice

Hillary is the Best Choice

✦

Ten Top Historical Voting Patterns that Show Americans Are Ready to Pick a Woman President

Benjamin Franklin L. Camins, Ph.D. & Catherine Lien, Washington High, Fremont, CA

iUniverse, Inc.
New York Lincoln Shanghai

Hillary is the Best Choice
Ten Top Historical Voting Patterns that Show Americans Are Ready to Pick a Woman President

iUniverse books may be ordered through booksellers or by contacting:

iUniverse
2021 Pine Lake Road, Suite 100
Lincoln, NE 68512
www.iuniverse.com
1-800-Authors (1-800-288-4677)

Because of the dynamic nature of the Internet, any Web addresses or links contained in this book may have changed since publication and may no longer be valid.

The views expressed in this work are solely those of the author and do not necessarily reflect the views of the publisher, and the publisher hereby disclaims any responsibility for them.

ISBN: 978-0-595-47453-0 (pbk)
ISBN: 978-0-595-91778-5 (cloth)
ISBN: 978-0-595-91727-3 (ebk)

Printed in the United States of America

Contents

Foreword

"It's one thing to have good intentions, another thing altogether to change the reality of people's lives. **Hillary has been changing people's lives for as long as I've known her** (emphasis in the original).

She did it in Arkansas when she made major improvements to our schools. She did it in the aftermath of September 11, when she helped first responders get the medical care they needed. She's done it in the U.S. Senate, where she has worked to make sure we fulfill our promises to our troops, veterans, and their families.

She has never let setbacks stop her. When our health care reforms didn't pass in the 90's, she rolled up her sleeves and got right back to work on the Children's Health Insurance Program, which insures six million kids in America today.

That's Hillary, the best combination of heart and mind, of leadership ability and feel for the problems of other people I've ever known. **She's also our best candidate to beat the Republicans for one reason: because she would make the best president** (emphasis in the original). She's got great plans for universal health care, good jobs, access to college, ending the war in Iraq, and restoring

America's position in the world; and she's been tested in the kind of campaign they always run.

You know, even if I weren't married to Hillary, I would still be enthusiastically supporting her. Her experience, her compassion, and her great ideas for the future make her the right candidate.

America is ready for change. After seven years of failed policies, it's time for a new beginning, led by someone who has spent her life making a difference for others.

If you want to know the kind of changes she'll make for you, you only have to look at what she's already accomplished for others for 35 years (emphasis in the original)."

The Hon. WILLIAM "BILL" JEFFERSON CLINTON
43rd President of the United States of America
New York, New York
Jan. 1, 2008

Dedication

This book, *HILLARY IS THE BEST CHOICE* is proudly dedicated to the Hon. U.S. Sen. Dianne Feinstein (*D, CA*), who herself would have been one of the best presidents of America, the greatest country in the world, had an opportunity presented itself for her to run for that highest office.

Because I was born and destined to help the election of the first woman president of America, as Benjamin Franklin (after whom my Irish-Hispanic-Filipino parents named me) of Philadelphia helped George Washington to become our first president, within 24 hours after I became a U.S. citizen on June 1, 1995 in San Francisco, CA, I wrote Ms. Dianne Feinstein to ask "if she was interested to be the first woman president of our country. If so, I suggested that she should run for California governor first because that would tremendously increase her chances!"

Ms. Feinstein wrote me back before the month was over to say that she had no plan to run for California governor, but she said that "since you have such creative ideas about the future of our beloved country, do you mind if I appoint you as a Democratic political consultant effective immediately? I am also enclosing with this letter my direct telephone line to my Senate Office in Washington, D.C., so you can easily communicate to me other concerns you might have to benefit our people."

It is now the year 2008, just barely 12 years following my suggestion, and I have invited one of my own protégées, Catherine Lien, a Vietnamese American, and a straight-A student at Washington High School, Fremont, CA 94536 to co-author this book in support of the presidential candidacy of the first viable female candidate for U.S. president in the person of the Hon. Sen. Hillary R. Clinton (*D, NY*) an esteemed senatorial colleague of Ms. Feinstein and whom the latter has also wholeheartedly endorsed.

BENJAMIN FRANKLIN CAMINS, Ph.D.
Democratic Party Political Consultant
P.O. Box 1604
Newark, CA 94560
New Year's Day, 2008

Preface

Dear Readers:

I'm Catherine Lien, a 15-year-old sophomore student at the Washington High School, Fremont, CA 94536. My mentor and co-author is an *Emeritus* Professor with a Ph.D. in History from Toronto, Canada; 2 Masters Degrees in Religion from Yale, New Haven, CT; a degree in Law (*magna cum laude*); a B.A. in Political Science (*summa cum laude*), and a Math teaching credential from Mills (Women's) College, Oakland, CA.

His newly-spawned home-business is: *"3StageActs1Price Entertainment: Hillary Herstories, Rodham Rhapsodies, and Clinton Comedies."* For one fee, your group can invite him to speak, to sing from his own lyrics (a future book: *"101 HILLARY CLINTON-Inspired Lyrics on Lifelong Love, Forever Friendships, and Deathless Dreams"*), and to tell the funniest jokes about current events. Please book him at his e-mail address: <u>Bfranklincamins@aol.com</u> or you may phone him at (510) 565-5777.

CATHERINE LIEN
Washington High School,
Fremont, CA
Jan. 1, 2008

(This is Benjamin Franklin Camins, my co-author).

Acknowledgements

(1) To the Hon. William "Bill" Jefferson Clinton, 43rd U.S. President for the FOREWORD

(2) To the Hon. Senior Sen. Dianne Feinstein (*D,* CA) for the DEDICATION

(3) To the Wikipedia: the source of the images of Hillary, the Hon. Democratic Senator from NY, the Hon. 43rd U.S. President Bill Clinton, and the Hon. Senior Sen. Dianne Feinstein (D, CA),

(4) To Dr. Carolyn Scott, principal of the Newark Adult School, NUSD, Newark, CA, for giving me a year's leave of absence to co-author this book, and

(5) Last but not least, to *iUniverse* for publishing this book (with special mention to Ms. Brenda Kluck who served as our Publishing Services Associate)

Introduction

The traditional view of politics is pessimistic in that it is considered as a "dirty" activity. That view includes the definition of an election as a matter of "choosing the lesser of two evils."

Also, when there are two equally strong presidential aspirants of a major political party and neither one is willing to concede the nomination to the other they compromise on a third nominee who is then called a "dark horse."

Hillary is the Best Choice presents a more balanced view of politics. To start with, politics is neither good nor bad. It is neutral. It can either go good or bad depending on the politicians who are involved. For the first time in American presidential politics, for example, we have a woman candidate. In previous elections, when only men were presidential contenders, the tendency to play "dirty" was always a great temptation. With Hillary Clinton, Democratic Senator from New York and our country's former First Lady, as one of the current leading presidential aspirants, it is our hope that the old pattern of negativity will be replaced by a new pattern of political civility. Politics can be a clean activity. And elections, especially presidential ones, ought to be a matter of choosing the better of two goods (when an independent or third party candidate is running, it will be a matter of choosing the best of three).

Books that have recently been written about the presidential election of 2008 are mainly focused on the comparative qualifications of Hillary Clinton and her potential opponents. Those who like Hillary emphasize her strong points, but those who do not, emphasize her weak points. Of about a dozen books about her possible presidency in the last 6 years, one of the best is U.S.C. Law Professor Susan Estrich's *the Case for Hillary Clinton* that refutes Peggy Noonan's earlier *the Case against Hillary Clinton.* Just as excellent is Carl Bernstein's *A Woman in Charge: the Life of Hillary Rodham Clinton* that describes in great detail the marital problems that Hillary had to overcome in order to be a winning example to her own family, to our nation of millions of families, and even to the families of the other "villages" in the world. Competing with Bernstein's book but critical of Hillary is Jeff Gerth and Don van Natta, Jr.'s *Her Way: The Hopes and Ambitions of Hillary Rodham Clinton.*[1]

An improvement on the comparative approach is the polling of sample voters the result of which is used as evidence for or against a particular candidate. The weight of the evidence gathered by polling is as good (or conversely, as bad) as the one conducting the poll.[2] The Gallup Poll can be considered the best polling organization, for it has a long history of being the most accurate in its results. In January, 2007, Gallup Poll released the result of its nation-wide random survey of Americans as to who is their most admired man or woman in our country this year. The most admired man is George W. Bush, and in close second is Bill Clinton. And the most admired woman of the year? Who else but Hillary Clinton! This is the 11th time that she was chosen most admired American woman by the same opinion poll of Americans since 1993.

To commemorate its 25th year of publication on September 15, 2007, the prestigious USA Today *selected the 25 most influential people in the world. It included 3 U.S. presidents: Ronald Reagan, George W. Bush, and Bill Clinton. Right behind Bill Clinton is his wife U.S. Senator Hillary Rodham Clinton (D, NY) the only former American First Lady.[3]*

Hillary is the Best Choice employs a totally fresh approach to this presidential contest. It neither presents the debatable, comparative qualifications of the prospective candidates, nor polls the opinion of potential voters as to their choice for the presidential election of 2008. Rather, it examines the history of the voting behavior of our American predecessors in the past 220 years, after which it makes a scientific projection as to who among the current presidential aspirants fits most, if not all, of the patterns of such behavior and therefore will quite likely receive the mandate of our people as our next, and hopefully first woman, president.

The study of Electoral Behavior is a well-established branch of Political Science which also incorporates the insights of History and Psychology. Several books on American Electoral Behavior had been published for the past 35 years, including J.H. Silbey et al, *The History of American Electoral Behavior* (1978); E. H. Rosenbloom, *A History of Presidential Elections* (3rd ed. 1970), and J. M. Clubb (ed.) *Electoral Change and Stability in American Political History* (1971). The most relevant to the subject-matter of this book in general, without reference to the presidential candidacy of a woman like Hillary Clinton, is the work of 3 scholars, Warren L. Mason, Kay Phillips, & Mostafa Rejai, titled *Demythologizing an Elite: American Presidents in Empirical, Comparative, and Historical Perspective* published in 1993 concerning the 40 presidents who had served up to that time.[4] *Hillary Is the Best Choice* includes all presidents from George Washington to the incumbent George W. Bush.

Human Behavioral Science is not as objective as Natural Science. The subjective element in the study of Electoral Behavior has mostly to do with a writer's choice of the patterns of voting on the part of the American electorate. Nevertheless, though it is not possible to predict anything with 100% accuracy, we resort to this method because as a whole humans are creatures of habit whose behavior is fairly consistent. For example, the American electorate has the tendency to vote according to certain patterns which are fully observable. Therefore, scholars can predict with a certain degree of certainty that as the American electors had constantly voted in the same way in the past, they will do so again in the future. They will only depart from their established habits of voting, if they are convinced that there is a strong reason or reasons to do so.

The 10 Top Historical Voting Patterns for Continuity

The main thesis of *Hillary Is the Best Choice* is as follows: the voting habits of Americans who had elected 42 (43, if Grover Cleveland who had been elected 2 nonconsecutive times is counted twice) presidents reveal 10 top patterns that form the chapters of this book:

- They had always selected a white male president, but this can change on 11/04/08

- They had elevated mostly vice-presidents, governors, and senators to the presidency

- They had favored presidents who were named after western heroes

- They had opted for presidents whose last names have consonant-sound endings

- They had given their blessings to presidents with a Protestant heritage

- They had not picked a president younger than 43 or older than 68 years

- They had only chosen presidential candidates of 2 major parties, never independents

- They had wanted their presidents to marry and stay married

- They had preferred presidents who were law graduates of Ivy-League colleges

- They had voted for presidents indirectly through the Electoral College.

The foregoing patterns are expected to persist when the American electorate will vote for president on November 4, 2008. There are many indicators that this same electorate is now ready, willing, and able to depart from following pattern number 1 of always choosing 42 white male presidents for the last 220 years but will be picking a female president for the first time in 2008. The reasons why there will be a dramatic change are presented in chapter 1. When the change does occur, it will be an incremental rather than an abrupt one.

An Incremental Pattern of Change

What is an incremental change? An incremental change is a one-step change, that is, the American electorate that has been accustomed to voting for a white male candidate all the time, in the event of change is *always* followed by voting for a *white female* candidate, but voting for a white female candidate is not necessarily followed by voting for another female candidate or a candidate representing a racial minority.

For quick references, *Table 0.1* lists all presidents from George Washington to George W. Bush in chronological order, and *Table 0.2*, all presidents in alphabetical order.

Table 0.1 The Presidents of the United States in Order of Appearance:

1. Washington, George (1789-97)

2. Adams, John (1797-1801)

3. Jefferson, Thomas (1801-09)

4. Madison, James (1809-17)

5. Monroe, James (1817-25)

6. Adams, John Q. (1825-29)

7. Jackson, Andrew (1829-37)

8. Van Buren, Martin (1837-41)

9. Harrison, William H. (1841)

10. Tyler, John (1841-45)

11. Polk, James (1845-49)

12. Taylor, Zachary (1849-50)

13. Fillmore, Millard (1850-53)

14. Pierce, Franklin (1853-57)

15. Buchanan, James (1857-61)

16. Lincoln, Abraham (1861-65)

17. Johnson, Andrew (1865-69)

18. Grant, Ulysses (1869-77)

19. Hayes, Rutherford B. (1877-81)

20. Garfield, James (1881)

21. Arthur, Chester (1881-85)

22. Cleveland, Grover (1885-89)

23. Harrison, Benjamin (1889-93)

24. Cleveland, Grover (1893-97) (*See* #22)

25. McKinley, William (1897-1901)

26. Roosevelt, Theodore (1901-09)

27. Taft, William H. (1909-13)

28. Wilson, Woodrow (1913-21)

29. Harding, Warren (1921-23)

30. Coolidge, Calvin (1923-29)

31. Hoover, Herbert (1929-33)

32. Roosevelt, Franklin D. (1933-45)

33. Truman, Harry S. (1945-53)

34. Eisenhower, Dwight D. (1953-1961)

35. Kennedy, John F. (1961-63)

36. Johnson, Lyndon (1963-69)

37. Nixon, Richard (1969-74)

38. Ford, Gerald (1974-77)

39. Carter, Jimmy (1977-81)

40. Reagan, Ronald (1981-89)

41. Bush, George H. W. (1989-93)

42. Clinton, William J. (1993-2001)

43. Bush, George W. (2001-09)

Table 0.2 The Presidents of the United States in Alphabetical Order.

Adams, John (1797-1801)

Adams, John Quincy (1825-29)

Arthur, Chester (1881-85)

Buchanan, James (1857-61)

Bush, George H. W. (1989-93)

Bush, George W. (2001-09)

Carter, Jimmy (1977-81)

Cleveland, Grover (1885-89; 1893-97)

Clinton, William J. (1993-2001)

Coolidge, Calvin (1923-29)

Eisenhower, Dwight D. (1953-61)

Fillmore, Millard (1850-53)

Ford, Gerald (1974-77)

Garfield, James (1881)

Grant, Ulysses S. (1869-77)

Harding, Warren (1921-23)

Harrison, Benjamin (1889-93)

Harrison, William Henry (1841)

Hayes, Rutherford B. (1877-81)

Hoover, Herbert (1929-33)

Jackson, Andrew (1829-37)

Jefferson, Thomas (1801-09)

Johnson, Andrew (1865-69)

Johnson, Lyndon (1963-69)

Kennedy, John F. (1961-63)

Lincoln, Abraham (1861-65)

Madison, James (1809-17)

McKinley, William (1897-1901)

Monroe, James (1817-25)

Nixon, Richard (1969-74)

Pierce, Franklin (1853-57)

Polk, James (1845-49)

Reagan, Ronald (1981-89)

Roosevelt, Franklin D. (1933-45)

Roosevelt, Theodore (1901-09)

Taft, William H. (1909-13)

Taylor, Zachary (1849-50)

Truman, Harry s. (1945-53)

Tyler, John (1841-45)

Van Buren, Martin (1837-41)

Washington, George (1789-97)

Wilson, Woodrow (1913-21)

1

Electing America's Woman President Is Long Overdue

✦

Speaker Nancy Pelosi Paves the Way for Future President Hillary Clinton

On February 20, 2006, Presidents' Day, Ray Westbrook in the *Lubbock Advance Journal*[5] wrote an article titled "Scheppler's Children Are Very Presidential." All 7 children—4 girls and 3 boys—of Richard and Regina Scheppler were named after presidents: Regan, Madison, Harrison, Tyler, Grant, McKinley, and Kennedy. The story included McKinley's complaint to her Mom that while her classmates had an easier time writing their first names in kindergarten, she had to struggle to write hers. "Her sacrifice might be worth it," Westbrook concluded, "for, it might be a good training for another McKinley to become our country's president someday."

Upon reading the foregoing article, this writer wrote to Richard and Regina Scheppler that before their daughter McKinley's presidential dream can come true, the people of our country must first show that they can elect a woman president.

Hillary expressed a similar opinion when visiting the St. Rose Dominican Hospital in Henderson, Nevada. Sara Dort, 11, a daughter of the hospital administrator made a surprising remark on meeting the visitor, "I wanted to be the first girl president but you beat me to it." "Well, not yet," Hillary replied with a smile. "But that's going to make it easier for you."[6]

The *New York Daily News* tells the story of a local girl, Alexandra Desaulniers, who can't be commander-in-chief of the United States before 2024, when she turns 35. But, she's sure glad a woman may be warming up her seat in the Oval Office come 2008. "The 18-year-old high school senior declared her candidacy to

8

her mom and dad when she was just 9, after they took her on a White House tour. She was disappointed that all of the portraits were of men."

The election of a woman president can happen as early as November 4, 2008. When historians will write about the year 2008 in the future, will they say that it was the year our daughters' highest American dream was first realized with the election of our first woman president? Or, will they remember it the same way we remember 1984, the first time a woman vice-presidential candidate, Geraldine Ferraro, lost the election?

"Is it the right time to elect America's first woman president?"

And the answer in Hillary's own words spoken before a big crowd in Des Moines, Iowa, during her first visit following her decision to run for president is:

"It's about time, *if not past time*, we had a woman president" (emphasis supplied).[7]

Women had only won the right to vote in our country in 1920, more than 130 years since the election of our first president, George Washington in 1788, and after more than 70 years from the official launching of the women suffrage movement in Seneca, New York, led by Susan B. Anthony, Elizabeth Cady Stanton, and Lucretia Mott.[8] And more than 85 years had gone by since they had acquired that right, we have yet to elect the first woman president. Some of the arguments used against giving women the right to vote have been advanced against electing a woman president. Chief among these was the fact that only men had the prerogative to bear arms to defend our country. Initially, President Woodrow Wilson opposed women suffrage, but he had a change of heart when they showed him in the First World War 1914-1918 that they could *wo*man the munitions factories and support the war effort in other ways in the home front.

For the first time in our history, following the 9/11/01 terrorist invasion of America, we have decided to avenge the death of 2,986 Americans that day by sending our young women side by side with our young men to Iraq, Afghanistan, and other foreign battlefields to fight in defense of their beloved country. If women could help defend their country, they should have the right to vote for the leaders of their country. That was the argument of the women's suffrage movement prior to 1920. Today, the argument is: if women can die for their country, they should have the right to lead it. Almost 2 million women have now served in the armed forces of the United States, and thousands more in the armed forces of other countries.[9]

If they can become city councilors, mayors, judges, CEOs of Fortune 500 corporations, presidents of Ivy-League universities—including Harvard—representatives, governors, senators, Supreme Court Justices, and now Speaker of the U.S.

House of Representatives, why not vice-president and president? In 1984, the vice-presidential running mate of the Democratic presidential aspirant Walter Mondale was Geraldine Ferraro. If that ticket had won the election we should have had a woman who would "be only a heartbeat away from the presidency!" The lingering opposition to a woman serving as the Commander-in-Chief of the U.S. armed forces would have been moot.

Since 1970 when the first year women had been promoted to the rank of general and admiral, we have had fourteen women high ranking military officers: nine one-star generals and admirals, one 2-star general, and four 3-star generals and admirals in command of the branches of the armed forces of the United States, not counting more than 10 women astronauts (*see* Table 1.0 & 1.1).[10]

Table 1.0 American Women Astronauts in Alphabetical Order

Roberta Bondar	Christa McAuliffe
Eileen Collins	Ellen Ochoa
Bonnie Dunbar	Judith Resnik
Susan J. Helms	Sally Ride
Mae Jemison	Kathryn Sullivan
Shannon Lucid	

Table 1.1 American Women Officers of the Armed Forces

One-Star Women Officers:

Army—Brig. General Elizabeth P. Hoisington—1970

Navy—Rear Admiral Fran McKee—1976

Marines—Brig. General Margaret A. Brewer—1978

Air Force—Brig. General Jeanne M. Holm—1971

Army Nurse Corps—Brig. General Anna May Hays—1970

Navy Nurse Corps—Rear Admiral Alene B. Duerk—1972 (the first woman admiral)

Air Force Nurse Corps—Brig. General E. Ann Hoefly—1972

Coast Guard—Rear Admiral Vivien S. Crea—2000

Army Nurse Corps—Brig. General Clara Adams-Ender—1991

Navy—Admiral Grace Hopper—1985 (promoted by a bill of Rep. Philip Crane {D} in 1984)

Two-Star Woman Officer:

Air Force—Major General Jeanne M. Holm—1973 (*see* also 1-star women officers above)

Three-Star Women Officers:

Marine Corps—Lt. General Carol A. Mutter—1996

Army—Lt. General Claudia Kennedy—1997

Air Force—Lt. General Leslie F. Kenne—1999

Navy—Vice Admiral Patricia Tracey

Now, if these women generals and admirals can command branches of the armed forces, why not the entire armed forces of the United States of America?

"But, a woman president will most likely not have a military background?" someone might object. Neither did most of the 42 previous men American presidents. We did not expect them all to be a George Washington, an Andrew Jackson, a William Henry Harrison, a Zachary Taylor, a Ulysses Grant, a Teddy Roosevelt, or a Dwight Eisenhower, did we?[11] Every previous American president had the heads of all the branches of the armed forces to advise him. The same type of advice will be given to the future first woman president and other women presidents after her.

The leaders of our present government have also often proclaimed that one of the justifications for our going to war in Iraq and Afghanistan is to liberate the allegedly less-than-free women in those countries. As late as the beginning of

2006, remnants of the Taliban fundamentalists in Afghanistan were reported as beheading school teachers for trying to educate girls![12] It has sounded so convincing that such messages of liberation were often delivered by a woman Secretary of State. How much more poignant such messages would have been if they had been delivered by a woman President of the United States!

Since 1945, there have been 76 countries that were led by 96 women chief-executives. That amounts to 40% of the total number of countries that are represented in the United Nations which is 192. If the Vatican, a non-UN member, were added to the total, that would be 193 countries in all.[13] They have led countries around the world, i.e. in 5 of the 6 populated continents, excepting only Australia. (The 7th continent, Antarctica, is not included, for it has no population).

The post-1945 women chief-executives are of 4 types:

1. Reigning queens,

2. Presidents,

3. Prime ministers, and

4. Governors-general (*see* Table 1.2; 1.3; 1.4; 1.5, & 1.6).[14]

Table 1.2 Top Women Chief—Executives of Countries in the World since 1945

Reigning queens	11	individuals	8	countries
Presidents	35	"	26	"
Prime Ministers	39	"	35	"
Governor Generals	11	"	7	"
Total	96	"	76	"

Table 1.3 Eleven Reigning Queens of Countries in the World, 1945 to the Present

1. Wilhelmina (1880-1962) Netherlands 23 Nov 1890 to 4 Sep 1948

2. Salote Tupou III (1900-1965) Tonga 5 Apr 1918 to her death on 15 Dec 1965

3. Charlotte (1896-1985) Luxembourg (Grand Duchess) 15 Jan 1919 to 12 Nov 1964

4. Juliana (1909-2004) Netherlands 4 Sep 1948 to 30 Apr 1980

5. Elizabeth II (1926-) United Kingdom from 6 Feb 1952

6. Sisovath Monivong Kossomak Nearireath (1904-1975) Cambodia from 3 Mar 1955

7. 'MaMohato Tabitha 'Masentle Lerotholi (1938-2003) Lesotho from 5 Jun 1970

8. Margrethe II (1940-) Denmark from 14 Jan 1972

9. Beatrix (1938—) Netherlands from 30 Apr 1980

10. Dzeliwe Shongwe: Swaziland (Queen Regent) 21 Aug 1982 to 9 Aug 1983

11. Ntombi Thwala: Swaziland (Queen Regent) 18 Aug 1983 to 25 Apr 1986.

Table 1.4 Thirty-Five Women Presidents of Countries in the World, 1945 to the Present

1. Suhbaataryn Yanjmaa (1893-1962) Mongolia (Presidium Chair) 23 Sep 1953 to 7 Jul 1954

2. Song Qingling (Sung Ch'ing-ling) (1893-1981) 1980 China ("Honorary President")

3. Isabel Peron (1931-) Argentina 1 Jul 1974 to 24 Mar 1976

4. Lydia Gueiler Tejada (1926-) Bolivia (Caretaker President) 17 Nov 1979 to 18 Jul 1980

5. Vigdis Finnbogadottir (1930-) Iceland 1 Aug 1980 to 1 Aug 1996

6. Maria Lea Pedini-Angelini (1953?-) San Marino (Co-Captain Regent) 1981

7. Agatha Barbara (1923-2002) Malta 15 Feb 1982 to 15 Feb 1987

8. Gloriana Ranocchini (1957-) San Marino (Co-Captain Regent) 1984 & 1989 to 1990

9. Carmen Pereira (1937-) Guinea Bissau (Acting President) 14 May 1984 to 16 May 1984

10. Corazon (Cory) Aquino (1933-) Philippines 25 Feb 1986 to 30 Jun 1992

11. Ertha Pascal-Trouillot (1943-) Haiti (Interim President) 13 Mar 1990 to 7 Feb 1991

12. Sabine Bergmann-Pohl (1946-) German Democratic Republic (Volkskammer Chair) 1990

13. Violeta Barrios de Chamorro (1929-) Nicaragua 25 Apr 1990 to 10 Jan 1997

14. Mary Robinson (1944-) Ireland 3 Dec. 1990 to 12 Sep 1997

15. Edda Ceccoli: San Marino (Co-Captain Regent) 1 Oct 1991 to 1 Apr 1992

16. Patricia Busignani: San Marino (Co-Captain Regent) 1993

17. Sylvie Kinigi (1952?—) Burundi (Acting President) 27 Oct 1993 to 5 Feb 1994

18. Chandrika Kumaratunga (1945-) Sri Lanka 14 Nov 1994 to 19 Nov 2005

19. Ruth Perry (1939?-) Liberia (Council of State Chair) 3 Sep 1996 to 2 Aug 1997

20, Rosalia Arteaga Serrano (1956-) Ecuador (Caretaker President) 9-11 Feb 1997

21. Mary McAleese (1951-) Ireland from 11 Nov 1997

22. Janet Jagan (1920-) Guyana 19 Dec 1997 to 11 Aug 1999

23. Ruth Dreifuss (1940-) Switzerland 1 Jan 1999 to 1 Jan 2000

24. Rosa Zafferani (1960-) San Marino (Co-captain Regent) 1 Apr to 1 Oct 1999

25. Veira Vike-Freiberga (1937-) Latvia from 17 Jun 1999

26. Mireya Elisa Moscoso de Arias (1946-) Panama 1 Sep 1999 to 1 Sep 2004

27. Tarja Kaarina Halonen (1943-) Finland 1 Mar 2000 to 2006

28. Maria Domenia Michelotti (1952-) San Marino (Co-captain Regent) 1 Apr to Oct 2000

29. Gloria M. Arroyo (1947-) Philippines from 20 Jan 2001

30. Megawati Sukarnoptri (1947-) Indonesia 23 Jul 2001 to 20 Oct 2004

31. Valeria Ciavatta (1959-) San Marino (Co-captain Regent) 1 Oct 2003 to 1 Apr 2004

32. Nino Burdzhanadze (1964-) Georgia (Acting President) 23 Nov 2003 to 25 Jan 2004

33. Fausta Simona Morganti (1944-) San Marino (Co-captain Regent) 1 Apr to 1 Oct 2005

34. Ellen Johnson-Sirleaf (1939-) Liberia from 16 Jan 2006

35. Michelle Bachelet Jeria (1951-) Chile from 11 Mar 2006

Table 1.5 Thirty-Nine Women Prime Ministers of Countries in the World, 1945 to the Present

1. Sirimavo Bandaranaike (1916-2000) Sri Lanka 21 Jul to 27 Mar 1965, 29 May 1970 to 23 Jul 1977, & 14 Nov 1994 to 10 Aug 2000

2. Indira Gandhi (1917-1984) India 19 Jan 1966 to 24 Mar 1977 & 14 Jan 1980 to her assassination on 31 Oct 1984

3. Golda Meir (1898-1978) Israel 17 Mar to 3 Jun 1974

4. Elisabeth Domitien (1926-2005) Central African Republic 3 Jan 1975 to 7 Apr 1976

5. Margaret Thatcher (1925-) United Kingdom 4 May 1979 to 28 Nov 1990

6. Maria de Lourdes Pintasilgo (1930-2004) Portugal 1 Aug 1979 to 3 Jan 1980

7. Mary Eugenia Charles (1919-2005) Dominica 21 Jul 1980 to 14 Jun 1995

8. Gro Harlem Bruntland (1939-) Norway 4 Feb to 14 Oct 1981, 9 May 1966 to 16 Oct 1989, & 3 Nov 1990 to 25 Oct 1996

9. Milka Planinc (1924-) Yugoslavia (Federal Prime Minister) 16 May 1982 to 15 May 1986

10. Benazir Bhutto (1953-) Pakistan 2 Dec 1988 to 6 Aug 1990 & 19 Oct 1993 to 5 Nov 1996

11. Kazimiera Danute Prunskiene (1943-) Lithuania 17 Mar 1990 to 10 Jan 1991

12. Khaleda Zia (1945-) Bangladesh 20 Mar 1991 to 30 Mar 1996 & 10 Oct 2001 to the Present

13. Edith Cresson (1934-) France 15 May 1991 to 2 Apr 1992

14. Hanna Suchocka (1946-) Poland 8 Jul to 26 Oct 1993

15. Kim Campbell (1947-) Canada 25 Jun to 5 Nov 1993

16. Tansu Ciller (1946-) Turkey 25 Jun 1993 to 7 Mar 1996

17. Sylvie Kinigi (1952?-) Burundi 10 Jul 1993 to 11 Feb 1994

18. Agathe Uwilingiyimana (1953-1994) Rwanda 18 Jul 1993 to her death 7 Apr 1994

19. Chandrika Kumaratunga (1945-) Sri Lanka 19 Aug to Nov 1994

20. Reneta Indzhova (1953-) Bulgaria (Interim Prime Minister) 16 Oct 1994 to 25 Jan 1995

21. Claudette Werleigh (1944-) Haiti 7 Nov 1995 to 27 Feb 1996

22. Sheikh Hasina Wajed (1947-) Bangladesh 23 Jun 1996 to 15 Jul 2001

23. Janet Jagan (1920-) Guyana 17 Mar 1997 to 19 Dec 1997

24. Jenny Shipley (1952-) New Zealand 8 Dec 1997 to 10 Dec 1999

25. Irena Degutiene (1949-) Lithuania (Acting Prime Minister) from 4 to 18 May 1999 & 27 Oct to 3 Nov 1999

26. Nyam-Osoriyn Tuyaa (1958-) Mongolia (Acting Prime Minister) 22 to 30 Jul 1999

27. Helen Elizabeth Clark (1950-) New Zealand from 10 Dec 1999

28. Mame Madior Boye (1940-) Senegal 3 Mar 2001 to 4 Nov 2002

29. Chang Sang (1939-) South Korea (Acting Prime Minister) 11 Jul to 31 Jul 2002

30. Maria das Neves Ceita Baptista de Sousa: Sao Tome and Principe 7 Oct 2002 to 16 Jul 2003

31. Anneli Tuulikki Jaatteenmaki (1955-) Finland 17 Apr to 18 Jun 2003

32. Beatriz Merino Lucero (1948-) Peru 28 Jun to 15 Dec 2003

33. Luisa Dias Diogo (1958-) Mozambique from 17 Feb 2004

34. Radmila Sekerinska (1972-) Macedonia (Acting Prime Minister) 2004

35. Yuliya Tymoshenko (1960-) Ukraine 24 Jan to 8 Sep 2005

36. Maria de Carmo Silveira: Sao Tome & Principe 8 Jun 2005 to 21 Apr 2006

37. Angela Merkel (1954-) Germany (Federal Chancellor) from 22 Nov 2005

38. Portia Simpson Miller (1945-) Jamaica from 30 Mar 2006

39. Han Myung Sook: South Korea from 19 Apr 2006

Table 1.6 Eleven Women Governors-General of Countries in the World, 1945 to the Present

1. Dame Elmira Minita Gordon (1930-) Belize 21 Sep 1981 to 17 Nov 1993

2. Jeanne Mathilde Sauve (1922-1993) Canada 14 May 1984 to 29 Jan 1990

3. Dame Ruth Nita Barrow (1916-1995) Barbados 6 Jun 1990 to her death 19 Dec 1995

4. Dame Catherine Tizard (1931-) New Zealand 20 Nov 1990 to 21 Mar 1996

5. Dame Calliopa Pearlette Louisy (1946-) Saint Lucia from 17 Sep 1997

6. Adrienne Clarkson (1939-) Canada 7 Oct 1999 to 27 Sep 2005

7. Dame Sian Seerpoohl Elias (1949-) New Zealand (Chief Justice acted as governor-general) 22 Mar to 4 Apr 2001 & 4 to 23 Aug 2006

8. Dame Silvia Cartwright (1943-) New Zealand 4 Apr 2001 to 4 Aug 2006

9. Dame Ivy Leona Dumont (1930—) Bahamas 13 Nov 2001 to 1 Feb 2006

10. Monica Dacon: Saint Vincent and the Grenadines 3 Jun to 2 Sep 2002

11. Michaelle Jean (1968-) Canada from 27 Sep 2005

The United States is among 60% of countries in the world that did not have a top woman executive since 1945. These also include 6 other big countries: Australia, Brazil, China, Japan, Nigeria, and Russia. There is no excuse for any country in the 21st century to cling to an outdated male-only top leadership role. It is infinitely more inexcusable for us in the USA, because our country is the only remaining super power in the world. The U.S.S.R. that rivaled our country as another super power in the Cold War Era had ended in 1989. We want the Iraqis, Afghans, and others, to imitate us for being the freeest and most democratic people on earth. And yet, when it comes to choosing a woman as the top leader of our country, we lag behind almost half of the countries of the world!

The United Kingdom, from which we had won our independence, has had women monarchs since 1553, as for example, the nine—days Queen Jane (also known as Lady Jane Grey), Queen Mary I, Queen Elizabeth I, Queen Mary II, Queen Anne, Queen Victoria, and now,

Queen Elizabeth II. It also had its first woman prime minister in Margaret Thatcher from May 4, 1979 to November 28, 1990, the first woman ruler ever elected to that high position in Europe.

Cherie Blair, Hillary's counterpart in Great Britain as the First Lady of Prime Minister Tony Blair, welcomed the entry of "her friend" in the presidential election of 2008. "I think it's fantastic that a woman is standing for president of the United States," she told ABC television. "In fact, in Britain, of course, we had a woman prime minister. We have a woman head of state in the queen. So it would be great to see the most powerful nation in the world led by a woman."[15]

Canada was led by Prime Minister Kim Campbell from June 25 to November 1993 becoming the first woman elected as the highest ruler in North America.

New Zealand has the best record of all countries of the world: all four top heads of government were occupied by women from April 4, 2001 to August 4, 2006: Governor-general Dame Silvia Cartwright, Chief Justice Sian Seerpoohl Elias, Prime Minister Helen Clark, and Opposition Leader Mary Shipley.[16]

Others who had learned democracy from the U.S., like Liberia, Germany, and the Philippines had also elected top women leaders. Ms. Ellen Johnson Sirleaf, the first woman president of Liberia was a recent visitor to the United States. In her speech to the combined houses of the U.S. Congress—in which both Senator Hillary Clinton from New York and then still Minority Leader Representative Nancy Pelosi from San Francisco, California, were in attendance—she thanked our people for having sent freed American slaves to found her country whose people had risen to unprecedented progress to the point of having chosen her the first woman president of Liberia, as well as the first African woman ever to have been elected to that position.[17]

It was not long ago, just before the middle of the 20th century, that the male dictator of Germany in the person of Adolf Hitler had plunged Europe into the Second World War. America and her Democratic allies, including Britain, France, and Russia, had to beat the Axis powers and impose democratization on Germany along with a Marshall Plan to help her on the road to economic recovery. The result of that enlightened policy is the emergence of a new, powerful democratic German state that recently chose its first woman chief-executive, the incumbent Chancellor Angela Merkel.

The Philippines, after less than 50 years of American political and educational tutelage—1898 to 1946—had contributed not just one but two women presidents, previous *Time Magazine's* Woman of the Year Corazon Aquino (who nominated Angela Merkel in 2006 for the same honor that was previously conferred on her),[18] and the incumbent woman President Gloria M. Arroyo, a daughter of a former Philippine president.

Even Muslim countries that are supposed to learn more about men and women's equality from us had elected women chief-executives! Benazir Bhutto, following in the footsteps of her father, former president and prime minister Zulfikar Ali Bhutto of Pakistan in the 1970's, became the first woman prime minister of a Muslim country, having been elected not only once but twice as president of her country in the 1980's and 1990's. Megawati Sukarnoptri, daughter of the late president Sukarno, was a worthy modern successor of her father by becoming the first woman president of Indonesia—the biggest Muslim country in the world—at the beginning of this millennium. And Khaleda Zia, the Prime Minister of one of the smallest and poorest Islamic countries in the world, Bangladesh, has served her country twice from March 20, 1991 to March 30, 1996 and again from October 10, 2001 until now.

America's Ready for a Woman President, Are You?

The closest in the United States that a woman has come to the Oval Office is in the cancelled TV series starring Geena Davis titled "Commander-in-Chief." In other countries, you have seen that female leaders are not just the stuff of TV drama. Even in the legislature of other countries women abound, making the U.S. Congress rank as only the 68th in the world. The reason for the relative success of women leaders in other countries can be attributed to the stronger-willed efforts of their women.

But, the good news is that there are a lot of indications that American voters are now ready, willing, and able to choose our country's first woman president. The first major indicator was the year of the woman in 1992 when the number of women members elected to both houses of the U.S. Congress had increased more than ever before. One hundred six women ran for office compared to a previous high of 69. There were 24 newly elected women in the U.S. Congress, including both Senators Barbara Boxer and Dianne Feinstein, both Democrats of California.

Another very significant indicator that Americans are ready to elect a woman president is the number of women voters that outnumber their male counterpart, that is, by almost ten million as shown in the presidential election of 2004. Since no woman president ran at that time, the participation of many more women than men in the electoral process did not appear to make much of a difference. It is true, however, that there was a so-called gender gap, in that more women voted

Democratic, and more men voted Republican. Therefore, this trend should favor Hillary because she is running as a Democrat. It should doubly benefit her, since she also happens to be a woman!

One of the best pointers that Americans are ready to elect a woman president is that they said so. A recent *CBS-New York Times* poll found that 92% of Americans would vote for a woman president. This had increased steadily in the last 50 years. Gallup Poll recorded in 1955, that 52% of Americans were in favor of a woman president; in 1975, 73%, and in 1987, 82%. [19]

The best sign ever that American voters are now ready, willing, and able to choose America's first woman president was the election of Rep. Nancy Pelosi (*D, CA*) as the first woman speaker of the House of Representatives in 2006. Democrats won both Houses of Congress. Many women—both Democrats and Republicans—also won. The president and vice-president are elected by the American voters, but the Speaker is elected very much like the Prime Minister of the United Kingdom. The Representatives of the majority party elect their leader and he or she becomes the presiding officer of the whole House *(see* Table 1.7, 1.8, & 1.9).[20]

Table 1.7 November 7, 2006 Results of All 435 Seats in the House Up for Election

Party	Seats				Popular Vote		
	2004	2006	+/-	%	Vote	%	+/-
Democratic	202	233	+31	53.6%	39,673,226	52.0%	+5.4%
Republican	232	202	-30	46.4%	34,748,277	45.6%	-3.6%
Independents	1	0	-1	0	501,632	0.7%	+0.1%
Others	0	0	0	0	1,305,803	1.7%	-1.9%
Total	435	435	0	100.0	76,228,938	100.0%	0

Table 1.8 November 7, 2006 Results of 33 or 1/3 of Seats in the Senate Up for Election

Party	Breakdown			Total Seats			Popular Vote	
	Up	Elected	Not Up	2004	2006	+/-	Vote	%
Democratic	17	22	27	44	49	+5	33,134,651	53.8%
Republican	15	9	40	55	49	-6	26,127,486	42.4%
Independents	1	2	0	1	2	+1	878,486	1.4%
Libertarian	0	0	0	0	0	0	600,991	1.0%
Green Party	0	0	0	0	0	0	402,800	0.7%
Others	0	0	0	0	0	0	408,335	0.7%
Total	33	33	67	100	100	0	61,552,749	100%
Voter Turnout	29.7%							

Table 1.9 Election Results on November 7, 2006 Quick Summary of Women Winners

16 women will serve in the U.S. Senate (11D, 5R)

> 6 (4D, 2R) re-elected incumbents
>
> 2 (2D) newly elected women
>
> 8 (5D, 3R) holdovers

71 women will serve in the U.S. House (50 D, 21R)

> 61 (42D, 19R) re-elected incumbents

10 (8D, 2R) newly elected

76 women will hold statewide elective office (47D, 26R, 3 Non-partisan)

includes 9 (6D, 3R) women governors

1,734 women will serve in state legislatures (1,186 D, 535 R, 10 Non-partisan, 2 Progressives, 1 Independent)

Nancy Pelosi has every reason to be so proud considering she is the first woman speaker of the House of Representatives that has now 435 members. She is only the 52nd person to hold the office and the 60th in order of service (a number of Representatives served as Speaker in more than one Congressional session) after 218 years since the first one was elected in 1789. She is also the first Californian to become House Speaker although she is not the first one elected to that position from the Far West. That distinction goes to Tom Foley of the state of Washington. Other states were represented in that position many times, topped by Massachusetts, with a total of 8 *(see* Table 1.10 & 1.11).[21]

Table 1.10 House Speakers from 1789 to the Present in Chronological Order

# Speaker's Name	Political Party	State/District	Congress	Term
1. Frederick A.C. Muhlenburg	(Pro-Administration)	PA-1	1st	1789–1791
2. Jonathan Trumbull, Jr.	ditto	CT-4	2nd	1791–1793
3. Frederick A.C. Muhlenburg	(Anti-Administration)	PA	3rd	1793–1795
4. Jonathan Dayton	(Federalist)	NJ-AL	4th	1795–1797
			5th	1797–1799
5. Theodore Sedgewick	ditto	MA-1	6th	1799–1801

6. Nathaniel Macon	(Democratic-Republican)	NC-5	7th	1801–1803
		NC-6	8th	1803–1805
			9th	1805–1807
7. Joseph Bradley Varnum d	itto	MA-4	10th	1807–1809
			11th	1809–1811
8. Henry Clay	ditto	KY-5	12th	1811–1813
		KY-2	13th	1813–1814
9. Langdon Cheves	ditto	SC		1814–1815
10. Henry Clay	ditto	KY-2	14th	1815–1817
			15th	1817–1819
			16th	1819–1820
11. John W. Taylor	ditto	NY		1820–1821
12. Philip Pendleton Barbour	ditto	VA	17th	1821–1823
13. Henry Clay	ditto	KY-3	18th	1823–1825
14. John W. Taylor	(National Republican)	NY	19th	1825–1827
15. Andrew Stevenson	(Democratic)	VA	20th	1827–1829
			21st	1829–1831
			22nd	1831–1833
16. John Bell	ditto	TN	23rd	1834–1835
17. James Polk	ditto	TN	24th	1835–1837
			25th	1837–1839

18. Robert Mercer Taliaferro Hunter	ditto	VA-9	26th	1839–1841
19. John White	(Whig)	KY-9	27th	1841–1843
20. John Winston Jones	(Democratic)	VA	28th	1843–1845
21. John Wesley Davis	ditto	IN	29th	1845–1847
22. Robert Charles Winthrop	(Whig)	MA-1	30th	1847–1849
23. Howell Cobb	(Democratic)	GA	31st	1849–1851
24. Linn Boyd	ditto	KY-1	32nd	1851–1853
			33rd	1853–1855
25. Nathaniel Prentice Banks	(American/ Republican)	MA-7	34th	1856–1857
26. James Lawrence Orr	(Democratic)	SC	35th	1857–1859
27. William Pennington	(Republican)	NJ-5	36th	1860–1861
28. Galusha A. Grow	ditto	PA-14	37th	1861–1863
29. Schuyler Colfax	ditto	IN	38th	1863–1865
			39th	1865–1867
			40th	1867–1869
30. Theodore Medad Pomeroy	ditto	NY		1869–1869
31. James G. Blaine	ditto	ME	41st	1869–1871
			42nd	1871–1873
			43rd	1873–1875
32. Michael C. Kerr	(Democratic)	IN	44th	1875–1876

33. Samuel J. Randall	ditto	PA-3		1876–1877
			45th	1877–1879
			46th	1879–1881
34. J. Warren Keifer	(Republican)	OH	47th	1881–1883
35. John Griffin Carlisle	(Democratic)	KY-6	48th	1883–1885
			49th	1885–1887
			50th	1887–1889
36. Thomas Brackett Reed	(Republican)	ME	51st	1889–1891
37. Charles Frederick Crisp	(Democratic)	GA	52nd	1891–1893
			53rd	1893–1895
38. Thomas Brackett Reed	(Republican)	ME	54th	1895–1897
			55th	1897–1899
39. David B. Henderson	ditto	IA	56th	1899–1901
			57th	1901–1903
40. Joseph Gurney Cannon	ditto	IL	58th	1903–1905
			59th	1905–1907
			60th	1907–1909
			61st	1909–1911
41. Champ Clark	(Democratic)	MO	62nd	1911–1913
			63rd	1913–1915

| | | | 64th | 1915–1917 |

Name	Party	District	Congress	Years
			64th	1915–1917
			65th	1917–1919
42. Frederick Gillett	(Republican)	MA-2	66th	1919–1921
			67th	1921–1923
			68th	1923–1925
43. Nicholas Long-worth	ditto	OH-1	69th	1925–1927
			70th	1927–1929
			71st	1929–1931
44. John Nance Gar-ner	(Democratic)	TX-15	72nd	1931–1933
45. Henry T. Rainy	ditto	IL	73rd	1933–1934
46. Joseph Welling-ton Byrns	ditto	TN	74th	1935–1936
47. William Brock-man Bankhead	ditto	AL-6		1936–1937
			75th	1937–1939
			76th	1939–1940
48. Sam Rayburn	ditto	TX-4		1940–1941
			77th	1941–1943
			78th	1943–1945
			79th	1945–1947
49. Joseph William Martin, Jr.	(Republican)	MA-14	80th	1947–1949
50. Sam Rayburn	(Democratic)	TX-4	81st	1949–1951
			82nd	1951–1953

51. Joseph William Martin, Jr.	(Republican)	MA-14	83rd	1953–1955
52. Sam Rayburn	(Democratic)	TX-4	84th	1955–1957
			85th	1957–1959
			86th	1959–1961
			87th	1961–1961
53. John McCormack	ditto	MA-12		1962–1963
		MA-9	88th	1963–1965
			89th	1965–1967
			90th	1967–1969
			91st	1969–1971
54. Carl Albert	ditto	OK-3	92nd	1971–1973
			93rd	1973–1975
			94th	1975–1977
55. Tip O'Neill	ditto	MA-8	95th	1977–1979
			96th	1979–1981
			97th	1981–1983
			98th	1983–1985
			99th	1985–1987
56. Jim Wright	ditto	TX-12	100th	1987–1989
			101st	1989–1989
57. Tom Foley	ditto	WA-5		1989–1991
			102nd	1991–1993
			103rd	1993–1995

58. Newt Gingrich	(Republican)	GA-6	104th	1995–1997
			105th	1997–1999
59. Dennis Hastert	ditto	IL-14	106th	1999–2001
			107th	2001–2003
			108th	2003–2005
			109th	2005–2007
60. Nancy Pelosi	(Democratic)	CA-8	110th	2007–

Table 1.11 Number of House Speakers by States from 1789 to the Present

# Chronology & Name	State	Total
	Massachusetts	8
5. Theodore Sedgewick		
7. Joseph Bradley Varnum		
22. Robert Charles Winthrop		
25. Nathaniel Prentice Banks		
42. Frederick Gillett		
49., & 51. Joseph William Martin, Jr.		
53. John McCormack		
55. Tip O'Neill		
	Kentucky	4
8., 10., & 13. Henry Clay		
19. John White		
24. Linn Boyd		
35. John Griffin Carlisle		

	Virginia	4

6. Philip Pendleton Barbour

15. Andrew Stevenson

18. Robert Mercer Taliaferro Hunter

20. John Winston Jones

	Georgia	3

23. Howell Cobb

37. Charles Frederick Crisp

58. Newt Gingrich

	Illinois	3

40. Joseph Gurney Cannon

45. Henry T. Rainey

59. Dennis Hastert

	Indiana	3

21. John Wesley Davis

29. Schuyler Colfax

32. Michael C. Kerr

	Pennsylvania	3

1., & 3. Frederick A.C. Muhlenburg

28. Galusha A. Grow

33. Samuel J. Randall

	Tennessee	3

16. John Bell

17. James Polk

46. Joseph Wellington Byrns

	Texas	3

44. John Nance Garner

48., 50., & 52. Sam Rayburn

56. Jim Wright

	Maine	2

31. James G. Blaine

36. & 38. Thomas Brackett Reed

	New Jersey	2

4. Jonathan Dayton

27. William Pennington

	New York	2

11. & 14. John W. Taylor

30. Theodore Medad Pomeroy

	Ohio	2

34. Warren Keifer

43. Nicholas Longworth

	South Carolina	2

9. Langdon Cheves

26. James Lawrence Orr

	Alabama	1

47. William Brockman Bankhead

	California	1

60. Nancy Pelosi

	Connecticut	1

2. Jonathan Trumbull, Jr.

	Iowa	1

39. David B. Henderson

	Missouri	1

41. Champ Clark

	North Carolina	1
6. Nathaniel Macon		
	Oklahoma	1
54. Carl Albert		
	Washington	1
56. Tom Foley		

In her inaugural speech, Nancy Pelosi recognized that her becoming the Speaker of the U.S. House of Representatives is a great milestone in American history effectively cracking "the marble ceiling" to which women were previously subjected to.

"We waited over 200 years for this time," she said at the beginning of her reign over the lower House of Congress on January 4, 2007. "But we just didn't just wait—we worked hard for this.... Simply put, there wouldn't be a woman Speaker of the House without this magnificent array of women in the House." [22] The actual elapsed time that Pelosi was elected to her present position is 218 years since the first U.S. House Speaker was elected in 1789.

Is our country ready for a woman president? Ms. Janet L. Holmgren, president of Mills College, a top ranking undergraduate women's college in Oakland, CA, has no doubt that the answer is an "unqualified yes." She could not agree with former George W. Bush right-hand man Karl Rove's assessment that Hillary Clinton is a "tough, tenacious, fatally flawed candidate," but nevertheless destined to win the Democratic presidential nomination in 2008.

*This is her counter-argument: "If Rove's definition of 'tough' means strong and substantial, then Clinton is his candidate. If he defines 'tenacious' as steadfast and unshaken, then Clinton still hits the mark. But then we arrive at that curious 'fatally flawed' factor in which Rove attempts to glibly dismiss **the most viable female presidential candidate of our time** (emphasis supplied). We can assume, like humans, that she is imperfect—but why are her flaws considered 'fatal'? We often hear it said that now, more than ever, we need smart, powerful women to make the world a better place.... Could it be that in the mind of Mr. Rove, any woman lacks the right stuff? Will our country only tolerate a woman speaker of the House safely positioned two steps away from the White House?*

"Scanning the globe, we find numerous countries with current or past female heads of state: Chile, Iceland, Argentina, Nicaragua, Ireland, Israel, Switzerland, Pakistan, Panama, Finland, England, Germany, Indonesia and the Philippines, among others. Could these women possibly be tough? Tenacious? Flawed?

"What do we seek in our 21st century leader? I look for authenticity—leaders who are passionate in intention, fair in serving all of society, and open to well-informed change. For women, still a distinct minority in public leadership roles, authenticity also involves leading in a way that is neither imitation masculine nor defensive feminine....

"My work as the president of Mills College involves ensuring that women lesser known, but possibly just as talented as Clinton, have every opportunity to fulfill their potential and contribute their gifts to the world."[23]

First woman Speaker Pelosi paves the way for first woman President Hillary. Why not first woman speaker Pelosi paves the way for herself, or another Democrat? As for Pelosi, it is not a good idea for her to run for president on November 4, 2008. Pelosi is already 2 breaths away from the presidency, being the second person in succession to it immediately after the vice-president, as per the Law of Presidential Succession of 1947. It provides that if the president and vice-president become incapacitated or disqualified, the Speaker of the House—regardless of political party affiliation—becomes president.

If only the president or vice-president becomes disqualified or incapacitated, the remaining qualified one between the two can appoint someone else to assume the position of the vice-president. That was the case with Gerald Ford who was appointed by President Nixon to take the place of his Vice-President (Spiro Agnew) who resigned due to political corruption. And when President Nixon himself had to resign subsequently because of his role in the Watergate Break-in anomaly, Vice-president Ford became president.

The coincidence of both the President and Vice-president becoming disqualified or incapacitated in office while Pelosi is Speaker might be improbable, but not impossible. Nevertheless, why should she run for president and risk being beaten for that number 1 position, when she is already just a couple of steps away at number 3? She has one advantage over Ford, for she is the second person in line to the presidency. She is already House Speaker; Ford was not. Yet, Ford went on to become the first and only unelected president in U.S. history from the position of a minority party leader like Pelosi was before her election as Speaker.

Why should not Pelosi pave the way for another white male Democratic presidential candidate in 2008? No, for if American voters are ready for a change from voting for white men only to a white woman for the first time, then that would be a move backward. The potential white male presidential Democratic candidate includes former Vice-president Al Gore, Sen. John Kerry, Sen. Christopher Dodd, Sen. Joe Biden, Sen. Joe Liebermann, former Sen. John Edwards, former Alaska Sen. Mike Gravel, Rep. Dennis Kucinich, former Virginia Gov. Mark Warner, General Wesley Clark, or any other white male Democrat.

With the sole exception of Mark Warner and General Wesley Clark, all these White male Democratic potential presidential candidates come from the ranks of the U.S. Congress and most have had experience in the Senate. If you were to look at the background of all the 42 presidents of the United States, no more than half a dozen became president directly from the Senate (*see* more on this in chapter 2 below). But, in most cases their legislative background is only a component of their much wider political and related expertise. Most of them also had executive experience, along with leadership in diplomacy, national security, and the armed forces. Therefore, legislative experience alone, especially for those who had no more than one term or even worse—a mere fraction of a first term—when compared to our presidents, have a woefully inadequate preparation to want to become the head of this greatest country in the world. When the other Warner (John), a Republican, decided not to run for re-election for the U.S. Senate from Virginia, Mark Warner humbly decided to run in his place, to boost the Democratic majority in the upper house.

General Clark also decided not to run for president, and much more, he also endorsed Hillary's bid by saying: "Senator Hillary Clinton has earned the support of millions of Americans in her campaign for president—and today I am pleased to count myself among them. The world has reached a critical point, and we need a leader in the White House with the courage, intelligence and humility to navigate through many troubling challenges to our security at home and abroad. I believe Senator Clinton is that leader, and I whole-heartedly endorse her for President of the United States. Senator Clinton and I share a worldview in which diplomacy is the best first-strike tool in our arsenal; in today's complicated global system, the United States should be making more friends than enemies. Never before have so many Americans had our well-being so closely tied to world events. Our economic and national security has become more complicated than ever before, and we deserve a leader who draws on wisdom, compassion, intelligence and moral courage—in short, we need Hillary Clinton. She is tough but fair, a rock-solid leader equal to the many weighty challenges ahead of us."

Gore and Kerry have the added liability of having previously run for the U.S. presidency, and lost. It came as no surprise that Kerry announced early in 2007 that he will not run for the presidency, but only for re-election to his present seat in the U.S. Senate.

Gore did not make a similar announcement. He should. If Kerry decided not to run because he thinks he cannot win this time around, it would be harder for Gore to do so. For several reasons:

(1). It was really neither Florida voters nor the U.S. Supreme that prevented Gore from winning the presidency in 2000; it was his failure to win his own home-state of Tennessee, that was why he had to depend on another state to bail him out.

(2). Gore must realize that a similar situation took place in 1876 when Democratic presidential candidate Samuel J. Tilden won the nation-wide popular votes, but lost the total electoral votes according to the decision of a 15-person committee composed of members of the U.S. Congress and Supreme Court justices, giving the disputed state electoral votes of Florida by a narrow decision of 8 to 7 to the Republican Rutherford B. Hayes making the latter win the presidency. Following that most disputed presidential election in U.S. history up to that time, Tilden neither ran for the U.S. presidency again nor did he occupy a prominent elected position below it.

(3). For Gore to run in 2008 would only remind people very quickly that he was a previous loser. Never mind that he won the over-all popular votes which do not count. Everyone knows that only the total states' electoral votes do. Most likely, he will end-up a 2-time presidential loser like Dwight D. Eisenhower's nemesis in the 1950's Adlai E. Stevenson, whose AES initial is a favorite answer in cross-word puzzles.

(4). Ever since his defeat for the presidency in 2000, it seems like Gore has put on a lot of weight. He must realize that obese presidential candidates have as little a chance as cigarette smokers to win. Somehow there is a perception that obese people, like cigarette smokers, are not disciplined enough to take charge of their own personal lives. So, how can they be expected to take charge of the lives of millions of Americans? There was only one extra heavy president in American history, William H. Taft who was elected more than a century ago!

(5). The best thing Gore can do (after losing weight) is to duplicate Richard Nixon's feat, that is, return to his home-state of Tennessee, run for governor and lose, and return to the presidential race and win!

Richard Nixon (*R*, CA) was the only president in U.S. history who managed to bounce back and win after losing it. He was the vice-president of Dwight D. Eisenhower for 2 successive terms from 1952. He lost the presidency to John Kennedy in 1960, and he lost the governorship of California following that. He came back as the Republican presidential standard bearer in 1968, to beat Hubert Humphrey, the vice-president of President Lyndon Johnson. The latter did not seek re-election as U.S. president because he thought he could not win with his discredited policy in the Vietnam War.

Senators Joe Lieberman and John Edwards have even a worse liability than Gore and Kerry, for they were losers as vice-presidential candidates with Gore and Kerry respectively. No defeated vice-presidential candidate in a previous federal election ever subsequently ran for president and won.

Joe Lieberman was a Democrat when he ran for vice-president with presidential candidate Al Gore. In 2006, he won re-election to the U.S. Senate as an independent candidate. Sen. Hillary Clinton openly declared her support for the Democratic senatorial opponent of Lieberman in Connecticut in 2006. It is doubtful if Lieberman will want to run under the banner of the Democratic Party again. He can run for president as an independent, of course. Only if he wants to act as a spoiler, for no independent candidate for president ever won (*see* chapter 2 further on John Edwards and chapter 8 on the role of independent candidates).

A positive endorsement of Hillary can be implied from the current 10 other Democratic female Senators, not including the 5 female Republican senators, who defer to Hillary's prior claim, based on her exemplary record and political experience (*see* Table 1.12).

Table 1.12 Democratic Senators in Alphabetical Order of States

1. Blanche Lincoln of Arkansas

2. & 3. Dianne Feinstein and Barbara Boxer of California

4. Mary Landrieu of Louisiana

5. Barbara Mikulski of Maryland

6. Debbie Stabenow of Michigan

7. Amy Klobuchar of Minnesota

8. Claire McCaskill of Missouri

9. & 10. Patty Murray and Maria Cantwell of Washington

Hillary's co-female senators no doubt agree with Geraldine Ferraro's conclusion: "It's been 22 years since I became the first woman to run on a major-party ticket, and we're still asking whether a woman can be elected president. I don't think that's the right question. This isn't just about any woman. It's specific to Hillary Clinton, and we should be asking if she could do it.... *Hillary's been preparing for the presidency for a long time*" (emphasis supplied).[24]

As far as potential opponents are concerned, the best indicator of a smoother sailing for Hillary to become our country's first woman president is the absence of a sitting vice-president together with the absence of a president running for re-election on November 4, 2008. This kind of situation last happened in 1928, and a non-Protestant candidate, Catholic Al Smith almost won.

Will Hillary suffer the same fate as Al Smith? No, because the Al Smith for women is Geraldine Ferraro! Listen to what Ferraro the vice-presidential running mate of Walter Mondale the Democratic presidential candidate in 1984 said, "Though I was qualified, I was not the most qualified Democrat to be vice president, but I did bring a first: gender balance to the ticket. Sure, we lost, but Al Smith, the first Roman Catholic to run for president, opened the door for Jack Kennedy. And Fritz Mondale, when he decided it was time to bring down the MEN ONLY sign from the door of the White House did the same for a potential woman candidate."[25]

Apparently American voters did not agree in 1984 that "it was time to bring down the MEN ONLY sign from the door of the White House." It took Americans 218 years to elect Nancy Pelosi as our first woman Speaker of the U.S. House of Representatives—and it is now 24 years beyond 1984 when Mondale and Ferraro thought it was the right time to put a woman inside the White House—how many more years do you want to wait for the right time to elect our first woman president?

2

Top Presidents' Origins: Vice-Presidents, Governors, & Senators

◆

Hillary Clinton Outranks VP Dick Cheney Who Misfired; Arkansas Ex-Gov. Mike Huckabee Who Is No Bill Clinton, & Ex-Sen. John Edwards Who Was & Is Still "Green"

The most obvious opponent of Hillary would have been Dick Cheney, the incumbent vice-president of President George W. Bush. But, in a Sherman-like manner he announced during an interview at *Fox News* Sunday in 2004 that he would not run to succeed the latter: "I will say just as possibly know how to say … 'If nominated, I will not run,' 'If elected, I will not serve,' or not only no, but 'Hell no,' I've got my plans laid out. I'm going to serve this president for the next four year, and then I'm out of here."[26]

What Cheney had done is equivalent to a boxer who gives up the fight before it has begun. He must have realized that he has absolutely no chance to win because of one, or two, or a combination of three reasons:

(1) That the tide for change in favor of a woman president is so strong it is pointless to oppose it

(2) That he is not healthy due to a cardiovascular disease that led to 4 heart-attacks because of previous heavy cigarette smoking, and

(3) That as an incumbent vice-president he is a political failure

Nothing worse can portray Cheney's failure as the number two man in this administration than the picture of him mistaking a fellow-hunter for a quail. The wounded man was a Republican contributor, Harry Whittington, who landed in a hospital. The owner of the ranch where the hunting accident took place in Kingsville, 30 miles southwest of Corpus Christi, TX, Katharine Armstrong reported days after the accident that "Whittington was 'peppered' with birdshot ... in the face and chest, but he never lost consciousness.... I would shoot with Dick Cheney everywhere, anywhere, and not think twice about it," she continued. "The nature of quail shooting ensures that this will happen. It goes with the turf." [27]

Armstrong may be right in her assessment about the nature of quail-hunting in general.

Nevertheless, the accidental shooting was caused not by an ordinary hunter. It was made by the second highest official of our land, the U.S. vice-president! It was to be expected that following this unfortunate accident, Cheney was the butt of jokes by late-night show comedians to the effect that our country is in danger of having a future president "who cannot tell the difference between a flying bird and a man walking in the *bush*!"

The office of the vice-president is the most popular steppingstone to the presidency. There were 14 vice-presidents who became presidents half of whom or 7 were promoted from 1900 to the present (*compare* Table 2.0 & Table 2.1). But, there were more holders of that office who failed rather than succeeded in obtaining the ultimate prize, the U.S. presidency. Cheney would just have to be content in being counted among the vice-presidents who ended their political careers at number 2.[28]

Next to a vice-president, a state governor is the second most popular steppingstone to the presidency. There had been 10 governors who were elected president since 1789. Of that total, 7 state governors were directly promoted to the presidency from 1900 (*see* Table 2.1).

Table 2.0 Most Popular Routes to the U.S. Presidency since 1789

Vice-presidents	14
State Governors	10
U.S. Senators	6
Department Secretaries	6
Military heroes	5

U.S. Representative	1
Total	42

Table 2.1 Most Popular Routes to the Presidency Since 1900

Vice-presidents	7
State Governors	7
Senators	2
Department Secretaries	2
Drafted hero	1
Total	19

While more vice-presidents than governors were promoted to the presidency, becoming a vice-president has a major drawback: Nobody could really run for vice-president. It is always the presidential candidate who decides his or her own vice-presidential running mate.

Franklin D. Roosevelt in 1928 and John F. Kennedy in 1956 attempted to run for vice-president.

But the Democratic presidential nominees in those years: Alfred E. Smith and Adlai E.

Stevenson chose others as their running mates.

Fourteen vice-presidents of our country succeeded to the presidency in 4 ways:

(1) By running for it after the expiration of the term of the incumbent president

(2) By assuming the presidency due to the assassination of the incumbent

(3) By assuming the presidency upon the death of the incumbent due to natural causes

(4) By becoming president upon the resignation of the incumbent (see *Table 2.2*).

Table 2.2 Vice-presidents Who Became Presidents by Method of Succession

By winning in an election to succeed the president: 5	(All 5 won election)
John Adams VP of George Washington	(John Adams won vs. Thomas Jefferson)
Thomas Jefferson VP of John Adams	(Thomas Jefferson won vs. John Adams)
Martin Van Buren VP of Andrew Jackson	(Martin Van Buren won vs. William Henry Harrison)
Richard Nixon VP of Dwight Eisenhower	(Nixon lost to John Kennedy in 1960, but won vs. Hubert Humphrey in 1968)
George H.W. Bush VP of Ronald Reagan	(George H.W. Bush won vs. Michael Dukakis)
By succeeding an assassinated president: 4	(2 won election)
Andrew Johnson VP of Abraham Lincoln	(Did not run)
Chester Arthur VP of James Garfield	(Did not run)
Theodore Roosevelt VP of William McKinley	(Theodore Roosevelt won vs. Alton B. Parker)
Lyndon Johnson VP of John Kennedy (	Lyndon Johnson won vs. Barry Goldwater)
By succeeding a president who died of natural causes: 4	(2 won election)
John Tyler VP of William Henry Harrison	(Did not run)
Millard Fillmore VP of Zachary Taylor	(Did not run)
Calvin Coolidge VP of Warren G. Harding	(Coolidge won vs. John W. Davis)

Harry S. Truman VP of Franklin D. Roosevelt	(Truman won vs. George Dewey)
By succeeding a resigned president: 1	(Ran and lost)
Gerald Ford VP of Richard Nixon	(Ford lost to Jimmy Carter)
Total	14

Five vice-presidents became president by running for it after the expiration of the term of the incumbent president. The first vice—president who became president by running for it, following George Washington, was John Adams in 1796. When Federalist John Adams won the presidency in his own right, he did not carry his vice-president with him. The winning vice-president was Thomas Jefferson who belonged to the opposite party, the Democratic-Republicans or anti-Federalists. The latter favored the states' rights as the paramount source of all federal rights. In the year 1800, Jefferson ran for president against Adams, and the former won, becoming only the second vice-president to do so. The third vice-president, under President Andrew Jackson, to run for president successfully as a Democrat in 1836 was Martin Van Buren. The fourth vice-president, after losing the presidency in his first try against John Kennedy in 1960 and ran for president a second time in 1968 and winning against Hubert Humphrey, Lyndon Johnson's Democratic vice-president, was the Republican Richard Nixon. And the fifth vice-president who was elected president as a Republican was Ronald Reagan's vice-president, George H.W. Bush in 1988.

Four vice-presidents assumed the office of president after the assassination of the incumbent president. The first vice-president to become president on the assassination of the president, Abraham Lincoln in his second term, was Andrew Johnson in 1865. Lincoln was Republican, but Andrew Johnson was Democrat. The second vice-president who became president on the assassination of the president, James Garfield in his first term, was Republican Chester Arthur in 1881. The third vice-president who became president, on the assassination of the president, William McKinley in his second term, was Republican Theodore Roosevelt in 1901. Theodore Roosevelt won election in his own right as president in 1904. And the fourth vice-president who became president, on the assassination of the president, John Kennedy in his first term, was Democrat Lyndon Johnson in 1963. Lyndon Johnson won election in his own right as president in 1964.

Neither Andrew Johnson nor Chester Arthur ran for president in their own right after having served the unexpired term of their predecessors. Unlike his future fellow-surname sake, Andrew Johnson, a Southern Democrat, had a running feud with the Republican Party of Abraham Lincoln. The latter wanted the former Southern Confederates states to guarantee the civil rights of the freed slaves before sending representatives to the U.S. Congress. Andrew Johnson wanted the ex-Confederates to rejoin the U.S. without any strings attached. When his Secretary of War, Edwin Stanton, refused to enforce his southern policy, Johnson fired him. For this, Congress impeached him—the first president ever to be dealt with in this extreme way. In the impeachment trial in the U.S. Senate, Johnson was acquitted by just one vote! The Republican Party nominated Ulysses S. Grant, the nemesis of General Robert E. Lee the commander of the Southern Confederacy, as its presidential candidate in 1864. He easily defeated Horatio Seymour, the Democratic candidate, as the controversial Johnson was not wanted by both major parties. Johnson regained some sort of vindication when he was elected as Tennessee's U.S. Senator in 1874. He died the following year.

Chester Arthur was a member of the "Stalwarts" faction of the Republican Party that was controlled by big city machine politicians. The Reform faction, identified with the late Garfield, did not completely trust Arthur. He was once the head of the biggest Federal Customs House located in New York, and some of the employees he hired stole money from it, though he himself personally did not. Still he was fired as head of Customs House in 1878 for failing to control his subordinates. When he became president, he surprised even his critics in that he became a great supporter of the Pendleton Act that established the first Civil Service system in America. This offended his own "Stalwarts" faction, and the Reform faction did not completely trust him, so that he was not nominated for president in 1884. Arthur's Secretary of State, James J. Blaine received the Republican nomination, but he lost to Grover Cleveland, former Democratic governor of New York.

Four vice-presidents became presidents due to the death of the incumbent president through natural causes. The first vice-president who became president, after the death of President William Henry Harrison due to pneumonia for failing to wear a coat while delivering his first-and only term inaugural speech, was the Whig John Tyler in 1841. The second vice-president who became president, after the death of President Zachary Taylor because of exposure to extreme heat after serving two years of his first term was the Whig Millard Fillmore in 1850. The third vice-president who became president after the death of President Warren G. Harding three years into his first term due to heart thrombosis was the Republican Calvin Coolidge. Finally, the fourth vice-president who became president on the death of President Franklin D. Roosevelt caused by heart failure after serving less than one year of his fourth term was the Democrat Harry S. Truman in 1945.[29] Coolidge and Truman went on to win the election in their own right as president in 1924 and 1948 respectively.

Neither John Tyler nor Millard Fillmore ran for president after serving the unexpired term of their predecessors. Tyler lost the support of the Whig Party that wanted the Cabinet and Congress, led by Henry Clay, to take on the duties of president. Tyler insisted on ruling as president. His entire Whig-cabinet, save one, resigned. In the 1844 presidential election, Tyler thought of running as Independent or as a Democratic Party candidate, but he changed his mind when the latter nominated James K. Polk, who won against Henry Clay of the Whigs.

Millard Fillmore was not renominated by the Whig Party in 1852, because although personally he was against slavery, he supported Henry Clay's Great Compromise that allowed a state to decide whether it would allow or outlaw slavery. It nominated General Winfield Scott, who lost to the Democrat Franklin Pierce. The Whigs ceased to exist as a party ever since.

The only vice-president who became president after the resignation of the incumbent President Richard Nixon, because of the Watergate scandal, was the Republican Gerald Ford in 1974. He failed to win the election for president in his own right in 1976. He lost to Jimmy Carter (*D*), former governor of Georgia. Earlier, Ford was serving as the minority Republican leader of the House of Representatives, when he was appointed the new vice-president by President Nixon, to replace Spiro Agnew, the elected vice-president who previously resigned due to his involvement in another scandal. Thus, Ford was the only president who was neither elected to the vice-presidency nor to the presidency.

Out of 14 vice-presidents who became president only 9 won when they ran for it. Thus, the number of state governors outnumbered the vice-presidents who ran and won by one, that is, 10. If the comparison were made between vice-presidents and governors elected from 1900, they were tied at exactly 7 (*compare Table 2.0 & 2.1*).

Why is the position of state governor a very popular steppingstone to the Office of the U.S. President? The position of a state governor is very similar to that of the U.S. president in that they are both in-charge of executing the laws, in contrast with legislators who make the laws, and judges who interpret them. Somehow, there is a general positive perception that if you have been good enough to run the affairs of any state, then you are good enough to run the whole country!

All governors promoted directly to the presidency have had varied political experiences at other levels of government such as a member of a state legislature, a U.S. Senator, a U.S. Representative, a Cabinet secretary, a military service person, an ambassador abroad, or any other local political position.

Table 2.3 Governors Who Became Presidents

1845	James Polk (TN)
1877	Rutherford Hayes (OH)
1885	Grover Cleveland (NY)
1897	James McKinley (OH)
1913	Woodrow Wilson (NJ)
1933	Franklin D. Roosevelt (NY)
1977	Jimmy Carter (GA)
1981	Ronald Reagan (CA)
1993	Bill Clinton (AR)
2001	George W. Bush (TX).

But, not every state governor is automatically qualified to be promoted to the presidency.

More than a vice-presidential candidate whose closeness to the presidential candidate might be the most important factor, a state governor running for president must prove that he or she is qualified to be president. Only 8 of the 50 states are represented among governors-turned U.S. presidents, with New York and Ohio having 2 each. The 6 other states are Arkansas, California, Georgia, New Jersey, Tennessee, and Texas.

The first governor who was promoted to the presidency was the Democrat James K. Polk. Before becoming Tennessee governor, Polk started as a member of the Tennessee state legislature, then as Tennessee's U.S. representative for 14 years, the last 4 years of which he became the third most powerful man in the

Federal Government as the Speaker of the U.S. House of Representatives that Nancy Pelosi presently occupies. He served as the governor of Tennessee for only one term, and twice he ran for re-election but he lost. He thought of retiring from politics, but in the presidential election of 1844, he emerged as the first "dark horse" candidate ever. The Democratic Party was evenly divided into 2: the pro-Van Buren and anti-Van Buren factions. When no presidential candidate from either side could win the nomination in the convention, they agreed on James K. Polk as the compromise candidate in the ninth ballot. He went on to narrowly defeat Henry Clay of the Whigs.

Rutherford B. Hayes was the second governor to be elected U.S. president. Hayes was in the service of the Union Army, and when the Civil War was over, he served briefly in the U.S. Congress, after which he was elected governor of Ohio for 3 successive 2-year terms. He was serving his third term as Ohio governor when the Republican Party chose him as their presidential candidate in 1876. His Democratic opponent, Samuel J. Tilden, appeared to have won the over-all popular votes as well as the electoral votes. But, the Republicans contested the results. A 15-man committee composed of members of Congress and the Supreme Court decided by a vote of 8-7 to declare Hayes the winner in the state of Florida and the election (*see* above for an almost identical situation when the present occupant of the White House then Republican Governor of Texas George W. Bush won against Al Gore in Florida in 2000 by a decision of the U.S. Supreme Court).

Grover Cleveland was the third governor to be voted U.S. president. He started his political career as mayor of Buffalo, New York, in 1881. Gaining the reputation of a reformer after he cleaned up his city of corruption in one year, he was elected for 2 successive terms as governor of New York when he was nominated as the Democratic presidential candidate in 1884. When Chester Arthur was snubbed by the Republican Party from running for re-election, his Secretary of State James G. Blaine was put forward instead. Some Republicans, who called themselves the reformist "Mugwumps" opposed Blaine's candidacy as being too much identified with machine politics, so they sided with the Democrat Cleveland who won handily. He lost his bid for re-election as U.S. president in 1888 to Benjamin Harrison of the Republican Party. Then in a rematch against Benjamin Harrison in 1892, Cleveland won. He was the only president to have been elected 2 nonconsecutive terms, as the 22nd and 24th U.S. president.

James McKinley was the fourth governor to become U.S. President. He served for 14 years as a U.S. Representative from Ohio. Although he lost for reelection as a U.S. Representative, he was popular enough to be elected governor of the entire state of Ohio in 1892. He served as governor for two terms after which he won as the Republican nominee for president beating William Jennings Bryan of the Democratic Party in 1896. He became the 25th U.S. president.

The fifth governor to serve as U.S. president was Woodrow Wilson. He became Democratic governor of New Jersey in 1910. His accomplishments as governor led to his election as the 28th U.S. president in 1912. He was re-elected for a second term in 1916 in the middle of the First World War. He founded the League of Nations, but the Republican-controlled Congress voted against American membership in it. The most far-reaching policy of Wilson was probably the reversal of his opposition to and his subsequent support for the right of American women to vote that came in 1920.

Franklin D. Roosevelt was the 6th governor to be chosen U.S. president. He started his career as a member of the New York state senate in 1910. In 1921, he was stricken with polio, which made him practically paralyzed from the waist down. Despite his ailment, he was elected governor of New York in 1928. He became the Democratic nominee for president in 1932, which he won as the 32nd U.S. president. He was re-elected for president in 1936, 1940, and 1944 but he died in 1945. He was the first and last president to serve more than 3 terms. Following Franklin Roosevelt's lengthy presidential service, the U.S. Congress passed the amendment to the Federal Constitution to limit presidential service to 2-consecutive terms, a tradition established by George Washington. Roosevelt kept America out of the Second World War, but he was forced to enter it by the Japanese bombing of Pearl Harbor, Hawaii in 1941. He neither lived to see the end of the war nor the founding of the United Nations.

The 7th governor who was selected U.S. president was Jimmy Carter of Georgia. He began his political career as a member of the Georgia state senate in 1962, and then Georgia governor in 1972. He ran as the Democratic presidential candidate in 1976, beating the incumbent unelected president Gerald Ford of the Republican Party.

Ronald Reagan of the Republican Party was the 8th governor to be selected U.S. president. He won as California governor in 1966 and won re-election in 1970. He sought nomination for president on the Republican ticket in 1968 and 1976, but he did not win. In his third try in 1980, Reagan finally succeeded to be the Republican Party nominee and he went on to defeat the incumbent president, Jimmy Carter. He was re-elected in 1984.

The 9th governor to be promoted to the presidency was Bill Clinton. He started his career as Attorney General of Arkansas in 1976, and 2 years later, he won as governor. He lost when he ran for reelection for governor in 1980. He determined to return to the office of governor which he won for 4 more terms in 1982, 1984, 1986, and 1990. In 1992, he was nominated as the Democratic presidential candidate, and he won against then President George H.W. Bush. He won reelection as president in 1996.

The incumbent Republican George W. Bush of Texas was the 10th governor to ascend to the office of U.S. President in 2000 beating Al Gore. In 2004, he was reelected president at the expense of Democrat John Kerry of Massachusetts.

A far greater number of state governors have aspired to become president but failed in their endeavor—certainly more than the vice-presidents who did not make it. However, just because you have been a state governor does not automatically guarantee your elevation to the presidency by the American electorate. Take the case of former Governor Mike Huckabee (*R*) of the state of Arkansas. He might have been judged by the voters of Arkansas to be one of the worthy successors of Bill Clinton to that state's governorship, but the rest of the country might not agree to elevate him to the U.S. presidency as they did Bill. To achieve a similar promotion to the highest office of our land, Huckabee has to present as good a record or better than Bill Clinton in governing the state of Arkansas. Otherwise, he will just end up among the vast majority of state governors who had tried to run for the presidency and failed. Even the *Time Magazine's* choice of the 5 best governors of 2005 that included Huckabee, Kenny Guinn (*R*) of Nevada, Janet Napolitano (*D*) of Arizona, Kathleen Sebelius (*D*) of Kansas, and Mark Warner (*D*) of Virginia, began the article as follows: "When it comes to raw political talent, there's not a Bill Clinton in this group." [30]

Everyone—who is male and white—who is a potential candidate for president in the Democratic ticket in the election of November 4, 2008 should follow the example of former Governor Mark Warner of Virginia by announcing that he will not run for president. Were it not for the fact that the time has arrived for a woman to be the next president of our country, Warner would have been the ideal presidential candidate of the Democratic Party. He was rated by *Time Magazine* in 2005 as one among "top 5 governors," and *Governing Magazine* noted that "Virginia was the best governed state under [Mark] Warner's direction." Mark Warner's stock increased when he was successful in anointing his Democratic successor: the incumbent Virginia Governor Tim Kaine. He was also instrumental in the defeat of the re-election of Senator—and former Virginia Governor—George Allen, thus derailing the latter's Republican presidential dream. [31] Mark Warner has decided to run for U.S. senator from Virginia in place of the other Warner, John (*R*, VA) who announced in September 2007 that he was retiring.

Any other Democratic governor, therefore, cannot conceivably desire to run for president on November 4, 2008, since none of them can equal former Mark Warner's excellent record as governor of Virginia. The only 2 other top 5 Democratic governors rated by *Time Magazine* are women: Governor Janet Napolitano of Arizona, and Governor Kathleen Sebelius of Kansas. Neither has declared any interest in running for president in 2008 or at any other time. It can only be assumed that like Governor Warner, they are loyal Democrats and respectful of their being co-gender with Hillary, whom they wish to wholeheartedly support.

The next best strategy to that of a state governor as a steppingstone to the U.S. president is to be a U.S. senator. Following the state governor's route to the presidency, the senatorial route is the third in frequency, that is, 6 (See *Table 2.4*).

Table 2.4 U.S. Senators Who Were Promoted to the Presidency

1828	Andrew Jackson (TN)
1840	William H. Harrison (OH)
1880	James A. Garfield (OH)
1888	Benjamin Harrison (IN)
1920	Warren Harding (OH)
1960	John F. Kennedy (MA)

Table 2.5 U.S. Senators Who Were Promoted to the Presidency Since 1900

1920	Warren Harding (OH)
1960	John F. Kennedy (MA)

While there had been many senators who aspired to be the presidential standard bearer of one of the 2 major political parties, those who had made it to the presidency were very few. There had, of course, been U.S. senators who were later elected as either governors or vice-presidents and from there became presidents, and are therefore included under those separate categories. For example, Lyndon

Johnson was a senator from Texas for a long time when John Kennedy chose him as his vice-presidential running mate. Then, they won against Richard Nixon's Republican ticket. Vice-president Lyndon Johnson became president when Kennedy was assassinated in his first term. Johnson is not included among the senators that got promoted to the presidency, for he passed by the office of vice-president.

It is true that the more often a U.S. senator is re-elected, the better are his or her chances to be nominated for president or at least be chosen as a vice-presidential running mate. For purposes of comparison with the current crop of U.S. Senators who are aspiring for the presidency in 2008, it is instructive to observe the qualifications of the previous 6 winners to gauge the way the American electorate has previously voted, and will most likely vote the same way on November 4, 2008.

The first U.S. Senator to be promoted to the presidency was Andrew Jackson. He had a lot of previous political experience besides being a military hero with the rank of major general. He was first elected as a congressman from the new state of Tennessee in 1796, and became a U.S. senator for 2 separate terms. One year after his second senatorial election in 1823, he ran for president in 1824, but he lost to John Quincy Adams in a closely contested election that was decided by the House of Representatives. Andrew Jackson in his second try for the presidency easily beat John Quincy Adams the incumbent president in 1824. He co-founded the Democratic Party with Martin Van Buren of New York. Jackson replaced John C. Calhoun with Van Buren as vice-president when he ran for presidential re-election in 1832.

William Henry Harrison was the second U.S. senator to be elevated to the presidency. He began his political career in 1801 when he was appointed governor of Indiana territory, an office that he held for so many years. Like Jackson, Harrison was a war hero in 1808 against Native American Indians and in 1812 against the British and their Native American allies. He also served as ambassador to Colombia, as a member of the House of Representatives, and as U.S. senator. In 1840, he was nominated by the Whigs for president and won it with John Tyler as his vice-president. Harrison is mostly remembered for having served the shortest period as a president, from March 4, 1841 to April 4, 1841, or exactly one month. He also delivered the longest inaugural speech, i.e. one hour and forty-five minutes. As he wore no coat while giving his speech in cold weather, he caught pneumonia that led to his premature death.

James A. Garfield of Ohio was the third U.S. Senator to be elevated to the presidency as a Republican in 1880. Garfield was the only U.S. senator who became president without serving even one day in the Senate. Before the Senate could meet, he was nominated as a "dark horse" presidential candidate in the 1880 Republican convention, and won the election narrowly to become the 20th U.S. president.

Garfield's varied background included the presidency of a college, Eclectic Institute (now Hiram College), Ohio; a Civil War (1861-650) hero rising to the rank of major general in the Union Army, and he was elected to the U.S. House of Representatives 8 successive times from 1863 to 1880.

Benjamin Harrison was the fourth U.S. senator to become president. He served as senator of Indiana from 1881 to 1887, and is remembered for 2 things:

(1) He was the only president who was a grandson of a previous president, the 9th president William Henry Harrison, a hero of the Indian wars, and

(2) He was known as the "centennial president" because he was elected the 23rd president 100 years after the first president George Washington. He was also a hero of the Civil War, having commanded the 70th Indiana Volunteer Infantry, as a brigadier general.

Warren G. Harding was the fifth U.S. senator who was promoted to the presidency from the state of Ohio. When the Republican convention in 1920 was deadlocked between two candidates, Harding became the winning compromise or "dark horse" candidate. With Calvin Coolidge for his vice-presidential running mate, the ticket won. Harding's previous experience included being a teacher for a short time, then owner of the newspaper *Marion Star*, state senator, and lieutenant governor. When he ran for Ohio governor in 1910, he lost. But, when he ran for U.S. senator in 1914, he won.

The sixth and last U.S. senator who got promoted to the presidency was John F. Kennedy in 1960, to become the 35th president. Many U.S. senators keep on trying to run for U.S. president, because like a state governor, it is possible to do so. Senators have usually national recognition more than governors. It even has a distinct advantage, in that there is no term limit for the office of a U.S. senator, while there might be for a state governor.

In this forthcoming presidential election, more U.S. senators are running than governors or U.S. representatives. That is the case in spite of the fact that it is awfully hard to win the presidency from the position of a Senator as a stepping-stone. There were only 2 senators who were promoted to the U.S. presidency in the 20th century: Warren Harding and John F. Kennedy (*see* Table 2.5). And the last one, Kennedy, won it almost half a century ago in 1960.

The Senators that are running for the presidency in 2008 include Hillary Clinton, although she is more than just a U.S. Senator; she had also been a U.S.

first lady as well as a former first lady of the state of Arkansas. The other senators who are running do not have any exceptional positive circumstance in their favor, so that in general their chances to win are rather quite slim: incumbent U.S. Senators Barack Obama (*D*, IL), John McCain (*R*, AZ), Joseph Briden (*D*, DE), Sam Brownback (*R*, KA), Christopher Dodd (*D*, CT), Evan Bayh (*D*, IN), and Chuck Hagel (*R*, NE) as well as ex-Senators Mike Gravel (*D*, AK), Fred Thompson (*R*, TN), and John Edwards (*D*, NC).

But, far more U.S. senators do not even try to run for the higher offices of president and vice-president. They are quite happy to end their political careers in the service of our country as U.S. senators. This is not so in the case of ex-Senator John Edwards who has declared his decision to run for U.S. president. It would have been better for him if he did not previously run for vice-president. He would not have to carry forward to his presidential candidacy the tag of a loser. John Edwards also has a very limited experience at the federal governmental level. He had neither an executive, diplomatic, or military experience.

When John Kerry chose John Edwards as his Democratic vice-presidential running mate in 2004, the latter just completed his first term as U.S. Senator. Joe Johns, an African American correspondent for CNN, predicted then that "Edwards will be hit almost immediately with charges that he is green, that he is not ready, [and] that he is inexperienced."[32]

Edwards was "green" in 2004, and what makes him think that he is no longer green in 2008, just a bare 4 years later with him completely out of any governmental position? What makes him think that losing the election as a candidate for vice-president is enough lesson learned to make him move up to a higher level office, that of president? We do not want to disillusion Edwards, and his sympathizers, but it is a matter of historical record that no vice-presidential candidate ever lost the election for vice-president of the Unite States and subsequently run for president and won.

There is further his controversial decision to continue with his presidential campaign, in spite of the fact that his wife, Elizabeth, had a recurrence of her incurable cancer. There might be many couples out there, including us, who have arrived at a different decision, i.e. quit the presidential campaign and let him stay by his wife's side.

Add to that the fact as elicited by Katie Couric during a CBS interview of John Edwards and his wife that they have 2 very young children, i.e., only 8 and 6 years old. "What will happen to them?" Their reply was that their children, while still young, must learn to fly, which prompted Couric to remark, "They are awfully very young birds!" But, Edwards was insistent, "Though young, they must learn to start flying." Of course, but all young birds need the presence and assistance of their parents until such time that they are able to fly from the coup on their own. As for humans, that stage is not reached till at least when children are in their final teenage years! Because of John Edwards and his wife's failure to do what might be considered as a more sensible decision, you may be forced as voters to do the right thing for them and their own children's sake by casting your votes for someone else, like Hillary, for example. Her only daughter, Chelsea at 27 had flown the coup ever since she went to Stanford University. She now lives on her own in the district of Chelsea, Manhattan, New York City, apart from her parents.

John Edwards should not have run for president for another reason. He already had a chance to run for vice-president and lost. Had he and his presidential running-mate won in 2004, both of them would be running for re-election this time around. It is just as well that the Kerry-Edwards ticket did not win, for Kerry does not seem to have much regard for his former vice-presidential running mate. Kerry recently impugned Edwards's honesty on a very important matter: did Edwards read or not read the National Intelligence Estimate report prior to voting to authorize Bush's sending a force to Iraq? John Edwards's campaign staff declared that Edwards only read a declassified version of the National Intelligence Estimate, when in fact Kerry said that he was able to read the actual report, before voting to authorize the use of force in Iraq:

"That fall, as a vote loomed on the resolution giving Bush authority to go to war," John Kerry said, "Edwards convened a circle of advisers in his family room in Washington to discuss his decision. He was skeptical, even exercised about the idea of voting yes. Elizabeth was a forceful no. She didn't trust anything the Bush administration was saying. But the consensus view from both the foreign policy experts and the political operatives was that even if Edwards was on the Intelligence Committee, he was too junior in the Senate; he didn't have the credibility to vote against the resolution. To my continuing regret, I said he had to be for it. As I listened to this, I watched Edwards's face; he didn't like where he was being pushed to go."[33] One cannot help conclude that Edwards voted against his own better judgment even against the advice of the closest person to his heart, his own wife, not because it was the right thing to do, but purely as a matter of political expediency, i.e., to increase his chances of becoming vice-president.

Edwards is fond of saying that there had been rich presidential candidates who became president, and still managed to be of help to the poor as he is planning to do when he gets elected. That includes the Roosevelts and the Kennedys. The major difference between them and John Edwards is that the former inherited their wealth, whereas John Edwards had to work for it. The latter argues that if someone like him can rise to the top and become rich, so can other ordinary Americans whom he is asking to vote for him.

In the month of July 2007, as reported in *Newsweek,* John Edwards tried to emulate Robert F. Kennedy by going on a month "Road to One America" poverty tour, even ending it in Prestonburg, KY where Robert Kennedy concluded his own tour of impoverished Appalachia. "'I want you to join us,' Edwards told his audience, 'to end the work Bobby Kennedy started.'

Kennedy's crusade against poverty enthralled many Americans. [But], Edwards's crusade has not. "[34]

What is John Edwards doing that does not seem to favorably resonate with the American people? It can be said that Americans are not as poor as they used to be almost half a century ago in Robert F. Kennedy's time. If that is true, that is only half of the story. The other half has to do with John Edwards not being able to convince Americans that he is genuinely interested in alleviating their economic problems. This has less to do with Edwards exhorting Americans to imitate him in trying to become rich in America by working hard, but more to do with their perception about Edwards's lack of authenticity shown by his ostentatious display of an extravagant new lifestyle.

There is the matter of 2 expensive haircuts in a Beverley Hills, California haircutting place at $400 each that Edwards had promised to reimburse because it was billed to his campaign team. The only thing worse than this is the fact that "the Congress of the United States spends more money than Edwards spends in a beauty parlor" was pointed out in a presidential debate by—not a comedian—but a rival candidate for president, former Arkansas Governor Mike Huckabee. If Edwards needs a hair at least once a month, his yearly budget amounts to almost $5,000. If he has a haircut at least twice a month, that would be a whooping yearly budget of $10,000!

"Edwards … has undermined his passionate advocacy for ordinary Americans by seeming to be anything but ordinary himself," editorialized *the USA Today* in its May 30, 2007 issue: "Expensive haircuts reinforce the elitist image of a wealthy trial lawyer who owns a 28,000-square-foot home, worked for a high-dollar hedge fund after he left the Senate and last year charged a public university $55,000 for giving a speech—on poverty."[35]

In mid-July of 2007, Mrs. Elizabeth Edwards said in an interview that her husband, John, has done more for women than Hillary Clinton. Bill Clinton said the exact reverse is true (this is just one example of what a *Gallup* poll revealed from its respondents by a margin of 70% to 28% that Bill will be a great asset to Hillary).

(1) Who is right, Elizabeth Edwards or Bill Clinton? Both of them are, although Bill is much more (if there is such a thing as "more" right). Elizabeth was "standing by her man." This is expected of a loyal wife.

Her negative remark drew a rebuttal from former President Bill Clinton who said that it was Hillary, former First Lady and a current U.S. senator from New York (in a position to continue working to benefit women) who has done more and continuing to do more for women. Bill was "standing by her woman." This, too, is totally expected of a loving husband. But, Bill is not just any ordinary husband in relation to her woman. You will recall that he just happened to be one of the most successful among 42 presidents in America's two hundred and a quarter century.

Let Bill Clinton speak for himself during an interview on ABC's Good Morning America: *"If you look at the record on women's issues, I defy you to find anybody who has run for office in recent history who's got a longer history of working for women, for families and children than Hillary does."*

On Mrs. Edwards's charge that Hillary is behaving "as a man," Bill replied: "I don't think it's inconsistent with being a woman that you can also be knowledgeable on military and security affairs and be strong when the occasion demands it."

When Bill was given a chance to criticize Hillary's opponents, he refused to do so. "This is a good time for us Democrats," he says. "We don't have to be against anybody. We can be for the person we think would be the best President."[36]

---

(2) Elizabeth Edwards and Bill Clinton are both right from two different perspectives: the former is a traditional woman who looks up to a man to support her (the image of a woman who is used to being provided fish to eat by a fisherman [not fisherwoman, for that word does not exist]); the latter is a modern man who allows, if not teaches, a woman how to fish and is not threatened by a woman who can catch her own fish!

(3) The amazing thing is that while Hillary can do the fishing by herself, and she does not need a man to help her fish—as her mother or grandmother or their equivalents in the lives of other women—yet when there was some cause for her to have said to herself, "I do not need any aggravation from Bill, for after all I can fish for myself. Let's get a divorce," which some of Hillary's friends advised her to do.

But, miracle of miracles: she had the means to take care of herself (thanks to her parents who trained her androgynously, i.e., "to be able to do anything that a man can do (e.g. to fish), though a woman," she decided to stand by her [fisher]man! Hillary is only asking you—American voters—to give her one chance to fish like a man (be an American president like you gave more than one chance to Bill Clinton!)

(4) John Edwards has only a promise to provide some kind of comprehensive health care to families that will be most helpful to women and children; Hillary actually attempted to sponsor a universal health care plan for families, women, and children when she was First Lady of Bill Clinton, but she was not successful.

(5) "The end result for both Edwards and Hillary is the same," you might argue about the foregoing. No, we say, Edwards had not failed, true, but only because he did not even have an opportunity to try to provide it. Hillary's attempt was real, and she had learned a lesson which she can avoid when she decides to provide comprehensive health care for families, women, and children when she becomes president.

That was why when she unveiled her new comprehensive health care plan on September 17, 2007 in Des Moines, IA, she could confidently say that it avoids the pitfalls of her aborted proposal in 1993 and incorporates what is perfectly working in our current health care system. "I'm the decision-maker now," she said in an interview. "I have a plan that is 100% my plan—and it is a plan that comes out of my years of experience at both ends of Pennsylvania Avenue, [Washington, D.C.]." "I learned that people who are satisfied with their current coverage want assurances that they can keep it," Hillary said. "Part of our health care system is the best in the world, and we should build on it; part of the system is broken, and we should fix it."[37]

(6) If you want to bet between John Edwards and Hillary Clinton as to who would most likely be more helpful to women in other areas of life besides health care, whom would you bet on? If you say, Edwards, you would be betting on someone who does not have anything to offer but limited legislative—and no executive, no military, and no diplomatic—experience.

You will be better off betting on Hillary because she has twice the legislative experience of Edwards—including long-term membership in the Senate Armed Services Committee—the equivalent of a military experience, as well as executive and diplomatic experiences when she was First Lady of the U.S. for 8 years, and an additional executive experience as First Lady of Arkansas when Bill Clinton was that state's 4-term governor.

(7) John Edwards has not written something on the subject of helping women and their families; Hillary wrote *It Takes a Village* (updated in 2007) to propose how to properly provide for the needs of families, women, and children included. Hillary donated the millions of dollars earned by the book to non-profit organizations for children.[38] While the main thesis of Hillary's book is on the need for an entire village to help rear a child successfully, according to the *New York Times*, "it [also] takes a village" to take care of the needs of the elderly. There are now more than 100 "aging in place" self-help communities nationwide that are incorporated as non-profit organizations, led by 2 seniors husband-and-wife George and Anne Allen of Washington, D.C.[39]

(8) John Edwards as a family man has not yet helped rear a woman who is successful in her life; Hillary, with the assistance of her husband, Bill, has reared an extraordinarily successful woman in Chelsea Clinton, her daughter, a Stanford University, CA and Oxford University, England, alumna who is ready to inherit from her Mom, future president Hillary her former role as First Lady of the United States!

(9) To elect John Edwards, being a white male Caucasian at a time when Americans are ready for a woman president would be a backward move, and if he wins, he will be remembered as the man who prevented the election of America's first woman president; to elect Hillary is a progressive move, for it demonstrates that in the United States people are equal regardless of gender as a fact of life that the rest of the world can emulate.

(10) To vote for John Edwards as U.S. President does not have any effect on the future of our daughters and their children's daughters for generations to come; to vote for Hillary for president is at the same time voting for the future of our daughters and their children's daughters for countless generations!

Not unlike, though less serious than John McCain's implosion of his campaign as early as July 2007, John Edwards's presidential campaign seems to be following the same direction, that is, reducing his campaign staff, or re-assigning some from Nevada, for example, to Iowa and New Hampshire one month later than McCain, because of an identical reason: lack of financial support from the public (*see* chapter 6 below on McCain's implosion).

Senior Edwards adviser Joe Trippi also unleashed a strong attack on Hillary for holding a $500.00-a-plate dinner at the law offices of Jones Day, the largest law firm in the country, in the middle of September 2007 calling her "a Democratic insider [and] that event was a poster child of what is wrong with Washington." This was not ignored by Hillary's campaign, when spokesperson Phil Singer released through Politico.com, this reply: "Increasingly negative attacks against other Democrats aren't going to end the [Iraq] war, deliver universal health care or turn around John Edwards's flagging campaign."[40] Prof. Peverill Squire, professor of Political Science in the University of Iowa, echoed similar sentiments: "There is a sense that this endless campaign will be coming to an end with the Iowa caucuses not far off.... Edwards and other candidates are focusing their criticism on [Hillary] as a way to bring them from the back."

One of the two states that elected John Edwards as winner of a Democratic primary event prior to the 2004 presidential election was North Carolina. Its caucus gave him 52% of the votes while 27% went to John Kerry. It would have been reasonable to assume that during the 2004 presidential elections that followed the winning ticket would be the one that carried his name, considering that Mr. Edwards not only hails from North Carolina but also represented it in the U.S. Senate. Perhaps surprisingly, it was not the Kerry/Edwards ticket that won, but the incumbent President George W. Bush who won 56.02% of the votes versus the Democratic ticket with only 43.58%. Thus, Edwards would not make a good Democratic presidential standard bearer in 2008. He is not even good enough to repeat as the vice-presidential running mate of Hillary.

Equal to the number of U.S. senators that became presidents were Department Secretaries, at 6 (see Table 2.6). A department secretary is much more dependent on the president than the vice-president. The former is not elected but appointed by the president. Of the total department secretaries that became president, the position of secretary of state was formerly occupied by 4, and the secretary of war and secretary of commerce were represented by 1 apiece.

Table 2.6 Types of Department Secretaries Who Were Elected President since 1789

1809	James Madison	Secretary of State
1814	James Monroe	Secretary of State
1825	John Q. Adams	Secretary of State
1857	James Buchanan	Secretary of State
1909	William H. Taft	Secretary of War
1929	Herbert Hoover	Secretary of Commerce

Table 2.7 Types of Department Secretaries Who Were Elected President since 1900

Secretaries of State	0
Secretary of War	1
Secretary of Commerce	1
Total	2

The top-ranking position among department secretaries is the secretary of state. Dick Morris and Eileen McGann in *Condi vs. Hillary*[41] must have thought of this when they chose Condi Rice as someone who could beat Hillary. But, the period when the secretary of state was understood to be an anointed successor to the presidency was only during the very beginning of our republic.

If you think that the almost half a century that passed when the last U.S. senator had become president is too long, a Secretary of State was even much longer than that, i.e., three times as long, or 150 years ago, when Secretary of State James Buchanan became president in 1856! The 2 department secretaries who were elected president since 1900—William H. Taft and Hebert Hoover—were not secretaries of State, but of War and Commerce respectively in 1908 and 1928. Thus, taking into account the last 150 years, the chance for General Colin Powell and Condi Rice, former and incumbent Republican secretaries of states respectively to become president in 2008, is exactly zero.

Never is a department secretary drafted to run for U.S. president as suggested by Morris and McGann. Only military heroes are, such as Arkansan retired General Wesley Clark, a Democrat who decided not to run, but endorsed Hillary instead. The number of military heroes who were directly elected U.S. presidents followed closely that of department secretaries, at 5 *(see* Table 2.8). There were military heroes who had later been elected U.S. senators, state governors, and vice-presidents before becoming president. They are therefore included under those separate categories.

Table 2.8 Military Heroes Who Became President since 1789

1789	George Washington
1849	Zachary Taylor
1852	Franklin Pierce
1869	Ulysses S. Grant
1953	Dwight D. Eisenhower

Table 2.9 The Military Hero Who Became President since 1900

1953	Dwight D. Eisenhower

George Washington was the first drafted hero to serve as America's first president. He was promoted to the U.S. presidency directly from being Commanding General of the victorious American army at Yorktown against the British that resulted in the independence of our country on July 4, 1776. Although he was Lieutenant General at his death, President Gerald Ford in 1976 posthumously appointed Washington the number 1 full ranking general of America of all time. He was the only president who was a unanimous choice, or who became president without any opposition. He was also the only president who did not belong to any political party.

The second drafted hero to become America's 12th president was Zachary Taylor of the Whigs. Following in the footsteps of his father, who was a colonel in the Revolutionary War (1775-1783), Taylor was an able soldier who attained the 4th highest rank of major general in the army. He fought in the War of 1812, the Seminole War (1818) and the Mexican War (1846-1848). Although a slave owner, Taylor was dedicated to the preservation of the Union. Taylor had died only after serving 2 years of his term in 1850 after eating cherries and milk during the Independence Day Celebration in Washington D.C. The cause of death was exposure to extreme heat. The Missouri Compromise of 1850 which allowed slavery below the Mason-Dixon Line would have been vetoed by Taylor. Millard Fillmore, his successor, supported it.

Franklin Pierce was the third U.S. drafted hero to become president. Prior to his elevation to the U.S. presidency, he served in the New Hampshire state legislature from 1829 to 1833, the U.S. House of Representatives from 1833 to 1837, and the U.S. Senate from 1837 to 1842. Then, he became a hero of the American-Mexican war (1846-1848) attaining the 5th rank of Brigadier General of Volunteers. In 1852, he was the Democratic nominee for president who defeated General Winfield Scott of the Whigs to become the 14th president.

The fourth drafted hero to ascend to the presidency was Ulysses S. Grant of the Republican Party becoming the 18th president. He was a 4-star general of the army and the commander-in-chief of the Union Armed Forces during the Civil War and was the victorious general that effectively ended it with the surrender of the commanding officer of the Southern Confederacy, General Robert E. Lee, at Appomattox Court House, Richmond, Virginia in April 1865. Among U.S. presidents, only George Washington and Dwight D. Eisenhower outranked him.

The fifth and final hero to be drafted to the presidency was Republican Dwight D. Eisenhower who became our 34th president. Eisenhower was a 5-star general who served as the Commander of the Allied Forces in Europe that fought victoriously against Adolf Hitler's German armed forces during the Second World War (1941-1945). He was serving as first commander of the North Atlantic Treaty Organization (NATO) when he was drafted to run for president under the banner of the Republican Party in 1952. Most of the drafted heroes to become president served prior to the 20th century. Eisenhower was the only drafted hero to serve as president in the 20th century. Among U.S. presidents, no one else was higher ranking than he except George Washington.

What is unique about Abraham Lincoln besides being rated "the greatest U.S. president in history?" He was the only U.S. president who was promoted directly from the U.S. House of Representatives.

Table 2.10 The U.S. of Representatives—Final Source of the U.S. Presidency

1860   Abraham Lincoln

The lowest level of political office that any president had ever risen from is that of a U.S. representative. There was only one former U.S. Representative who was promoted directly to the presidency, Abraham Lincoln. And he was elected president almost as long ago as a secretary of state was elected, that is, 150 years ago. The major reason why a U.S. Representative is not a popular steppingstone to the U.S. presidency is that unlike a Governor who represents a whole state, or a U.S. senator who represents half of a state, a U.S. Representative represents less than half of a state, that is, only his own small congressional district.

The presidential aspirations of U.S. Representatives Dennis Kucinich (D, OH), Duncan Hunter (R, CA), Ron Paul (R, TX), Tom Tancredo (R, CO), and Newt Gingrich (R, GA) cannot completely be ruled out based only on historical precedent. But, it is highly unlikely that anyone of them can even be nominated by their political party. If any of them miraculously wins his party's nomination winning the presidency after that will practically be impossible. To be able to win, he will have to duplicate Abraham Lincoln's feat of ascending to the presidency from the office of a U.S. representative by showing our people that he has as good a record as Abraham Lincoln, "the greatest U.S. president ever!"

Early in the 1850's Lincoln engaged in a debate against Stephen Douglas for a U.S. senatorial seat from Illinois. Lincoln lost the election, but his performance in the debate, made him so popular that in the presidential election of 1860, he became the presidential candidate of the Union Party representing the Republican Party, with Andrew Johnson of the Democratic Party as his vice-presidential running mate.

"Senator" Is the Least of Hillary's Qualifications

Hillary does not have to be a governor or a vice-president, the two other most popular steppingstones to the U.S. presidency, for she is more than just an ordinary senator. Hillary's case is quite unique, for the simple reason that she was already both the First Lady of Arkansas when her husband Bill was governor for 4 terms and First Lady of the U.S. when he became president of our country for 2 successive terms. A combination of a virtual co-governorship and a co-presidency is more than the equivalent of a mere governorship or vice-presidency.

First ladies have always had a quasi-presidential role, for they have always served as the *de facto* adviser to their respective husbands, whether she was Abigail Adams, or Eleanor Roosevelt, or Jackie Kennedy, or Hillary Clinton, or even Laura Bush. Abigail, the First Lady of our second president John Adams, would perhaps be most remembered by a letter addressed to her husband when he was involved in helping to draft the Declaration of Independence of the United States from the United Kingdom:

"Remember the Ladies. Become more generous and favorable to them than your ancestors. Do not put such unlimited power into the hands of the Husbands. Remember all Men would be tyrants if they could. If particular care and attention is not paid to the Ladies we are determined to foment a Rebellion, and will not hold ourselves bound by any Laws in which we have no voice, or Representation."[42]

The position of First Lady Abigail Adams was so influential that one historian suggested that she be considered one of the founders of our country, i.e., a founding mother![43] Had Abigail Adams been the First Lady in our time rather than 200 years ago when women could not even vote, let alone run for office, she would have been an excellent candidate for U.S. president!

Eleanor Roosevelt was practically a co-president of FDR and for 3+ full terms until he died at the start of his 4th term. He was sick with polio all through his 4-term presidency and was confined to his wheel chair, so that First Lady Eleanor had to be his leg and arm. She traveled throughout the country and the world for him, to be his eyes and ears as well.

Another First Lady, who practically took charge of the federal government for 2 years, i.e. from 1919 to 1921 when her husband, President Woodrow Wilson, became an invalid, was Edith Bolling Galt Wilson. She refused to hand the administration of the government over to the vice-president, preferring to run it herself by consulting her husband who was still in complete possession of his mental faculties and to assign specific matters to the department heads. Her role was so dominant that some of her critics started calling her "the first woman president!"[44]

Hillary is simply trying to follow and implement what unparalleled forward-looking vision for the women of America that the First Lady Abigail Adams, wife of John Adams, America's second president, providentially had more than 200 years ago, and what both Eleanor Roosevelt and Edith Wilson virtually performed on behalf of their respective husbands.

She is also and at the same time "the most qualified candidate for president to hit the ground running," in her own words. More than just legislative she also has executive, diplomatic, and national security expertise. As First Lady of both the state of Arkansas when her husband Bill was governor, and of the United States when the same Bill was president, she demonstrated an extraordinary executive savvy as her husband's most intimate political adviser.

"What I bring to the table, in addition to my ideas and my experience, is that I'm battle-hardened," she told *CBS News* Early Show Harry Smith. "I've been there. I know how to overcome these kinds of political tactics."[45]

Byron York of the *National Review* writes that when Hillary says, "'I have the experience to get this country back in the right track,' she's not referring just, or even mostly, to her Senate experience. If she were, she would have scarcely more case to make for herself than Barack Obama or John Edwards. No, what she is saying is: I've been in the White House, I know the job, I've got the right executive stuff. In her memoir, *Living History,* Clinton wrote that during her husband's administration she and her staff were 'fully immersed in the daily operation of the West Wing'...." "People associate her with the White House because she was such a visible first lady," Democratic strategist Donna Brazile told York, "they give her *de facto* executive experience, even though she wasn't chief executive."[46]

Hillary was quite acquainted with America's diplomatic relations in the world, having visited 82 countries when she traveled either with her husband or even alone to represent our country in international meetings. She has also been active as a women's and children's advocate through private and government channels or the UNESCO, a branch of the U.N.

Time Magazine's Joe Klein, often a critic of Hillary had to admit that she has an expertise that she alone among present presidential candidates possesses, that is, in the field of national security. He writes that several Democratic presidential candidates can rival her in foreign affairs, such as Joe Biden, Christopher Dodd, and Bill Richardson, but Hillary's many years of membership in the Senate Committee of the Armed Services has given her an unparalleled knowledge of "the way military leaders think."[47]

3

All Presidents' First Names Are Of 4 Western Heroic Types

◆

Hillary Fits All 4 Types; Barack (Obama), Not Even 1

Democratic Daniel Inouye, 82, the third most senior of all U.S. senators representing Hawaii where Obama was born, speaks for most open-minded Americans that Obama's candidacy is quite untimely. He states that many senators—past and present—like Hillary Clinton and John Edwards are ready to be U.S. president. Some say also "Barack Obama, but he should wait. He has been in the Senate for [how long]? Two years? You can almost anticipate what they are going to do to him. It is so predictable...."[48] On another occasion Hillary received an unqualified endorsement from Inouye, who after looking at the field of possible presidential candidates said that he would "give you odds that on the Democratic stage, the person in the best position to be nominated is Hillary Clinton, because of her financial resources and organizational resources."

But, is there not a danger that the American electorate will choose Obama and not Hillary on November 4, 2008? No, because in the incremental principle of change in the history of American politics, it is always a white woman who gets elected following the election of white men into high political leadership. The most obvious example is Nancy Pelosi, the first woman Speaker of the U.S. House of Representatives. No less than 51 white men in 59 terms preceded her in 218 years of American history (*see* chapter 1 above).

A not-so-obvious example is the fact that 10 white women senators were popularly chosen prior to the first African American senator Edward Brooke of Massachusetts in 1967 (*see* Table 3.0).[49] This is really astonishing, considering African American men could vote as early as the 1860's following Abraham Lincoln's emancipation proclamation, whereas women could only vote starting in 1920!

Table 3.0 U.S. Women Senators from 1922 to 1967

Name	State	From	To	Party
Rebecca Latimer Felton	Georgia	1922	1922	Democrat
Hattie Wyatt Caraway	Arkansas	1931	1945	Democrat
Rose McConnell Long	Louisiana	1935	1937	Democrat
Dixie Bibb Graves	Alabama	19347	1938	Democrat
Gladys Pyle	South Dakota	1938	1939	Republican
Vera Cahalan Bushfield	South Dakota	1948	1948	Republican
Margaret Chase Smith	Maine	1949	1973	Republican
Eva Kelley Bowring	Nebraska	1954	1954	Republican
Hazel Hempel Abel	Nebraska	1954	1954	Republican
Maurine Brown Neuberger	Oregon	1960	1967	Democrat

There is one advantage which Gov. Bill Richardson (*D*, NM), has over Barack Obama in that the former who had a Mexican mother and a white American father ended up with a Western heroic first and last name. His American father who was working in Mexico City arranged for his pregnant Mexican wife to have their first born baby in Los Angeles, California, so that he will be a native-born American citizen. That simple move plus giving their son an American sounding first name to go along with his American last name are among the 2 most important reasons why Bill Richardson has come a long way politically.

Someone may say that there is nothing Obama could do about his family name, for he inherited it from his father. Of course, there was something he could have done, i.e. he could have his name legally changed in an American court. It is still a very strange coincidence that by changing one letter in Obama's last name we come up with the first name of the current number one enemy of the United States. If that were not bad enough, his middle name also happens to be Hussein, the last name of the former dictator of Iraq. For Obama to have dropped his middle name was the right decision. But he did not go far enough. He could have chosen a more American-sounding first name, especially as his mother is a Caucasian from Kansas. There was not a single presidential first name that ended with a–ck (*see* Table 3.1).

He could even have replaced Barack with Barry, the American nickname his Kansan mother gave him. He would have had an Americanized name with a western heroic meaning, i.e., a marksman. He missed out from using a slogan which could have been very meaningful: "Beat the Bull's Eye with Barry." Why not "Beat the Bull's Eye with Barack? No, because "Barack" does not mean marksmanship while Barry does!

Table 3.1 Presidential First Names in Alphabetical Order

1. Abraham Lincoln

2. Andrew Jackson

3. Andrew Johnson

4. Benjamin Harrison

5. Calvin Coolidge

6. Chester Arthur

7. Dwight D. Eisenhower

8. Franklin Pierce

9. Franklin D. Roosevelt

10. George H. W. Bush

11. George W. Bush

12. George Washington

13. Gerald Ford

14. Grover Cleveland

15. Harry S. Truman

16. Herbert Hoover

17. James Buchanan

18. James Garfield

19. James Madison

20. James Monroe

21. James Polk

22. Jimmy Carter

23. John Adams

24. John Quincy Adams

25. John F. Kennedy

26. John Tyler

27. Lyndon Johnson

28. Martin van Buren

29. Millard Fillmore

30. Richard Nixon

31. Ronald Reagan

32. Rutherford B. Hayes

33. Theodore Roosevelt

34. Thomas Jefferson

35. Ulysses S. Grant

36. Warren Harding

37. William J. Clinton

38. William Henry Harrison

39. William McKinley

40. William H. Taft

41. Woodrow Wilson

42. Zachary Taylor

In stark contrast with Obama's native Kenyan Swahili name, Barack, all the first names of American presidents are western heroic names: Nearly half of all presidential first names are religious—16 from the Bible and 4 from Christian Church History—for an over-all total of 20. Of the 16 biblical names, 13 were taken from the New Testament and 3 from the Old Testament. There were also 13 presidential first names in honor of western secular heroes, 5 associated with popular places, and finally 4 that describe positive personality (*see* Tables 3.2; 3.3; 3.4, & 3.5).

Table 3.2 Presidential First Names from the Bible and Christian Church History (20)

From the New Testament (13):

1. James (disciple of Jesus & a son of Zebedee) Madison

2. James Monroe

3. James Polk

4. James Buchanan

5. James Garfield

6. Jimmy (variation of James) Carter

7. John (disciple of Jesus & younger brother of James) Adams

8. John Q. Adams

9. John Tyler

10. John F. Kennedy

11. Andrew (disciple of Jesus & younger brother of Peter) Jackson

12. Andrew Johnson

13. Thomas (the doubting disciple of Jesus) Jefferson

From the Old Testament (3):

14. Abraham (the father of the Jewish people) Lincoln

15. Benjamin (the youngest of the 12 sons of Jacob) Harrison

16. Zachary (variation of Zechariah) Taylor

From Christian Church Saints (4):

17. Martin (after a Catholic saint or the Protestant Reformer Martin Luther) van Buren

18. Calvin (after the Protestant Reformer John Calvin) Coolidge

19. Theodore (early saint's name meaning God's gift) Roosevelt

20. Herbert (early saint's name meaning illustrious warrior) Hoover

---

Table 3.3 Presidential First Names Derived from Western Secular Heroes (13):

21. William (after William the Norman Conqueror of England) H. Harrison

22. William McKinley

23. William H. Taft

24. William (Norman Conqueror) Jefferson (a former U.S. president) Clinton

25. George (the Dragon-Slayer of England) Washington

26. George H. W. Bush

27. George W. Bush

28. Franklin (after "the First American" Benjamin Franklin[50]) Pierce

29. Franklin D. Roosevelt

30. Harry (variation of Henry, one of many kings of England) Truman

31. Richard (after Richard, also among many kings of England) Nixon

32. Ulysses (after the Greek hero Ulysses) S. Grant

33. Rutherford (in honor of King Ruther of Scotland) Hayes

Table 3.4 Presidential First Names Associated with Popular Places (5)

34. Millard (guardian of the mill) Fillmore

35. Warren (park warden) Harding

36. Chester (city of Chester, capital of Chesire, England) Arthur

37. Woodrow (from the lane in the woods) Wilson

38. Lyndon (linden tree hill) Johnson

Table 3.5 Presidential First Names that Describe Positive Personality (4):

39. Gerald (spear ruler) Ford

40. Ronald (ruler's counselor) Reagan

41. Grover (one who carves or engraves) Cleveland

42. Dwight (white or blond) Eisenhower

Hillary is definitely a western heroic name, unlike Barack (Obama). As Hillary's admirer, you would be delighted to have her name classified with one of the 4 types of presidential western heroic first names. Would you be pleasantly surprised, along with Hillary herself, to find out that her name can be classified with not just 1, or 2, or even 3, but all 4 types of western heroic names?

(1). It is the name of a *Christian Church hero*, for Hilary (the original form of Hillary) was the name of an early male saint and an early Catholic pope. St. Hilary of Poitiers, France (formerly Gaul) lived in c.315-367. His real Latin name was Hilarius (one "l"), but he was often referred to as Hillarius (double "l," a French variation?). Pope Hilarius was born in Sardinia and he served in 461-468 succeeding his famous mentor, Pope Leo I the Great.

(2). It is *the name of a secular hero*, Sir Edmund Hillary. He is a New Zealander who became famous as the first man who climbed Mt. Everest in 1953 (this famous New Zealander died early in 2008, as if to say that another Hillary, that is, Mrs. Clinton will take over!)

(3). It is *associated with a popular place,* since there is a "hill" (not to mention Mt. Everest, the highest hill in the world) as part of her name, and

(4). It is *a description of a positive personality,* for her name is derived from the Latin name "Hilarius" meaning hilarious or cheerful.

What could well be Hillary's theme slogan for "HillCorps," the official name of her campaign, is as follows: "It's Mt. Everest-Climbing Time with Hillary." It was inspired by Deborah Lopez, a Tex-Mex American who serves as a banker for Wells Fargo in Lubbock (again!), Texas. She made these comments over the telephone when this writer was following up a bank transaction: "You know climbing Mt. Everest is easier for women than becoming president of the United States. Many women had already physically climbed Mt. Everest, but no woman has yet become U.S. president." To date, there were in fact more than 2,000 men and women from at least 64 nations who had climbed Mt. Everest, the world's tallest mountain, measuring 29,029 feet.

Ms. Lopez's inspiring comments are not specially predicated on the claim of Bill Clinton in his best-selling book, *My Life,* that his wife, Mrs. Hillary Clinton, nee Hillary Rodham, was named after Sir Edmund Hillary of New Zealand for being the first man to have climbed earth's tallest mountain, Mt. Everest in 1953.[51] That could not be literally, but only symbolically true, for Hillary was born in 1947, or six years before Sir Edmund became internationally famous for his unprecedented conquest of Mt. Everest. "The beauty of this country is that America is a place where anyone, regardless of propriety, prominence or genetic makeup, can climb to the top of whatever metaphorical mountain they choose."[52]

Did Bill Clinton lie about the origin of Hillary's first name? No, because he was only repeating what Hillary herself claimed in person. Did Hillary Clinton lie? Neither, for she was just repeating what her parents told her.

Did Hillary Clinton's parents—Hugh Ellsworth Rodham and Dorothy Emma Howell Rodham—lie for telling their daughter that she was named after Sir Edmund Hillary? No, and if they did, it was not for a deceptive purpose. What happened was a matter of parental foresight as to their daughter's future destiny. Hillary's parents intentionally named their daughter after Hilary, the name of an early saint and a Catholic pope—both males—because they wanted her to grow up androgynously and be able to do what any man can do, as a woman!

They could have named her Hilary—like Hilary Swank one of our famous actresses or Hilary Duff one of our favorite female vocalists—which is the original English derivative of the Latin name Hilarius. But, they chose Hillary, derived from "Hillarius," the French modified version of the original Latin name. Was it mere coincidence that it was not a man with the family name Hilary (single "l") but rather a man with the family name Hillary (double "l") that climbed Mt. Everest 6 years after the birth of Hillary Clinton nee Rodham? No, it was not mere coincidence; it was a matter of destiny for Hillary Clinton!

It will not be Nancy Pelosi but Hillary who will have to pave the way for Obama to become U.S. president at least 8 years down the road. It will give him some time to be cured of his cigarette-smoking habit. He promised his wife, Michelle, to quit smoking again. He tried to quit once before, but he resumed the habit. Dick Armey, former Republican majority floor leader of the U.S. House of Representatives, cannot understand why Obama does not have enough determination to please his wife. "I was just thinking about my wife one day," he said, "and I realized that of all the things I could do on this Earth that would make her happy is to quit smoking."[53] And he did.

A promise to quit smoking with success this time around on the part of Obama is not good enough. This is one more reason why his presidential bid in 2008 is quite untimely. First, he must show that he has licked his bad smoking habit, and then run for president. Of the score of presidential hopefuls from both the Democratic and Republican Parties, none but Obama smokes.

The last time we had a daily smoker in the Oval Office was Lyndon Johnson in the 1960's. Both John F. Kennedy and Richard M. Nixon were once smokers, but successfully quit prior to going to the White House. Gerald Ford did only occasionally smoke a pipe. Ronald Reagan was not a smoker when he entered the White House. The most recent presidents were totally smoke-free: Carter, Clinton, and the Bushes. To elect cigarette-smoking Obama as president on November 4, 2008 therefore would be a complete backward step!

There is a real bad news for Obama for smoking: early in January 2007, a Harvard study concluded that certain tobacco manufacturers had increased the nicotine content of their product, for in the words of Sen. Ted Kennedy who promised to investigate, "they are addicted to addicting the young people of America."

There is a second bad news for Obama on his cigarette-smoking. In the week following the Harvard study released in January, 2007, it was reported that the best cure for tobacco addiction is by causing an injury to the head. Some tobacco smokers who had suffered accidents that involved injuries to their heads did not crave smoking after that.

There is a third bad news on cigarette-smoking for Obama. A government advisory panel named the Institute of Medicine came out with its initial report on May 25, 2007 proposing to Congress to give drastic powers to the FDA to regulate tobacco business as much as alcohol, such as:

(1) Requiring all insurers—including Medicare and Medicaid programs—to cover smoking-cessation programs.

(2) Licensing retailers that sell cigarettes, just as states issue licenses to sell alcohol.

(3) Raising cigarette taxes as much as $2 a pack.

(4) Banning smoking in all non-residential indoor areas. The report's authors say that "tobacco ... kills more Americans annually than AIDS, alcohol, cocaine, heroin, homicides, suicides, car accidents and fires combined.[54] *The New York Times* in its editorial on May 30, 2007 estimates that tobacco kills 440,000 smokers every year.[55] Almost half of the USA's 44.5 million adult smokers [21% of all adults] will die prematurely of a tobacco-related illness if they don't stop.

There is a fourth bad news about cigarette smoking for Obama. It is not only detrimental to his personal health; it is also hazardous to other people in society. There are about 126,000,000 Americans and about 22,000,000 children ages 3 to 11 exposed to secondhand smoke. And tobacco also kills 50,000 bystanders who have inhaled secondhand smoke every year! According to Richard H. Carmona, M.D., 17th U.S. Surgeon General (2002-06), "Prior to publication of 'the Health Consequences of Involuntary Exposure to Tobacco Smoke: A Report of the Surgeon General [my office],' many people didn't know that non-smokers exposed to second hand smoke increase their risk of developing heart disease by 25%-30% and lung cancer by 20%-30%. Secondhand smoke exposure is also a known cause of sudden infant death syndrome (SIDS), respiratory problems, ear infections and asthma attacks in infants and children. These [scientific] findings are of major public concern because nearly half of all non-smoking Americans is regularly exposed to secondhand smoke."[56]

There is a fifth bad news about cigarette smoking for Obama. Cigarette smoking is also a fire hazard! Not only is it the cause of the burning of million dollars worth of property; it also causes the death of some 700-900 peoples by fire every year, according to Jim Shannon, head of the National Fire Protection Association as reported in the *USA Today*.[57]

There is a sixth bad news for Obama about smoking even so-called "smokeless tobacco." "The American Cancer Society, in a study of 116,000 men published in February [2007] says, male smokers who gave up cigarettes for smokeless tobacco still had higher death rates from lung cancer, heart disease and strokes than men who quit all tobacco or never smoked." The *USA Today*has added its voice to the proposal that the FDA must be empowered by Congress to ban the so-called "smokeless tobacco" for it is not any less harmful as the original product. "Cheerios are regulated," it argues, "why not cigarettes?"[58]

There is a seventh bad news for Obama for smoking. According to a study of 7,000 people aged 55 and over in Holland, it was found that smokers are 50% more susceptible to developing dementia or Alzheimer's disease than non-smokers and those who quit smoking.[59]

Will Obama assure the American people that he would not be beholden to the powerful tobacco lobby? Will he appear before Ted Kennedy's senate committee to make his declaration? Will Obama promise to help Sen. Ted Kennedy pass the necessary legislation as recommended by the IOM? Will he add his voice to those who are clamoring for Hollywood to stop glamorizing the smoking of cigarettes by movie stars that easily influences young people, the number one source of new smokers?

No less than Martin Luther King, Jr., the number 1 leader of the civil rights movement, acknowledged the incremental principle that white women have a priority over African-American men when he delivered his speech, "I Have a Dream." [60] He said,

"I have a dream that ... little black boys and girls will be able to join hands with little white boys and white girls as sisters and brothers." If he meant for an African American man to follow a white man, he should have said, "I have a dream that little black boys will be able to join hands with little white boys as brothers and then little black girls will be able to join hands with little white girls as sisters." If the latter were Martin Luther King, Jr.'s message, then Senator Obama would be the logical immediate successor to President George W. Bush. But, since the real message of Dr. King was the former, therefore, Hillary Clinton (or any other white woman) will be the right successor to the incumbent President Bush.

No African American ever won the presidential nomination of a major political party. That has been the sad experience of the Rev. Jesse L. Jackson who tried twice to join the Democratic primary in 1984 and in 1988. In both cases, he lost the nomination: he only won 5 primaries in the first try and 11 primaries in the second. This is his conclusion about his over-all experience: "It wasn't uncommon for voters to come up to me in Iowa or New Hampshire and tell me they liked what I had to say, but that they weren't 'ready' for a black president.... I liken my campaigns to swimming upriver. It's possible to do it, but the undercurrents—often unseen—can drag you under. For Obama, the undercurrent will be more subtle, but it will be there."[61]

Should Obama aspire to be the vice-presidential candidate, if Hillary were the Democratic presidential nominee? No, Hillary as a presidential candidate will be better off to team up with a white male candidate. For her to team up with a minority person like herself, a woman, or a racial minority sends the wrong message of being a rebellious leader. No, far from being a disgruntled leader Hillary, like Nancy Pelosi, desires to represent the mainstream and lead the entire people of our country and not just women or other racial minority.

What will prevent the vice-president of Hillary from running to succeed Hillary once she is elected president? Nothing will. Obama must just have to rack up good records starting now, as U.S. Senator to show to the American electorate that he would be the best presidential successor to Hillary in 2016. Had Obama listened to the good advice of Senator Daniel Inouye (D, HI), and patiently waited for Hillary's presidential term or terms to end, he would have been in her good graces, and would help him when his turn to run for president will come after her. And after 8 years, Obama would only have become 55 years old, and even after 16 years, he would have become only 63 well within the age range of all American presidents.

Obama's political future would have been assured, for hopefully after Hillary's victory in 2008 with his help, he could rely on the power and influence of 2 former U.S. presidents to better prepare him as their successor! In a Hillary Clinton administration, he could have asked to be appointed to the office of the Secretary of State or to any other high position that suits him.

Obama's innate sense of propriety, if not outright gratitude, for what the Clintons did for him as a neophyte in Washington D.C. should have directed him in the direction of further learning from the mentorship that the Clintons were beginning to provide. "When Obama was running for the Senate in 2004, Mrs. Clinton once sat on the tarmac waiting out a lightning storm to fly to Chicago for a fund-raiser on his behalf. After he arrived in Washington in 2005, he studied her first year in office and worked to keep a similarly studious and low profile. After Hurricane Katrina, he [was invited and] joined Mrs. Clinton and former President Bill Clinton as they visited storm evacuees in Houston."[62]

But, instead, he is now trying to run prematurely against Hillary. This kind of wrong choice of the direction of his political career by itself is enough reason for him *not* to deserve the presidency. Because of his impatience, his almost certain defeat on November 4, 2008's presidential election could ruin his political future irreparably!

Admirers often compare Obama to John Kennedy. It must be admitted that outwardly, Obama may be positively compared to Kennedy:

(1). Obama is as eloquent as Kennedy. Eloquence is a method of speaking. Anyone can learn how to speak eloquently. More important than how to speak is what to speak. In this Kennedy has more substance and experience, so does Hillary, to speak eloquently about.

(2). Obama is a writer like Kennedy. Kennedy, however, was a Pulitzer Prize winning author; while Obama is not.

(3). Obama is an alumnus of Harvard University as was Kennedy.

(4). Obama's wife, Michelle Robinson is as attractive as Kennedy's wife, Jacqueline Bouvier.

(5). Obama has 2 lovely children, 2 daughters, Malia and Natasha; Kennedy had also 2 lovely children, a boy, John Jr. and a girl, Caroline. Jacqueline Kennedy was as much a working mom with 2 young children, but she was never heard to complain about the combination of her roles. Michelle Obama complained to *the Los Angeles Times* about the fact that "When people told me, 'You can do it all. Just stay the course, get your education, and you can raise a child, stay thin, be in shape, love your man, look good and raise healthy children.' That was a lie."[63]

What Mrs. Obama said is not entirely true. She acknowledged that she worked for the University of Chicago Medical Center that accommodated her being a multi-task worker even to the extent of allowing her to take one of her young children, Shasha, to her job interview, and still managed to get the job. Furthermore, she said that she got promoted to a managerial position in the same medical center she started to work for. She also admitted that when her husband, Barack Obama declared his intention to run for U.S. President that she was able to cut back on her hours at the center, so that she could help her husband campaign. She even said that she was satisfied with her decisions. "God help those who don't feel the same way about their own [choices]. I know who I am," she said. "I'm a grown up now. Maybe if I were 20 going through this, it would be hard. But these discussions aren't about me. I know why I made my choices. I know what I need to sustain myself, and Barack is the same way."[64]

"... On the campaign trail," the *Los Angeles Times* went on, "[Michelle Obama] has carved out a niche connecting with women over shared daily schedules: to get the kids up, their hair brushed and out the door; to have a job and a family and not go crazy; *to hope for better for their daughters when they grow up* (emphasis supplied)."[65]

If Mrs. Obama meant what she wished for her daughters, then she should discourage her husband from running for president to oppose Hillary. It is not too late for Barack Obama to withdraw. She must realize that if her husband beats Hillary in this coming election, it will not only be a personal defeat for the latter, but it will also be a terrible setback for—in her own words—"the better future of her daughters."

The negative comparisons are much more significant, for they definitely prove that Barack Obama does not possess the qualities of an American president that John F. Kennedy did:

(1) Kennedy did not have to make his wife Jacqueline give up her career just to help him campaign for the presidency. Obama has not only ruined his own political future by being too impatient for wanting to run this time (when he could have waited up to 16 years and will still be young enough to run for president), but he has also dragged down his wife, Michele, with him.

The strangest thing about this is that Michelle Obama is seemingly of the idea that her chosen path is superior to others, including that of her husband's rival, Hillary Clinton. She boasted that "our view is that if you can't run your own house, you certainly can't run the White House."[66]

Michelle Obama's way is not a superior lifestyle that can be commended because she has retreated to the old style of a woman totally depending on her husband for support. She had given up 6 directorships in corporations and scaled down her former full-time job as Vice-President of Community and External Affairs of the University of Chicago Hospitals. She had to interrupt her promising multi-faceted careers and be jobless just so that she can campaign for her husband for U.S. president too prematurely. She should have resigned from her jobs when her husband shall have already become the official Democratic presidential nominee. That is too much of a reckless gamble. If he wins the Democratic presidential nomination, that will be well and good. But, if he does not (his chance is rather quite slim) both of them will be begging for jobs after the Democratic national convention in summer 2008. You would not recommend this as a model for your daughter or your daughter's daughters to follow, would you?

Anyone can be critical about Bill Clinton on something, but nobody can fault him for totally subordinating his wife Hillary's future just so that she could help him succeed in his chosen career. If Bill did not stand by his woman in the best possible way, we would not have at the present time an exciting presidential candidacy of his wife, Hillary, who most likely will be the first woman president of our country! The Clinton model is a win-win situation and therefore very highly commendable not only to your daughter or children's daughters, but also to your son and your children's sons to emulate and pass on to future generations.

(2) Kennedy was at the end of his first term as a U.S. senator after having served for 3 successive terms as a U.S. Representative from Massachusetts when he ran for president, whereas Obama has barely completed 2 years of his first 6-year term as senator from Illinois.[67]

As we saw previously (chapter 2 above), an African-American CNN correspondent Joe Johns said that John Edwards having had just completed his first term as U.S. Senator was too "green" to be John Kerry's Democratic vice-presidential running mate in 2004. If this yardstick were applied to Barack Obama, who has not even completed half of his first term as a U.S. senator, then he is not just ordinary green but really "green green."

How could such "greenness" possibly do any harm? It does, and it will when Obama becomes president. For example, in the Democratic presidential debate on CNN-YouTube in Charleston, SC on July 23, 2007, Hillary called Obama's suggestion that as president he would personally meet with the head-of-states of Iran, Syria, North Korea, Cuba, and Venezuela rather "irresponsible and naive." Hillary said that she would not meet with such leaders without preconditions because they might use such commitment on the part of our country's leader "for propaganda purposes." She said she would not rule out a face-to-face meeting, but she would ascertain what any state leader's intentions are first by sending one of our diplomatic representatives.

In early August 2007, no doubt as a counter-move against Hillary's comment that Obama was "irresponsible and naïve" on his suggestion at the debate the week before, decided to announce hypothetically that if President Pervez Musharraf of Pakistan did not do anything to stop the sympathizers of Al Qaeda from operating in the tribal zones of his country that Obama as president, will send American troops there to take them out. His remarks did not only offend the intended target, but also the friendly government of Pakistan, which used to strongly support the Talibans but stopped that support following 9/11 and switched sides with the United States.

"It's a very irresponsible statement, that's all I can say," remarked [Pakistan's] Foreign Minister Khusheed Kasuri practically repeating Hillary's own words of criticism to the *AP Television News.* "As the election campaign in America is heating up, we would not like American candidates to fight their elections ... at our expense."[68]

There is nothing worse than a bull-headed one-sided policy in foreign affairs that George Bush, along with McCain, is pursuing in Iraq than a confused alternative foreign policy presented by Obama, if and when hypothetical events happen, which may not. His announced policy regarding Pakistan is too hawkish as to amount to trying to out-Bush (ambush?) Bush. His policy announced during the CNN-YouTube debate on July 23, 2007 was too dovish, i.e. to meet with the presidents of anti-U.S. nations without pre-conditions. This confused Obama foreign policy was pointed out by Mitt Romney during the Republican presidential debates in Des Moines, IA on August 5, 2007: "... In one week, he went from saying he's going to sit down, you know, for tea, with our enemies, but then he is going to bomb our allies," Romney said. "He's gone from Jane Fonda to Dr. Strangelove in one week."[69]

To add more to the confusion, sometime earlier, Obama sounded like John F. Kennedy when he said about Darfur, Central Africa that the United Nations must police it (which incidentally the U.N. had subsequently done!). Which only goes to show that if you have what amounts to a shotgun hit-or-miss approach to foreign policy, even if contradictory to one another, that sooner or later, you can accidentally strike the right target with one of the straying bullets! But, which one is the true Obama foreign policy? Perhaps, because he is "too green," he does not even know that he is contradicting himself. You might have noted that in every case, Obama delivered his messages eloquently. But, because his messages have contradictory meanings, nobody will know which one to follow!

On the subject of whether to use or not to use nuclear weapons against suspected strongholds of Al Qaeda, Hillary had to remind Obama in a subsequent debate before the AFL-CIO in Chicago, "you should not always say *everything* you think if you're running for president, because it has consequences across the world (emphasis supplied)."[70] Obama's utterances were made by him as one of the candidates for president of our country, and he had done considerable damage to our foreign relations. You can just imagine how much more damage he can cause when he becomes U.S. president!

Much of what Obama has been doing in his presidential campaign is making a lot of promises about what changes he plans to make in Washington, D.C., once he is elected president. How can we be sure that he will fulfill even one promise, since he has no national track record to back up any of his promises? Most likely, he will not keep his promise. In spite of his almost total lack of national—not to say executive—experience, and his just serving the beginning of his first term in the U.S. Senate, he has already shown a lack of party discipline (*See* number 3 immediately following).

(3) Kennedy was always a loyal Democrat throughout all his years of service; Obama must be disqualified from running under the Democratic Party banner because he had not been totally loyal to it when he successfully supported the re-election bid of an independent party senatorial candidate, Joseph Lieberman, at the expense of a fellow-Democrat (Hillary supported the latter). Obama has only a 2-year record in the U.S. Senate but it is more than enough to show that he is inconsistent, for he claims to be against the Iraq War from the beginning throughout his presidential campaign so far, and yet he supported the successful senatorial re-election bid of Connecticut's Joseph Lieberman one of the strongest backers of Bush's Iraq war! This is one of the major reasons why Obama despite all his vaunted eloquence could not convince Rev. Al Sharpton to endorse him (*see* below in this same chapter).

Another evidence of Obama's disloyalty to the Democratic Party is that he cannot see anything good that Bill Clinton did for 8 years! If Bill did not do any-thing good for the country why was he re-elected? The last time someone ran for president ignoring the achievements of Bill Clinton resulted in that someone los-ing to the incumbent George W. Bush. Yes, that someone was Al Gore. Is there any doubt in anybody's mind that Obama's disloyalty to such a good Democratic record as Bill Clinton's will not end up with the same disastrous result as Gore's?

Hillary, according to the *U.S. News & World Report*, "is the rare candidate who is *not* (sic.) playing the Outsider card. In fact, she's actually out there defending the expediency of knowing how to play the Inside game. That's her story and she is sticking to it."[71] Hillary is the first presidential candidate who is proudly running on Bill Clinton's previous successful Democratic record as pres-ident—with an end-of-presidency approval rating of 65%, the highest since the end of the Dwight Eisenhower administration in the 1950's—and should there-fore result in victory for her come November 4, 2008!

(4) Kennedy who had an executive experience as a naval officer during the Second World War never said that serving our country in the armed forces is a "waste"; Obama who did not serve in an executive or even at the lowest rank in any branch of the armed forces said that going to war in Iraq is a "waste of American lives."

(5) Kennedy was 1 of 2 youngest presidents when he was elected at the age of 43, whereas Obama is not as young at the age of 47.

(6) Kennedy had a western religious hero's first name, John, and an American consonant-sounding last name; Obama has neither. Kennedy had an American nickname, Jack that he was proud to bear; Barack refused to use his American nickname Barry that his Kansan white mother gave him. Otherwise, instead of being an unknown to begin with, he would have been in the company of well-known and beloved western heroic people, such as African American Barry Bonds (the baseball batting champion of all time), Barry Manilow (popular international singer), and Dave Barry (famous author and humorist). Kennedy was proud to bear his mother's family name as his second name "Fitzgerald" signing his name at least with a middle initial, John F. Kennedy; Obama dropped his second name although he is a junior and Barack Hussein Obama, Sr. was his father's name.

(7) Kennedy's parents belonged to the Catholic religion, a sister of Protestant denominations of which 97 ½ % of all presidents' parents were members; the parents of Obama were atheist on the mother's side and Moslem on the father's side, neither of which was the religion of a parent of any American president ever!

(8) Also, John Kennedy's parents were among 97 ½ % of all presidential parents who were married for life (the only exception being Gerald Ford's parents who were divorced once) thus providing real stability in the life of their children; Obama's parents would be the first presidential parents, if he wins, who were divorced more than once (this may partly explain Obama's lack of discipline having been raised by white grandparents who might have "spoiled" him and allowed him to do whatever he wanted as a child as well as the explanation for his anxiety about wanting to become president at an inopportune time, ignoring the advice of those who know better about his almost total lack of experience in any field of government). A major reason why Obama is not ready to become U.S. president is that he carries so much extra family baggage that no other previous American president had to, or any other present presidential aspirant, like Hillary, has to.

(9) Kennedy never inhaled marijuana or cocaine; Obama inhaled marijuana and cocaine "in his youth," he says. Does his admission of these, along with his

on-going cigarette-smoking make these habits any less objectionable, and qualify him better to serve as U.S. president?

(10) Kennedy was not involved with questionable characters, but Obama was involved with Antoin "Tony" Rezko who was indicted for influence peddling. Two investigative reporters of the *Chicago Tribune*, Ray Gibson and David Jackson wrote that "the Obamas and the Rezkos bought property in a fashionable [Chicago] South Side neighborhood next to each other on the same day, from the same lot, and the Obamas came out the winners. Obama bought his home at a $300,000 discount. Rezko bought the adjoining lot from the same sellers at full price. One got a juicy bargain. The other overpaid." [72]

When Obama tried to appear innocent, making it look like he did not know Rezko well, and that he was returning or giving to charity the contributions to his presidential campaign of Rezko and his associates, it was the turn of 2 investigative reporters of the *Chicago Sun-Times*, Chris Fusco and Tim Novak who exposed "the truth" that Obama lied:

"During his 12 years in politics, Sen. Barack Obama has received nearly three times more campaign cash from indicted businessman Tony Rezko and his associates than he has publicly acknowledged.... Obama has collected at least $168,308 from Rezko and his circle. Obama has also taken in an unknown amount of money from people who attended fund-raising events hosted by Rezko since the mid-1990s. But 7 months ago, Obama told the *Sun-Times* his 'best estimate' was that Rezko raised 'between $50,000 and $60,000' during Obama's political career."[73]

Compare further the foregoing stories about Obama that was the result of just a couple of years of investigation that expose his pretense at "lecturing Africans and Republicans about corruption, while privately dancing with Tony Rezko" with the investigative methods of the authors of the book *Her Way*, Jeff Gerth and Don von Natta, who spent more 15 years trying "to discover the [awful?] truth" about Bill and Hillary Clinton and they still came up empty!

Obama's Rezko connection cannot be analogous to Hillary's dealing with Norman Hsu, who recruited 260 donors to give about $850,000 to her campaign for 2 reasons:

(1) She did not knowingly cooperate with Mr. Hsu's wrongdoing, and

(2) She refunded all the money where they came from once she had known about their tainted sources. Should any of the donors be able to show that the source of their initial contribution is from their own private bank account rather than from funds funneled by Mr. Hsu, then they may safely remit back their

refund, along with any new contribution they wish to give, to support Hillary's presidential run.

Just like Al Gore in 2000, Obama does not have a firm home-base. He represents Illinois in the U.S. Senate, but Hillary has a better claim on Illinois, for that is where she was born, grew up, and where her parents and relatives continue to live and participate in business and civic affairs. It is doubtful if Kansas where Obama's mother came from or Hawaii where he grew up will rally behind him as his 2 alternatives home-bases. The people of Kansas who had just elected a woman governor in Kathleen Sibelius, one of *Time Magazine's* top 5 governors in 2005, are no doubt equally eager to have another woman in the highest office of our land, Hillary. Hawaiians, who are mostly Pacific Islanders and Asian Americans, cannot possibly fully identify with African American Obama. Besides, Hawaii's Democratic senator Inouye is strongly opposed to Obama's presidential candidacy, as being "too premature" (*see* the beginning of this chapter 3).

Talk of having multiple bad luck, or should we say ancestral sabotage? Obama on his mother's side had ancestors who were slave-owners. Is this a case of the biblical warning that "the sins of the fathers being visited upon their children and children's children for many generations?" If so, in spite of his claim that he has a share in the legacy of Martin Luther King, Jr. and the other civil rights leaders from the 1960's, he cannot be a recipient of it because his father, though black was never a slave. His claim to a civil rights inheritance should be replaced with a deep apology for his slave-owning white ancestors along the lines of a resolution passed by the Virginia state legislature in February, 2007, that "present-day Virginians deeply regret a part of their history in which some white ancestors were slave-owners and that the state resisted the freedom of slaves till it lost the [American] Civil War to be forced to do it."

Obama declared his candidacy in Illinois on February 10, 2007 "the same day as the State of the Black Union, an annual event organized by Tavis Smiley to gather prominent African Americans. It drew 10,000 people and would have been a perfect venue" [for him, but he snubbed it].

New York's Rev. Al Sharpton who ran for president in 2004 said: "We cannot put our people's aspirations on hold for anybody's career, black or white," he said. "Just because you are our color doesn't make you our kind."[74] Sharpton was also angered by Obama's lack of consistency in saying that he was against Bush's Iraq war from the beginning, but he went on to support the successful re-election in 2006 of Connecticut Sen. Joe Liebermann, a strong Iraq-war backer!

Democratic African American Rep. Charles Rangel from Harlem, New York, told of a story about his having a problem remembering the name of a male presidential candidate. When the person concerned heard about it, he personally approached Rangel and said: "I heard you over the air say that if your life depended on it, you didn't know the name of the guy that was running against Hillary Clinton," Rangel recalled. "He says, 'Well, it's me'." A few days later, Rangel admitted genially that he still can't remember the candidate's name. "It ends with a vowel," he offered.

"Sen. Hillary Clinton (*D*, NY), presented the Founder's Award to TV maven Oprah Winfrey at the 39th annual International Emmy Awards in New York. In accepting her award … Winfrey drew loud applause when she said to Clinton: 'I hope you do us the privilege of running for office'," reported the *Daily Variety*.[75] Winfrey was, of course, alluding to Clinton's seeking the Democratic presidential nomination in 2008.

But Oprah, for reasons of her own, decided to back Obama in the primary phase of the election does not change the fact that she was one of those who encouraged Hillary to run for president in the first place. Hopefully, when the primary season would have been over, and Hillary will be left as the sole presidential nominee of the Democratic Party, Oprah will be most welcome back!

Obama talked of asking Oprah to go to South Carolina to campaign for him, too. The fund-raising in her home in California was probably the best that Oprah could do for him. But, for her to campaign for Obama is not logical. It will be completely a waste of time, money, and energy. The appeal of Oprah in her highly rated show is to white Americans, not to African Americans. Granted that she will be able to energize the African Americans of South Carolina, the white Americans outnumber them there by a huge number. As residents of a red-leaning state, most of the South Carolinians will very likely vote Republican in the presidential election any way.

For Hillary to campaign among African Americans in South Carolina would make more sense, because the African American vote is only a component of her entire appeal. As a white candidate, she can appeal to the majority white South Carolinians. As a woman, she can appeal to the women voters who outnumber men. And as a red-leaning state, Hillary can point to her 20-year achievements as a resident worker, public servant, and former First Lady of a sister southern state of Arkansas. A similar approach will work well for Hillary throughout the rest of Dixieland.

Hillary who enlisted both basketball star "Magic" Johnson, record producer Quincy Jones, Motown founder Berry Gordy and music industry executive Clarence Avant to co-host a fundraiser for her in Hollywood, CA in mid-September 2007 made more sense. The endorsement of these big guns in the African American entertainment industry will help keep most of the African American voters who mostly supported Bill Clinton for president in the 1990's.

Nothing is more telling about the unacceptability of Obama as a presidential candidate in that the group with which he is most identified with, African Americans, prefer Hillary Clinton by a margin of 40 points, as per a *Washington Post-ABC* poll published in the *Time Magazine* in mid-February 2007.[76] She is just continuing the positive political record among African Americans that her husband, Bill, had established during his 2-term presidency, to the point that Nobel and Pulitzer Prize-winning author Toni Morrison jokingly called him, "the nation's first black president."[77]

"Hillary Has a Lock on the Nomination of the Democratic Party"

Dick Morris and Eileen McGann's opinion expressed in *Condi vs. Hillary* that "Hillary has a lock on the nomination of the Democratic Party" must be completely correct considering they are Republicans who are not expected to favor her. Before leaving office in August 2007, another Republican Karl Rove, the right hand man of incumbent President George W. Bush, also grudgingly predicted that Hillary will definitely be the nominee of the Democratic Party.[78]

That is the same conclusion that we have arrived at. There is a very strong trend that American voters are now willing to depart from following the historical pattern number 1 of always voting for a white male presidential candidate. Mrs. Elizabeth Edwards complained as early as mid-August that her husband John does not seem to be able to attract people as much as Hillary or Obama. "What can John do?" she asked rhetorically. "[He] cannot be black or female."

The answer to Elizabeth's question is quite simple: John's *timing* in running for president this *time* around is *untimely*! Her husband represents the white male presidential candidate that the American voters elected at least 42 different times in the last 220 years. All of a sudden, in this presidential election, the same American voters have expressed in poll after poll that they prefer a female and an African American president to a white male! The right order of their preference is: female first before an African American male.

Obama is trying to show that American voters are now ready to elect an African American presidential candidate like himself. Granting but not admitting that Americans are ready to vote for an African American; we have demonstrated in many ways that Obama is not ready to become America's president. Even if he were, we have also proved by clear historical examples that the next incremental step after departing from the pattern of always voting for a white male presidential candidate, is to vote for a white female one.

Over-all, according to a *CBS News* poll, putting to rest the issue of electivity or non-electivity of Hillary completely to rest, is the fact that she received the highest favorable rating among all declared presidential candidates in this 2008 federal election, that is, no less than "43% of Americans have a favorable opinion" of her.

If the gender gap were to be taken into account, Hillary would benefit even more. The gender gap should greatly favor her presidential candidacy, taking into account the fact that there are at least 10 million women more than men voters as of the 2004 election. That will be a major factor in favor of Hillary during the federal election on November 4, 2008 when she will have been the Democratic presidential nominee against her male Republican presidential opponent and perhaps even another male independent candidate.

Surprisingly, it appears that this gender gap is also going to be very helpful to her during the nomination process to choose the Democratic presidential candidate vis-à-vis her 2 closest rivals: Barack Obama and John Edwards. In a *Washington Post-ABC News* poll taken on June 1, 2007, Hillary led Obama by more than 2 to 1 margin among women voters. The women favored her 51% to Obama's 24% and Edwards's 11%. Hillary's lead among men is a slim 1%, i.e. 32% to Obama's 31%, but her lead over Obama among women is 27%. Edwards's percentage of votes from men was not recorded (*see* Table 3.6).[79]

Table 3.6 Washington Post-ABC *Poll by Gender among Top Democrats on June 1, 2007*

Support among Women	*Percentage Points*
Hillary Clinton	51%
Barack Obama	24%
John Edwards	11%
Support among Men	
Hillary Clinton	32%

| Barack Obama | 31% |
| John Edwards | (Not available) |

In a *USA Today/Gallup* poll of Democrats and Democratic-leaning independents during the first weekend of August, 2007, Hillary as expected, significantly
widened her lead over Sen. Barack Obama for the Democratic presidential nomination. "The survey ... puts Clinton at 48%—up 8 percentage points from three
weeks [before]—and Obama at 26% down 2 points. Among Democrats and
independents who lean Democratic, former North Carolina senator John
Edwards is at 12%.

"The 22-point gap between the two leaders is nearly double the margin found
in the July 12-15 [2007] poll. 'People are seeing her as the one ready to be president,' says Mark Penn, Clinton's chief strategist, a perception he says, was 'accel-
erated' by the recent debate."[80] Not just in 1, but in all 4 different aspects of
foreign policy, Hillary leads Obama by very wide margins (*see* Table 3.7).

**Table 3.7 August 2007 USA Today/Gallup *Poll on Who Can Better
Handle US Foreign Policy***

	Hillary	*Obama*
1. International terrorism	60%	33%
2. Relations to nations unfriendly to the USA	60%	35%
3. The war in Iraq	56%	36%
4. The role of commander-in-chief the military	56%	36%

A *CBS News* poll of 1,072 registered voters from Aug. 8-12 [2007] "shows
that voters perceive Mrs. Clinton as being more qualified than Mr. Obama, and
it says that both people who plan to vote in a Democratic primary or caucus ... as
well as voters over all believe she has a much better chance of becoming president.... Most strikingly, 80% of Democrats say Mrs. Clinton has 'the right kind
of experience to be a good president,' while 41% say that of Mr. Obama. Of all
voters, 59% say she has such experience, twice as many as believe Mr. Obama has

it.... Now, 76% of Democrats and 62% of voters over all say she could win the presidency if she wins her party's nomination."[81]

"Obama Campaign Retreats in the Face of Gaffes" is the title of *American Thinker* blog dated August 19, 2007 with this observation: "In what appears to be tacit acknowledgement of recent embarrassing blunders, Barack Obama will be cutting back on his appearances in candidate forums. When Obama has been asked to *think on his feet* about such weighty issues as meeting with foreign despot enemies in his first year as president and invading our ally Pakistan, the results have not been pretty. And Obama has fallen sharply in the polls, to the benefit of Hillary Clinton (emphasis supplied)"[82]

It is not only what Obama is doing wrong that he is so far behind. It has even more to do with what Hillary is doing right that she is so far ahead. Hillary is the prohibitive favorite to win the 2008 Democratic nomination for president. Her dominance is not surprising, as she starts with several advantages:

- *"Name Recognition.* Having been at the center of national attention for over 14 years, Clinton has very high name recognition.

- *Money & Organization.* Clinton has the campaign infrastructure to run an effective race. Clinton has also assembled a team of top campaign professionals, who have been plotting strategy for months.

- *Party network.* She is in high demand as a speaker at Democratic functions across the country, giving her an opportunity to establish personal relationships and cement friendships.

- *'True believers.'* Clinton benefits from the strong emotional support of many Democrats."[83]

In these very early stages of the Democratic primary campaign, she has formed a nation-wide organization appropriately called "HillCorps," an army of volunteers that has branches in every state that call themselves "Hill-Stars." According to Averill "Ace" Smith, Hillary's California campaign womanager, the first target of the "HillCorps" is California for the simple reason that "as many as half of the state's 6.7 million registered Democrats could be absentee voters" who will start casting their votes on January 7, 2008. "We have a 29-day election that starts before the current Jan. 14 schedule for the Iowa caucus and the Jan 22 New Hampshire primary," Smith said (*see* Table 3.8). It calls for unprecedented organization and innovation in California to make sure that those who are absentee voters send their ballots in, and those who are not to be motivated to go to the polls, said Clinton senior adviser Ann Lewis. For the first serious female presidential candidate, Lewis added, "the power of the networks, the growth of social networks, will be the strength of this campaign."[84]

Table 3.8 Shuffling the Presidential Primaries

A look at the political calendar of primaries and caucuses to choose convention delegates for 2008, as it stands [on August 27, 2007]. Because South Carolina Republicans have moved up their primary to Jan. 19, Iowa and New Hampshire are likely to move up their expected dates.

Some other states haven't set dates or are considering changes. Florida's plan for a January 29 primary has led the Democratic Party to threaten to strip that state of its convention delegates.

To be	IOWA caucuses are set for Jan. 14, but by state law must be eight days before
Set	voting elsewhere which would put them on Jan. 4, or earlier.
To be	NEW HAMPSHIRE primary was expected to be Jan. 22, but by state law it must
Set	be seven days before any other primary, putting it on Jan 12 or earlier.
Jan. 19	NEVADA caucuses, SOUTH CAROLINA Republican primary
Jan. 22	WYOMING Republican conventions
Jan. 29	FLORIDA primary, SOUTH CAROLINA Democratic primary
Feb. 1-3	MAINE Republican caucuses

Feb. 5	ALABAMA primary, ALASKA caucuses, ARIZONA primary, ARKANSAS primary, CALIFORNIA primary, COLORADO Democratic caucuses, CONNECTICUT primary, DELAWARE primary, GEORGIA primary, IDAHO Democratic caucuses, ILLINOIS primary, KANSAS Democratic convention, MICHIGAN Republican primary, MISSOURI primary, NEW JERSEY primary, NEW MEXICO Democratic primary, NEW YORK primary, NORTH DAKOTA caucuses, OKLAHOMA primary, TENNESSEE primary, UTAH primary, WEST VIRGINIA Republican convention
Feb. 9	LOUISIANA primary, MICHIGAN Democratic primary, NEBRASKA Democratic caucuses, WASHINGTON caucuses
Feb. 10	MAINE Democratic caucuses
Feb. 12	DISTRICT OF COLUMBIA caucuses, MARYLAND primary, VIRGINIA primary
Feb. 19	WISCONSIN primary, HAWAII Democratic caucuses, WASHINGTON primary*
March 4	MASSACHUSETTS primary, OHIO primary, RHODE ISLAND primary, TEXAS primary, VERMONT primary
March 8	ARKANSAS Democratic convention, WYOMING Democratic caucuses
March 11	MISSISSIPPI primary
March 13-15	ALASKA Republican convention
April 3-6	NORTH DAKOTA conventions
April 22	PENNSYLVANIA primary
May 6	INDIANA primary, NORTH CAROLINA primary
May 13	WEST VIRGINIA primary
May 20	KENTUCKY primary, OREGON primary
May 27	IDAHO primary*
June 3	MONTANA primary, NEW MEXICO Republican primary, SOUTH DAKOTA Primary

Aug. 25-28   Democratic National Convention

Sept. 1-4   Republican National Convention

Nov. 4   Election Day

*   Washington and Idaho decisions are not binding on the Democratic Party.

There was a time, the campaign staff of Hillary, recommended that she bypass the Iowa caucus because John Edwards had been to Iowa many times, that is, for at least 4 years during the time he ran as John Kerry's vice-presidential running mate and 3 years more in the current presidential campaign. Hillary decided to go against her staff's advice, and started her first campaign in Iowa. She, of course, brought her not-so-secret weapon, Bill, to introduce her everywhere she spoke, making sure that he did not upstage her main messages. The combination is quite potent, so that what Hillary could do in Iowa as a testing ground, she could very well do in any other state, and thus, throughout the country. She outdid what Edwards did in Iowa in 7 years with just a few visits! She is now at least tied head-to-head in the lead with Edwards in Iowa voters' preference, or even slightly ahead! Her extraordinary performance in so short a time has relegated Obama in Iowa to a distant third.

Both Rudy Giuliani and Hillary Clinton both hold double-digit leads in at least ¼ of the "Super Duper Tuesday" states that will hold primaries on February 5, 2008 and help determine each party's nominee, as per the *New York Post*.

"Hillary Is Pulling Away from Field" is the headline of *Democratic Underground.Com* on September 15, 2007. "Polls, polls, and more polls over the last few days, *and they uniformly paint a bright picture for Sen. Clinton* and a dim picture for Obama/Edwards/rest of the candidates (emphasis supplied).

CNN—national primary—Clinton 46%, Obama 23%, Edwards 16%. *CBS/NYT*—roughly the same numbers. Add the new *WashPost/ABC* poll to the list: Clinton leads Obama, 41-27. The *LA Times* is out with new polls in the early three states (IA, NH, SC) which show Clinton climbing. 'If Hillary can pull out a win in Iowa, it's over for the rest of them. If she finishes second but wins NH and SC, it's over for the rest of them too. It's hard to envision a scenario in which she loses this nomination'."[85]

4

Forty-One Presidents' Surnames Have Consonant-Sound Endings

◆

Mrs. Clinton Will Most Likely Be the 20th Presidential Last Name Ending in a Vowel+n; Like Obama's Consonant+a, Giuliani's Consonant+i Ending = Zero

Many Americans whose ancestors crossed the Atlantic Ocean to immigrate to America have unpleasant recollection about the eastern port of entry, Ellis Island which opened for business in 1890 during the presidency of Benjamin Harrison. Their ancestors told them that they were practically forced to change their original names into what the immigration officials there thought sounded more American. They—both immigrants and their descendants—might have had a sigh of relief when Ellis Island was finally closed for business in 1954 during the presidential administration of Dwight D. Eisenhower.

According to Marian Smith, INS historian, such a literal interpretation is more likely fiction. She urges us to consider another and more plausible "interpretation of 'Ellis Island.'

That immigrant is remembering his initial confrontation with American culture. Ellis Island was not only immigrant processing, it was finding one's way around the city, learning to speak English, getting one's first job or apartment, going to school, and adjusting one's name to a new spelling or pronunciation. All these experiences, for the first few years, were the 'Ellis Island experience'. When recalling their immigration decades before, many immigrants referred to the entire experience as 'Ellis Island'."[86]

However, there might be a few Americans who have second thoughts about that closure of Ellis Island as a port of entry. They could include politicians who may regret that their not-so-Americanized last names are now a real liability when running for office, especially the highest governmental position of president of our country. Take Rudy Giuliani, although he had been a former mayor of New York City, yet his not-so-Americanized last name does not show that his ancestors had an "Ellis Island" experience, literal or composite.

But, no U.S. president had ever been elected who did not have an Americanized last name. What exactly is an Americanized last name? Judging from the names of all 42 U.S. presidents elected by our people, an Americanized last name must be either one of two types:

(1) It must end with a consonant letter, and

(2) If it ends in a vowel, it must be the silent vowel letter "e."

There are 41 presidential last names with consonant-sound endings including three that end with the silent letter–e: Pierce, Coolidge, and Fillmore. Only one presidential last name ends with a vowel sound-o because the last letter–e is also silent: Monroe. Apart from the final "o" sound in Monroe, therefore, all Americanized last names of presidents have consonant ending sounds (*see* Table 4.0 & 4.1).

Table 4.0 Presidential Last Names with Consonant-Sound Endings (41)

Presidential Family Names Ending in Consonant Letters (38)

1. Garfield, James

2. Cleveland, Grover

3. Ford, Gerald

4. Harding, Warren

5. Bush, George H. W.

6. Bush, George W.

7. Polk, James

8. Reagan, Ronald

9. Truman, Harry

10. Buchanan, James

11. Van Buren, Martin

12. Lincoln, Abraham

13. Madison, James

14. Harrison, Benjamin

15. Harrison, William Henry

16. Jackson, Andrew

17. Wilson, Woodrow

18. Johnson, Andrew

19. Johnson, Lyndon

20. Jefferson, Thomas

21. Washington, George

22. Clinton, William J.

23. Nixon, Richard

24. Tyler, John

25. Carter, Jimmy

26. Hoover, Herbert

27. Eisenhower, Dwight D.

28. Taylor, Zachary

29. Arthur, Chester

30. Hayes, Rutherford B

31. Adams, John

32. Adams, John Quincy

33. Taft, William H.

34. Roosevelt, Franklin D.

35. Roosevelt, Theodore

36. Grant, Ulysses S.

37. Kennedy, John F.

38. McKinley, James

Presidential Last Names Ending with Consonant-Sounding Silent-e Letter (3)

39. Pierce, Franklin

40. Coolidge, Calvin

41. Fillmore, Millard

Table 4.1 Presidential Family Name with a Vowel-o Sound Ending (1)

1. Monroe, James

Hillary Rodham Clinton's name by destiny, rather than mere coincidence, happens to have the same vowel+n sound ending as the last name of the first president George Washington (shared with 18 other presidents). A second fortuitous matter of family genealogy is the fact that the Rodhams came from Durham, northeast England originally, which also happens to be where the ancestors of George Washington came from.[87]

Against candidates whose last names end in a vowel sound, Hillary Clinton has a winning edge of 41 out of 42 against 1 for last names ending in "oe" (i.e. Monroe) or none for the opposition! There was never a president with a surname that had any of these other vowel ending sounds: "a" as in Obama, "e" pronounced as in Huckabee, "i" as in Giuliani, "o" as in Tancredo, or "u" as in Stephanopoulou (not a presidential candidate).

(1) The number 1 handicap that Giuliani has is the "i" ending of his family name. It is unlikely that Giuliani will be elected president because of the not-Americanized spelling of his surname, although it is only one of the negative factors that can be held against him. According to the Wikipedia, Giuliani's relatives included police officers, firefighters, and criminals. It goes on to say that his father, "Harold Giuliani had been convicted of felony assault and robbery and served time in Sing Sing; after his release he served as a Mafia enforcer for his brother-in-law Leo D'Anza, who ran an organized crime operation involved in loan sharking and gambling at a restaurant in Brooklyn, [New York City]."[88] For this one reason alone, it will be most unlikely that American voters will choose him as our next president. No one among all 42 presidents in 220 years of American history ever had a parent who was a convicted criminal.

There are several other formidable obstacles to Giuliani's fulfillment of the highest American dream, the presidency of the United States, the greatest country in the world:

(2) It is almost, if not impossible, for Giuliani to climb all the way to the presidency from that of an ex-mayor of New York City. The lowest governmental position that served as a steppingstone to the presidency was that of U.S. representative, and even that was quite rare. Only 1 former U.S. Representative ever became president, and that was Abraham Lincoln.

Excepting drafted heroes, no vice-governors, other state officials, city mayors, or lower-level city officials had ever been elected president of the United States. There is therefore a zero chance that Rudolph Giuliani, ex-Mayor (*R*) of New York City, will be the very first U.S. president that will directly come from the rank of local officials below that of a U.S. Congressman.

(3) May Giuliani not be considered as a hero in the performance of his duties as New York City mayor during the 9/11/01 terrorist attacks? No, for several reasons:

All the drafted heroes who became president had the minimum military rank of Brigadier General which Giuliani, being civilian, has not and will not be able to attain. That is true of all 5 of them: George Washington, Zachary Taylor, Franklin Pierce, Ulysses Grant, and Dwight D. Eisenhower (*see* table 2.8 *in* chapter 2 above).

Newsweek reports that "as Rudy Giuliani's presidential campaign rolls along, there are more and more voices protesting that he's not the 9/11 hero America considers him to be."[89] The earliest to criticize Giuliani were the rescuers affiliated with the International Association of Firefighters (IAFF) when they accused him of not only being neglectful of the welfare of firefighters prior to 9/11/01 in which 343 of their members died, but even his actions following it were judged wholly inconsiderate. They blame Giuliani for outdated radios that failed on 9/11. The lack of radio contact was directly responsible for the death of 121 of their comrades, for failing to receive 2 evacuation orders that day prior to the collapse of the North Tower. The federal 9/11 commission faulted Giuliani for not only those antiquated radios, but also for failing to make the police and fire departments to work together, and even for locating the emergency command center in the 23rd floor of the Trade World Center that was a target of a terrorist attack some 5 years back![90]

Lorie van Auken, whose husband, Kenneth, died in the Trade World Center, voiced the resentment of many of surviving relatives when she said: "As people so directly affected, what we would want as a presidential candidate is someone whose record is pristine, not someone who's made terrible mistakes, not owned up to terrible mistakes and is now claiming a fabulous record."[91]

To add insult to injury, Giuliani subsequently said in September 2006 in an *Associated Press* interview, "he spent as much time, if not more, at ground zero exposed to the same health risks as workers combing the site after the Sept. 11 attacks" which was contradicted by some firefighters and police officers who demanded an apology which they got, with Giuliani admitting, "I misspoke."[92]

In spite of his previous apology for "misspeaking" 1 month short of 1 year before, in August 2007, Giuliani repeated almost the same words on 3 different occasions during his mid-West campaign. "I was at ground zero as often, if not more, than most of the workers," he said in Cincinnati, OH. "I was there working with them. I was there guiding things. I was there bringing people there. But I was exposed to exactly the same things they were exposed to. So in that sense, I'm one of them." And once again, he had to apologize to Mike Gallagher, a talk show host for the "tone of his remarks, but reiterated the substance of them"[93]

So, how many hours did Rudy Giuliani spend at Ground Zero during and following the events of September 11, 2001 and how did it compare with the hours spent by the firefighters and others involved in the rescue and recovery efforts? Unfortunately, there is no known record of the 6-day period following the attacks, but there exists a detailed account of the mayor's archive for the dates September 17 to Dec. 16, 2001, according to the *New York Times*: "It shows he was there for a total of 29 hours in those 3 months, often for short periods or to visit locations adjacent to the rubble. In that same period, many rescue and recovery workers put in daily 12-hour shifts."[94]

Michael J. Palladino, president of the Detectives' Endowment Association of New York City said that "It's unfair for [Giuliani] to characterize himself as being in the position as the first responders." Mr. Palladino said "many of his members logged 30 hours in the first two days after the attacks, and most averaged more than 400 hours at ground zero and in the debris at the Staten Island landfill. They are among the thousands who claim long-term health damage from the exposure."[95]

"A sample by Mount Sinai Medical Center of 1,138 participants in its study of health problems among rescue, recovery and debris removal workers found that they had spent a median of 962 hours at the Trade World Center site, or the equivalent of 120 eight-hour days!"[96]

In the "presidential forum" hosted by the IAFF in the middle of March 2007, most of the presidential frontrunners among candidates of the Democratic Party, Hillary Clinton, Barack Obama, and John Edwards, and the Republican Party, John McCain and Chuck Hagel, among others were invited to speak, except Rudy Giuliani. They wrote on February 2, 2007 to explain why Rudy was snubbed, "His actions post 9/11 rise to such an offensive and personal attack on our brother and sisterhood—and directly on our union—that the IAFF does not feel Rudy Giuliani deserves an Audience of IAFF leaders and members at our own Presidential Forum.... He valued the money and gold and wanted the site cleared before he left office at the end of 2001 more than he valued the lives and memories of those lost.... The fundamental lack of respect that Giuliani showed our FDNY members is unforgivable—and that's why he was not invited."[97]

(4) Giuliani had demonstrated a lack of flexibility that is necessary for anyone to occupy the position of the highest office in the world, the U.S. presidency. The officers of the IAFF mentioned in the preceding paragraph subsequently changed their minds and decided to send a letter of invitation to Giuliani anyway (as a gesture of letting bygones be bygones). Would you believe that Giuliani (who has also been known to have a temper as bad as another presidential wannabe John McCain), replied: "Thanks, but no thanks?" (*See* chapter 6 below on McCain).

(5) How can we prove to you that Giuliani is highly temperamental? Just this one quote from T.A.B.A.C.C.O (*Truth about Business and Congressional Crimes Organization*) should be proof enough: "The night he was defeated for mayor of New York [he did not always win!] by David Dinkins, he was on the podium to give a concession speech. His own supporters filled the room. They shouted 'No.' They did not want him to give up just yet. Rudy, in demonstration of his dictatorial persona, told them with the TV cameras rolling, 'Shut up!' And he said that to his supporters. If you think George W. Bush is stubborn and incorrigible,

what will you get if Mr. Giuliani becomes president of the United States? Rudy Giuliani's high character perception is totally undeserved."[98]

(6) Giuliani must also be disqualified for U.S. president because of his total failure in his family life. All previous American presidents, except 1, had never divorced. But, Giuliani is trying hard to work on his third marriage. No wonder he prevented his current wife from being involved with his campaign; people kept getting reminded that she is not Rudy's first wife, not even his second! And some might even know that "he was carrying on with number 3 while still married to number 2." And if that were not enough, he announced to the press that she was separating from wife number 2—the mother of his children—without the courtesy of informing her first.[99]

The only president who was divorced and remarried was Ronald Reagan. The American electorate could tolerate one marital mishap; anyone is entitled to receive the benefit of the doubt when committing only one misstep. But, we doubt if they will tolerate 2 marital failures Giuliani cannot even raise obedient children who are respectful of his authority as a father. In contrast with his desire to keep his current wife away, he would have wanted his children to campaign for him. But, they refused to do so, and he has not found a way to convince them to change their minds. If he cannot positively influence his own children as a father, how can he aspire to be president and be a role model for all the millions of children in America? When that question was asked by someone in his audience when he was speaking in New Hampshire in mid-August, 2007, the best answer he gave is not good enough, "Leave my family alone, as I leave yours." There is a great difference, is there not? Giuliani is running for president, but you the voter, are not. You have the right to a reasonable answer to a very reasonable question. If Giuliani cannot even manage his own small personal family affairs, how can he fix the ills of millions of families in America, not to say even the problems of families in other "villages" in the world?

(7) Giuliani furthermore suffers from a disadvantage in his presidential campaign in that evangelical leader Dr. James Dobson and his large constituency cannot be relied upon to support his bid. Dobson has gone on record as totally opposed to Giuliani's presidential candidacy. He said that under no circumstances will he vote for Giuliani if he were the Republican nominee.

(8) But, of course, Giuliani is a Catholic, like Alfred Smith, John F. Kennedy, and John Kerry. Will he turn out to be another winning president like Kennedy? We doubt it very much. Kennedy came out openly that he would observe the strict separation of church and state, and that he would not allow his church to interfere in the way he was going to govern our country as president. Neither

would his governmental policies interfere in the affairs of any church, Catholic or otherwise. And he was able to convince the American electorate to elect him as the first and only Roman Catholic president of our predominantly Protestant country! Giuliani did not even have a chance to promise the same thing that Kennedy did, because the present leaders of the American Catholic Church on its own went out of its way to interfere in this election by declaring that they do not support the candidacy of Rudy Giuliani!

(9) Giuliani is not even as good as Mike Bloomberg in being top executive of New York City, how can he be "the best choice" for the top executive of the U.S., the greatest country in the world? We do not think that Bloomberg will eventually run for president, for as an independent candidate, he cannot win *(see* chapter 7 below as to the reasons independents have no chance).

According to Alec Macgillis of *the Washington Post*: "Simply having [Bloomberg] in the picture calls into question some of the assumptions underlying Giuliani's appeal.... Bloomberg ... has shown that the city of 8 million can be run successfully in a far more understated fashion—that a mayor can reduce crime without cultivating a sheriff's swagger and antagonizing minorities, protect against terrorism without overly fixating on security, and tackle deeply rooted urban problems without getting into public spats with top appointees. 'Bloomberg shows it's possible to manage New York without offending people,' said Peter Kostmayer, a former Democratic congressman who is president of Citizens for New York City, a nonprofit group.... 'You're able to compare. You have one mayor [Giuliani] who was successful and turned off lots of people and one [Bloomberg] who was successful and has turned on lots of people'.... This extends even to the response to the Sept. 11 attacks, the heart of Giuliani's national appeal. Giuliani won acclaim for the resolve he showed on Sept. 11 and the days and weeks following, but Bloomberg ... [reminds] voters that Giuliani was out of office within four months of the attacks, that most of the city's resurgence has been presided over by someone else—and that many New Yorkers were ready to be rid of Giuliani before Sept. 11."[100]

(10) Finally, Giuliani has no home base. He shares the situation of Al Gore who could not win in his home state of Tennessee, and Florida was not willing to bail him out in 2000. The last time Giuliani had a chance to prevent Hillary from winning her first election as senator from New York he pulled out at the last minute (due to personal health reason as he was afflicted with prostate cancer) leaving the weak opposition to Rick Lazio who promptly lost. He could not run for senator because of a serious health problem, but he is able to run for president in spite of the same health problem compounded by additional exposure to seri-

ous health hazards posed by the 9/11 bombed out World Trade Center buildings? These things do not seem to add up, do they?

Do you blame New Yorkers for showing their deep loyalty to Hillary by re-electing her as their U.S. Senator with almost 70% of the votes? Does Rudy Giuliani, like Al Gore, expect another state to bail him out for his failure to have a home state? Compare that with Hillary who has at least 7 home states to start with including New York (*see* chapter 10 below on Hillary's Electoral College advantage for having multiple home states).

Against opponents whose last names end in a consonant sound like Hillary's, she still has a formidable advantage. There are 19 presidential last names with a vowel+n ending like her, whereas the possible opponents (unless their last names also have a similar vowel+n sound to tie her) will not have more than up to half a dozen out of 42 odds to win (*see* Tables 4.2 ; 4.3; 4.4; 4.5; 4.6 ;4.7, & 4.8).

Table 4.2 Presidential Last Names with Vowel+n Sound Endings (19)

1. Reagan, Ronald

2. Truman, Harry

3. Buchanan, James

4. Van Buren, Martin

5. Lincoln, Abraham

6. Madison, James

7. Harrison, Benjamin

8. Harrison, William Henry

9. Jackson, Andrew

10. Wilson, Woodrow

11. Johnson, Andrew

12. Johnson, Lyndon

13. Jefferson, Thomas

14. Washington, George

15. Clinton, William J.

16. Nixon, Richard

17, Cleveland, Grover

18. Harding, Warren

19. Grant, Ulysses S.

Table 4.3 Presidential Last Names with "r" Sound Endings (6)

1. Tyler, John

2. Carter, Jimmy

3. Hoover, Herbert

4. Eisenhower, Dwight D.

5. Taylor, Zachary

6. Arthur, Chester

Table 4.4 Presidential Last Names with "s" Sound Endings (5)

1. Bush, George H. W.

2. Bush, George W.

3. Hayes, Rutherford B

4. Adams, John

5. Adams, John Quincy

Table 4.5 Presidential Last Names with "t" Sound Endings (3)

1. Taft, William H.

2. Roosevelt, Franklin D.

3. Roosevelt, Theodore

Table 4.6 Presidential Last Names with "d" Sound Endings (2)

1. Garfield, James

2. Ford, Gerald

Table 4.7 Presidential Last Names with "y" Sound Endings (2)

1. Kennedy, John

2. McKinley, James

Table 4.8 Presidential Last Name with a "k" Sound Ending (1)

1. Polk, James

No other announced candidate can duplicate the last name of a previous president except Hillary Clinton, that of her own husband, Bill Clinton. She will also establish the record of being the first First Lady and the first woman to become president. She will also increase the number of vowel+n pairings of presidential last names from 2 to 3. The pairing of John Adams and John Quincy Adams, like George H.W. Bush and George Bush are father and son respectively. William Henry Harrison is the grandfather of Benjamin Harrison. Theodore Roosevelt is the fifth cousin of Franklin D. Roosevelt (incidentally First Lady Eleanor Roosevelt's name was exactly the same even before marrying Franklin, as they are also cousins!). Andrew Johnson and Lyndon Johnson just happen to have the same last names, but they are not related (*see* Table 4.9).[101]

Table 4.9 Pairs of Presidential Last Names that Favor the Vowel+n Sound Ending:

Two Pairs of "n" Endings:

William Henry Harrison & Benjamin Harrison

Andrew Johnson & Lyndon Johnson

Two Pairs of "s" Endings:

John Adams & John Quincy Adams

George H.W. Bush & George W. Bush

One Pair of "t" Ending:

Theodore Roosevelt & Franklin D. Roosevelt

What Is So Right about Being a Clinton?

Which is better: being stuck with a not so Americanized family name that ends in a vowel and not doing something about changing it, or having an acceptable Americanized family name that ends in a consonant and improving on it?

Giuliani's parents did not anticipate that their original last name which was useful in the Old World where they came from became a real handicap in America. But, be that as it may, they are not really exclusively to blame for Giuliani's unacceptable not American-sounding family name. Just like we wrote about Obama in chapter 3 above, Giuliani did not do anything to Americanize the sound of his family name, to be in sync with the names of all our presidents.

In May 2007, it was negatively reported in the Internet that Hillary was so ambitious that she decided to even drop her maiden name Rodham which was her second name as a married woman and to stick with her husband's last name Clinton. There are two things that can be said in defense of Hillary's move:

First, Hillary does not have anything to be ashamed about Rodham. It is an honored last name that his parents and relatives continue to be known in Illinois as well as the name with which Hillary received her outstanding academic degrees at Wellesley College in Massachusetts and at Yale University in Connecticut. In earlier times, it was taken for granted that a woman upon marriage replaces her maiden surname with that of her husband's. But, today, a married woman has the choice of retaining her own name that she was born with. There was nothing wrong with Hillary's initial decision to include Rodham as her second name. It was her privilege as a modern married woman. When she decides instead to use her husband's last name alone,—as in the old days—(and she does not have to), she should be applauded rather than criticized!

Second, Hillary was in fact not dropping Rodham. Because she is so famous, whenever the name Hillary is mentioned in America, it is usually understood to mean Mrs. Hillary Clinton (unless you accompany it with another surname). An example of this is Dick Morris and Eileen McGann's *Condi vs. Hillary* that omits any surname (which incidentally we imitated in the title of this book). Thus, Hillary Rodham Clinton was in reality not dropping Rodham. Hillary was restoring Clinton—that Morris and McGann dropped—in front of her name where it (he) belongs!

5

Forty-One Presidents Were Protestants & Only 1 Catholic

◆

Methodist Hillary Raises Protestant Presidents to 42; Romney's Mormon = Zero

Those who support Barack Obama claim that he is a John Kennedy. Later in the Conclusion, you will read that Hillary also claims that she is in reality the "JFK of 2008." In both cases, both Hillary and Obama can justify their claim, by analogy: "there never was a Catholic president before Kennedy ran," in the same way that there was never an African American who ran for president before Obama (at least by 50%) or there was never a woman who ran before Hillary.

Why does not Mitt Romney campaign similarly? If Kennedy's uniqueness was his being non-Protestant by religion, why does not Romney emphasize that his uniqueness is his not being a traditional Christian?

All presidents of the United States, except 1, were Protestants. That exception was John F. Kennedy who was a Catholic. Hillary when she will have become elected with your votes on November 4, 2008, will be the 42nd Protestant president. She will be the 6th Methodist, the third most in number among the presidents' Protestant denominations. Ahead of Methodists were 12 Episcopalian and 7 Presbyterian presidents. Right behind the Methodists were Baptists and Unitarians at 4 each. Three were non-denominational Protestant Christians (Thomas Jefferson, Abraham Lincoln, and Andrew Johnson), followed by 2 Quakers, 2 Disciples of Christ, 1 Dutch Reformed, and 1 Congregationalist. Based on her religion, Hillary has 41 out of 42 chances to become our next president (*see* Table 5.0, 5.1 & 5.2).

Table 5.0 Religions of Presidents

Protestants		41
Catholic		1
	Total	42

Table 5.1 Protestant Presidents (41)

Episcopalians (12)

1. George Washington

2. James Madison

3. James Monroe

4. William Henry Harrison

5. John Tyler

6. Zachary Taylor

7. Franklin Pierce

8. Chester A. Arthur

9. Theodore Roosevelt

10. Franklin Delano Roosevelt

11. Gerald Ford

12. George H. W. Bush

Presbyterians (7)

13. Andrew Jackson

14. James Buchanan

15. Grover Cleveland

16. Benjamin Harrison

17. Woodrow Wilson

18. Dwight D. Eisenhower

19. Ronald Reagan

Methodists (5)

20. James Knox Polk

21. Ulysses S. Grant

22. Rutherford B. Hayes

23. William McKinley

24. George W. Bush

Baptists (4)

25. Warren G. Harding

26. Harry S. Truman

27. Jimmy Carter

28. William Jefferson Clinton

Unitarians (4)

29. John Adams

30. John Quincy Adams

31. Millard Fillmore

32. William Howard Taft

No Specific Christian Denomination (3)

33. Thomas Jefferson

34. Abraham Lincoln

35. Andrew Johnson

Disciples of Christ (2)

36. James A. Garfield

37. Lyndon B. Johnson

Quakers (2)

38. Herbert Hoover

39. Richard M. Nixon

Congregationalist (1)

40. Calvin Coolidge

Dutch Reformed (1)

41. Martin Van Buren

Table 5.2 Catholic President (1)

1. John Kennedy

Based on his religion, Mitt Romney has a zero chance to become our president. His denomination, the Church of Jesus Christ of Latter day Saints or Mormon Church is not represented among all the 42 presidents. It is unlikely that Romney will be the first Mormon president just as John Kennedy was elected the first Catholic president in our predominantly Protestant country.[102] The Protestant churches that have positive ecumenical relations with one another include all the denominations that 41 American presidents belong to (*see* table 5.0). These Protestant denominations also have a similar positive ecumenical attitude to the Catholic Church. John Kennedy had always been a devout Catholic. He fulfilled his promise not to allow the Catholic Pope to advise him on American governmental policy. "I don't speak for my church," he said, "and my church does not speak for me." And he never ceased to be a practicing Catholic until he died.

Evangelical Protestants are also less anti-Catholic as they used to. Thanks to the leadership of the late Jerry Farwell, who founded the Moral Majority, evangelicals discovered what they had in common with Catholics. They found out that Catholics are in agreement with them on the sanctity of human life, including the unborn. It is not strange, therefore, that the 5 majority members of the U.S. Supreme today are Catholics, and they were all appointed by non-Catholic presidents who were supported by evangelicals.

In 1994, some 40 Roman Catholic and evangelical leaders, including Chuck Colson (founder of Prison Ministries), Bill Bright (founder of Campus Crusade for Christ), and James I. Packer (evangelical theologian) signed a document of unity titled "Evangelicals and Catholics Together: The Christian Mission in the Third Millennium."[103] We are very hopeful that with time and positive experience of relating on personal and official bases that as Christians together, we will continue to re-discover what we have in common!

On the international level, the World Evangelical Alliance to which the National Alliance of Evangelicals in the United States belongs had agreed in the middle of August 2007 to meet with the World Council of Churches to which the U.S. National Council of Churches and the Eastern Orthodox Churches are a part, and the Vatican on behalf of the Roman Catholic Church, "to create a common code of conduct for religious conversions to preserve the right of Christians to spread their religion while avoiding conflict among faiths."[104]

Just in perfect time for the 2008 election, America's evangelicals are experiencing a transition of leadership that is even broader and more positive in its approach to politics. This transitional leadership includes: (1) Rick Warren, author of *the Purpose-Driven Life;* (2) Joel Hunter, pastor of Northland Church, outside Orlando, FL and next year's author of *A New Kind of Conservative;* (3) Bill Hybels, pastor of the Pioneering Willow Creek Community Church, outside Chicago, IL; (4) T.D. Jakes, pastor of the Potter's House in Dallas, TX; (5) Frank Page, the newly re-elected president of the Southern Baptist Church; (6) Richard Cizik, chief lobbyist for the 30-million-member National Association of Evangelicals, and (7) Barry H. Corey, the newly elected president of Biola University, La Mirada, CA.

Being directly church-based rather than para-church or semi-independent arm-of-the-church organized groups, the new evangelicals are not identified with any single political party, such as the GOP as the earlier evangelicals tended to be in the past. Barry H. Corey made these comments in July 2005: "Evangelicals are not defined by a political party, by their views on when life begins or their justification for the war in Iraq.... Evangelicals are Democrats, Republicans and independents; they are conservatives, liberals and moderates; Catholics, Protestants and Orthodox Christians; members of churches large and small."[105]

While the evangelical Old Guard's opposition to abortion, gay marriage and stem cell research is continued by the New Guard leadership, the latter "want to broaden the evangelical agenda beyond what Hunter calls 'below the belt issues' linked to sexuality. For them, people of faith should engage issues such as AIDS, Darfur, economic justice, war and peace, prison reform and human trafficking."[106]

Friction between Mormons and other Christians has been present throughout the history of the Church of Jesus Christ of Latter-day Saints since it began in 1830. Most Christians had many reasons for rejecting the Mormon movement during the 19th century, among which were:

"(1). Their religious exclusivity, communal lifestyle, and 'Mormons first and for themselves' lifestyle were criticized....

(2). Some of [Joseph Smith's] theological teachings about the nature of God, structure of heaven, requirements for salvation, history of the Americas, etc. were rejected as heresy.

(3). Plural marriage in particular was considered totally unacceptable behavior.

(4). Smith's elevation of three writings to equality with the Bible was considered offensive.

(5). Smith's new translation of the Bible was viewed as heretical.

(6). Smith's political goals were viewed as threatening to his neighbors. They feared that he wanted to establish a theocracy."[107]

According to Sally Denton, "In fact, in 1844, Smith announced his candidacy for the U.S. presidency, advocating theocratic rule for the entire nation. Challenging the Whig and Democratic parties, he advocated what he called 'theo-democracy where God and the people hold the power to conduct the affairs of men in righteous matters.'

"Smith was the commander-in-chief of an 'army of God,' composed of well-trained and armed church members that was nearly one-quarter the size of the U.S. Army.... He prophesied the overthrow of the U.S. government.

"But Smith's candidacy came to an end that summer [of 1844] when he was shot to death in Illinois by an anti-Mormon vigilante mob. 'I am going like a lamb to slaughter.... My blood shall cry from the ground for vengeance,' he said before his death."[108]

Today many of the above points of conflict continue. During the early years, opposition by other Christians was violent. Much blood was shed. Now, the battle is mainly a war of words.

Leaders of the Roman Catholics regard Romney's Mormon Church as a cult. They are used to calling their own church "the only true church" and do not look with favor—to say the least—on Mormons claiming that it is the Church of Jesus Christ of Latter-day Saints that is "the only true church."

The Methodist Church (of which Hillary Clinton is a member), the Southern Baptist Church (of which Bill Clinton is a member), and the Presbyterian Church (U.S.A.), among other Protestant Churches, agree with the Roman Catholic Church that the Mormon Church is a cult, but they do not agree that any particular denomination—Christian or otherwise—can claim to be "the only true church." The general meetings of the United Methodist Church, the Presbyterian Church (U.S.A.) and the Southern Baptist Convention have stated, in their opinion, that the Church of Jesus Christ of Latter-day Saints—despite its name—is a denomination that is separate from the Christian religion.

The general conference of the United Methodist Church approved a document in 2000 that states: "the Church of Jesus Christ of Latter-day Saints, by self-definition, does not fit within the bounds of the historic, apostolic tradition of Christian faith.... [Mormons] explicitly [profess] distinction and separateness from the ecumenical community."[109]

According to a document issued by the Presbyterian Church (U.S.A.): "... Mormonism is a new and emerging religious tradition distinct from the historic tradition of the Christian Church, of which Presbyterians are a part.... Latter-day Saints understand themselves to be separate from the continuous witness to Jesus Christ, from the apostles to the present affirmed by churches of the 'catholic' tradition. Latter-day Saints and the historic churches view the canon of scriptures and interpret shared scriptures in radically different ways. They use the same words with dissimilar meanings. When the Church of Jesus Christ of Latter-day Saints speaks of the Trinity, Christ's death and resurrection, and salvation, the theology and practice related to these set it apart from the Orthodox, Roman Catholic, and Protestant churches."[110]

Tom Elliff, president of the Southern Baptists, said: 'The Christ that the Mormons speak about is not, in our minds, identified with Christ solely in scriptures.... When we (Mormons and Baptist) try to talk about a belief in Christ, we're really comparing apples and oranges. We're not talking about the same Christ. It's a different Christ [altogether].[111]

LA Times, reporting on Governor Mitt Romney's possible bid for the U.S. presidency, wrote: "Pastor Ted Haggard, [at the time] president of the *National Association of Evangelicals* (NAE) in Colorado Springs, CO said: 'We evangelicals view Mormons as a … cult group. A cult is a group that claims exclusive revelation. And typically it is hard to get out of these cult groups. And so Mormonism qualifies as that.… When Romney says that he accepts Jesus Christ as his savior, we appreciate that,' Haggard said. 'But very often when people like Mormons use terms that we also use, there are different meanings in the theology behind those terms'."[112]

The major reason why Christian denominations call the Mormon Church a cult is that it has an extra-biblical or extra-canonical book of Mormons which it considers of equal doctrinal value to the Bible. How come if the Mormon Church is "the only true church" that it is so wrong about its teaching on race? The book of Mormons declares that only white people from whom the American Indians are supposed to have descended (DNA evidence and historical anthropology have been scientifically used to prove the falsity of this claim) are God's chosen people. Such teachings are incompatible with the Christian scriptures. "2 Nephi 5:21 refers to God cursing some of the early inhabitants of America, the Lamanites: 'And he had caused the cursing to come upon them, yea, even a sore cursing, because of their iniquity. For behold, they had hardened their hearts against him, that they had become like unto a flint; wherefore, as they were white, and exceedingly fair and delightsome, that they may not be enticing unto my people the Lord God did cause a skin of blackness to come upon them'."[113]

Perhaps, the most controversial aspect of Mormonism is its insistence that polygamy is the only acceptable form of marriage. Joseph Smith justified the practice as being in agreement with the Old Testament in which God's anointed kings had many wives. He neglected to take into account the teaching of Jesus, Who is the number 1 authority on Christian faith and practice to the effect that marriage is only intended to be between one man and one woman here on earth. Besides Jesus's teaching, common sense tells us that polygamy is not conducive to the health and happiness of the parties to the marriage. Perhaps, the only advantage goes to the polygamous man, but we doubt if even he can be truly happy with so many women and their children wanting to be favored, along with all the jealousies and quarrels that such competitions entail.

For sure, polygamy does not redound to the health and benefit of the wives in a polygamous marriage. Todd Compton of UCLA has written a book titled *In*

Sacred Loneliness: the Plural Wives of Joseph Smith claiming that in general, the women lived sad and unfulfilling lives:

"Beginning in the 1830's, at least thirty-three women married Joseph Smith, the founder of Mormonism. These were passionate relationships which also had some longevity, except in cases such as that of two young sisters, one of whom was discovered by Joseph's first wife, Emma, in a locked room with the prophet. Emma remained a steadfast opponent of polygamy throughout her life.

"The majority of Smith's wives were younger than he, and one-third were between fourteen and twenty years of age. Another third were already married, and some of the husbands served as witnesses at their own wife's polyandrous wedding. In addition, some of the wives hinted that they bore Smith children—most notably Sylvia Sessions's daughter Josephine—although the children carried their stepfather's surname.

"For all of Smith's wives, the experience of being secretly married was socially isolating, emotionally draining, and sexually frustrating. Despite the spiritual and temporal benefits, which they acknowledged, they found their faith tested to the limit of its endurance. After Smith's death in 1844 their lives became even more 'lonely and desolate.' One even joined a convent. The majority were appropriated by Smith's successors, based on the Old Testament law of the Levirate, and had children by them, though they considered these guardianships unsatisfying. Others stayed in the Midwest and remarried, while one moved to California. But all considered their lives unhappy, except for the joy they found in their children and grandchildren."[114]

Starting in the 1890's, under pressure from the United States government and the state of Utah (where most Mormons went to dwell), the Church of the Latter-day Saints under the leadership of prophet Wilford Woodruff began to "suspend" indefinitely the practice of polygamy. The suspension of plural marriages has thus been in effect for over a century now.

However, a fundamentalist group of the Church of Latter-day Saints refuses to abandon polygamy, for it was prescribed by Joseph Smith (and practiced by him as the founder), and so they kept to themselves isolated in the Utah, Colorado, and Arizona corner (the members of this fundamentalist Mormon church suffer from a hereditary disease not found in the rest of the American population, due to too much inbreeding).

The fundamentalist Church of the Latter day Saints under the leadership of Warren Steed Jeffs had been more strict and abusive of members, especially women. He had allegedly:

"(1). Forbidden members to use television sets, VCRs, video games or connections to the Internet.

(2). Banned boating, fishing and other water activities.

(3). Instructed parents to throw away most children's books including the Bible and Book of Mormon story books.

(4). Terminated community and holiday celebrations, such as observing the birthdays of previous church leaders and Pioneer Day.

(5). Stopped further dances, socials and other get-togethers.

(6). Warned members that laughter causes the spirit of God to leak from their bodies.

(7). Urged older men to take child brides before the girls are attracted to boys of their own age. It is for this reason that Jeffs is being tried in court today as an accessory to rape because he influenced a 14-year old girl to marry her cousin. The girl complained that she was practically forced to marry, because Jeffs told her that it was part of her religious duty as a believer in the Church of Christ of Latter-day Saints to do so.

(8). Drove male youths out of the community so as to leave a surplus of females.

(9). Made plural wives apply for government assistance as single mothers.

(10). Expelled hundreds of men and reassigned their wives and children to other men."[115]

Matthew Smith, the Mohave County, Arizona Attorney who had Warren Jeffs indicted by a grand jury, said: "This isn't about religious persecution. This has nothing with polygamy. It has to do with underage marriage. It has to do with leaving these young girls alone so that they can have a little more maturity and make their own decisions." Gary Engels, a Mohave County investigator who helped in the capture of Jeffs on August 29, 2006 was hopeful: "It has all the makings of coming apart. People are scattering all over the place. Most of Warren's faithful are moving on to somewhere else, where there is less focus on them…. It's my hope and dream that this place comes back into America, where these people have the same rights as anyone, and where the government isn't run by a religious organization."[116]

Mitt Romney is not married to more than one wife. In fact, it is part of his campaign's message that he is more committed to monogamy than Giuliani, McCain, Gingrich, or Fred Thompson who had multiple marriages (though not at the same time). But, Romney has not disavowed the Mormon religion in its entirety. Compound this with the fact that he was a Mormon missionary to France in his youth. If Romney no longer practices polygamy because American law prohibits it, not just because Wilford Woodruff, the one of the successor-prophets to Joseph Smith had a new revelation to "suspend," not abolish, the practice of polygamy in 1890, does he still believe that polygamy is right and the forced temporary suspension of it wrong?

Or, does Romney now believe that his Mormon Church was totally mistaken about the true nature of marriage? If so, whose view regarding the ideal practice of and teaching about marriage did he replace it with? And when he becomes president, he will be a role model for all American families and of the families of the world, what authority will he cite as the basis of the right practice of monogamy or having only one wife, instead of many? Will he say then that Joseph Smith, the founder of his church, was in error in his polygamous view of marriage? Will he exert his influence as American president on Mormon leaders not just to "suspend" but to outlaw polygamy forever? How can the Mormon Church to which he belongs be "the only true church" and be so wrong about the right practice of and teaching about marriage?

May we not consider Mitt Romney as someone like Thomas Jefferson, Abraham Lincoln, and Andrew Johnson who were considered Christians, though they were not affiliated with any one denomination? No, because, the Church of Jesus Christ of the Latter-day saints is not a Christian denomination. Thomas Jefferson, Abraham Lincoln, and Andrew Johnson were reared in Christian denominations, although they later declared themselves independent of any particular Christian denominational label.

The founding fathers, aware that they and their ancestors fled the Old World because they were persecuted by a union of the church and the state, created a Constitution that declared that "Congress shall make no law regarding the establishment of religion." Mitt Romney's Church of Jesus Christ of Latter-day Saints which began in New York State did not have this historical background to draw upon. As such, his church tends to want a union of church and state, or worse the subordination of the state to the dictates of the church, i.e., a theocracy, as Joseph Smith wanted to establish when he ran for U.S. president in 1844.

The Church of the Latter-day Saints teaches that only its members are saved. God has destined Mormons alone to go to heaven. This belief was what made Romney a Mormon missionary to France in the first place. That Romney has not departed from his strong Mormon faith is evidenced by the fact that he even converted his wife, nee Ann Davies formerly an Episcopalian, to Mormonism. Also he saw to it that all his 5 children—all sons—were brought up in the Mormon religion. He also brought them up to avoid American military service.

Romney's adherence to a one-sided theocratic-oriented Church of Jesus Christ of Latter-day Saints is totally irreconcilable with the flexibility that is needed in the president of the people of the United States of many churches, creeds, and colors. When Romney becomes president, there is no guarantee that because of his deep religious beliefs that he will not give an unwarranted preference to his own Mormon Church.

In the online magazine, *Slate*, editor Jacob Weisberg called Joseph Smith, Mormonism's founder, an "obvious con man" and wrote, "Romney has every right to believe in con men, but I want to know if he does, and if so, I don't want him running the country."[117]

Hillary Is an Exceptional Timothy-Type Christian Woman

Our country needs a president who recognizes the validity of other Christian persuasions, the kind of flexibility that Hillary offers. In a rare interview by Soledad O'Brien of CNN on the campus of Georgetown University on June 4, 2007, as to how she managed to survive the infidelity of her husband, Hillary replied, "I could not have gotten through it without my faith." She assured her audience that she took her faith "very seriously and very personally." At the same time, she made it clear that she came from a faith tradition, Methodism that is "perhaps a little too suspicious of people who wear their faiths on their sleeves." She admitted that talking about her faith in public "doesn't come naturally to me," saying she often flashed back to "the Pharisees and all of the Sunday School lessons and readings I had as a child."

She expressed gratitude for close friends and others who she said ... were praying for her, describing them as "prayer warriors" who "sustained me through a very difficult time." "I am very grateful I had a grounding in faith that gave me the courage and strength to do what I thought was right, regardless of what the world thought," she said.[118]

That Hillary desires to communicate her genuine Methodist Christian faith and practice is evidenced by the fact that at the beginning of her announcement to seek the U.S. presidency, she appointed Burns Strider, a top evangelical staffer on Capitol Hill to be part of her campaign staff.

"Over the years, Senator Clinton has expressed her faith often in speeches and books," says Strider, "and I've always been impressed with its authenticity." Strider says that the campaign will focus on both "social justice" Democrats and on socially Conservative Democrats, too. Hillary "raised eyebrows in 2005 by calling for fewer abortions before an audience of family planning providers with the focus on preventing unwanted pregnancies in the first place."[119]

When Hillary wore a crucifix, some critics said that it was a religious put on, but as a matter of fact, many pictures in her family album had shown that she was in the habit of doing so, way before she became a presidential aspirant. This is a practice which "high church" Methodists have in common with "high church" Episcopalians and, Catholics of course.

Hillary is among the most religious Protestants seeking the presidency on November 4, 2008. "I got deluged from calls from New York Reporters who had this view of her as a nonreligious person," says John Greenberg at the Pew Forum on Religion and Public Life. "But, she's actually the real deal, a very serious social-justice Methodist."[120]

Susannah Meadows had written earlier in *Newsweek* that Hillary in her early teens met a Methodist Church youth minister named Rev. Don Jones who has been her religious mentor until today at 75 years of age. "Though she's been accused of adopting a religious patina for political gain," continues Meadows, "[Hillary's] relationship with Jones shows that from the time she was young, Hillary was thinking seriously about her faith. She clearly talks more about religion these days, as many politicians do—but her connection to Jones reveals that her Christianity has always been at the center of her identity. 'She's not using the language of prayer and God for the first time,' says Jones. 'While there may be a political dimension, it's authentic.'

"Jones describes Hillary's beliefs as falling, like her politics, somewhere in the middle of the spectrum. Unlike the extreme left, she understands the limitations of human being, he says. And unlike the extreme right, he argues, she believes in humanity's potential. She does take seriously the doctrine of original sin. And after [almost] a lifetime in politics, she's seen plenty of it."[121]

Since birth, Hillary's major religious influence were her parents, Hugh Ellsworth Rodham and Dorothy Emma Howell Rodham, especially her mother who had been a Sunday School teacher in the Methodist Church in Park Ridge, Illinois. So, she is a Timothy-type Christian, in contrast with one who is a newly converted "born again" Christian. The basis of the former is found in the introduction of Paul's letter to Timothy: "I thank God, whom I serve from my forefathers with pure conscience, that without ceasing I have remembrance of thee in my prayers night and day; Greatly desiring to see thee, being mindful of thy tears, that I may be filled with joy; When I call to remembrance the unfeigned faith that is in thee, which dwelt first in thy grandmother Lois, and thy mother Eunice; and I am persuaded that in thee also" (2 Tim. 1:3-5 *KJV*).

Hillary, of course, recognizes that some Christians are "born again" or Nicodemus-types—those who were converted to Christianity. The phrase "born again" comes from Jesus in answer to the question of Nicodemus, a leader of the Jews, on how one can be saved: "Verily, verily, I say unto thee, Except a man be born again, he cannot see the kingdom of God" (John 3:3 & 5 *KJV*).

That appropriate balance between Timothy-type and Nicodemus-type Christians has been struck in the ministry of the premier evangelist of our time, Billy Graham who conducts crusades in major cities of the world, and at the same time, he enlists the cooperation of members of all Christian churches, including the Roman Catholic Church. Graham also refused to conduct crusades "for the conversion of the Jews." New evangelicals may be surprised to know that Graham had been a registered Democrat, although he exercised the right to vote for a non-Democratic presidential candidate if he thought that the latter would make a better leader of our country. Nevertheless, in 1981 he advised that "Evangelicals can't be closely identified with any particular party or person. We have to stand in the middle to preach to all the people, right and left. I haven't been faithful to my own advice in the past. I will in the future."[122] That is probably quite far into the future, for the presidential election of 2008 is now, and he has violated his advice once again, for he has practically endorsed the candidacy of Hillary. He said that he was keeping a close eye on the candidacy of Hillary whom he knows best of all the candidates: "I keep up with her," he said of his old friend. "I think a lot of Hillary." And the feeling is mutual. She had known Graham since she was First Lady of Arkansas, and when she became First Lady of the United States, they became even closer especially during the time when she needed his pastoral care at the height of the Monica Lewinsky affair.[123]

It is true that Graham tried his best to be neutral. Graham did serve as counselor to presidents who belonged to different political parties. He visited with presidents Harry S. Truman (briefly), Dwight Eisenhower, Lyndon B. Johnson, Richard Nixon, Gerald Ford, Jimmy Carter, Ronald Reagan, Bill Clinton, and the Bush family.[124]

There was a time Graham was called upon to sort of arbitrate between the incumbent President George W. Bush and his Mom, Barbara Bush, on the request of the latter, because the former based on his own reading of the Bible insisted that "only born-again believers can go to heaven." She disagreed, so would Billy Graham please give a definitive answer? "Technically, George W. is right," Graham replied. "But be both warned that no one should try to play God—for [He] alone knows who has or has not received Christ as their Saviour."[125]

How does Hillary's United Methodist Church compare with Romney's Mormon Church?

The original Methodist Church was founded by John Wesley, along with his prolific hymn-writer brother, Charles Wesley. The former used to be a priest of the Anglican Church in England. One day, he "felt strangely warm" all over his body, something like a "born-again" experience,—although he did not call it that, since he grew up in a Christian Church already—that led him to dedicate his life to a deeper commitment to God and to found the new Christian denomination called Methodist Church (sometimes informally called Wesleyan Church in honor of its founder or co-founders). Thus, because of their former connection with Anglicans (Episcopalians in the U.S.), Methodists are composed of both "low church" and "high church" members in faith and practice just like Anglicans or Episcopalians. Some "high church"-influenced Methodists, for example, use crucifix and rosary just like their Episcopalian counterparts.

(1) Unlike Romney's Mormon Church, Hillary's Methodist Church does *not* claim to be "the only true Church."

(2) Unlike Romney's Mormon Church, Hillary's Methodist Church does *not* teach that only white people are blessed and colored peoples, cursed by God.

(3) Unlike Romney's Mormon Church, Hillary's Methodist Church does *not* sanction plural marriages. The teaching about polygamy as the preferred union of a man and many women has not been changed in the Mormon Church, only its practice had been "suspended" since 1890 under pressure from the government of the United States.

(4) Unlike Romney's Mormon Church's founder, Joseph Smith, who had wives from anywhere from 33 to 48 (depending on who is doing the counting, and including minors and even women who already had husbands!), Hillary's Methodist Church's John Wesley and Charles Wesley had only one biblically ordained wife each respectively.

(5) Unlike Romney's Mormon Church that had allowed minor women to be married, Hillary's Methodist Church has always allowed only women of age to be married. Warren S. Jeffs, the latest leader of the Fundamentalist wing of the Church of Jesus Christ of Latter-day Saints, has been imprisoned by the state, and is now being tried for being an accessory to the crime of rape, for making a "minor" girl marry her adult cousin!

(6) Unlike Romney's Mormon Church that was founded in New York State, U.S.A., that intentionally isolated itself from other churches, referring to all of them as "apostates," Hillary's Methodist Church that was founded in England had apostolic connection through its bishops with Jesus's apostles of the Bible.

(7) Unlike Romney's Mormon Church that produced a book of Mormons making it equally authoritative as the Bible; Hillary's Methodist Church has the Bible alone as the basis of its faith and practice.

(8) Unlike Romney's Mormon Church that is considered a cult because of its exclusive claim that only its members are saved; Hillary's Methodist Church teaches that all believers in Christ of any Christian Church are saved and destined by God to go to heaven.

(9) Unlike Romney's Mormon Church which does not cooperate with any other Christian group, Hillary's Methodist Church cooperates ecumenically with all Christian denominations, including the Episcopal Church that produced the most number of American presidents, the Roman Catholic Church, and evangelicals of what ever church, creed, or color, as defined by Barry H. Corey of Biola University, La Mirada, California (*see* above this chapter). That is why Hillary, a Methodist, continues to maintain her membership with her local church Methodist Church in Little Rock, Arkansas, and currently attends with her Baptist husband, Bill, the Protestant ecumenical Riverside Church in New York City.

(10) Unlike Romney's Mormon Church that promotes theocracy wherever it spreads, Hillary's Methodist Church resists theocracy and supports the separation of church and state.

Hillary is a firm believer in the separation of church and state as defined by the Constitution that "Congress shall make no law respecting the establishment of religion." The state will allow all Christian denominations to practice and propagate their own brand of the Christian faith, without outlawing the existence of any Christian religion, or non-Christian religion, or even an atheistic religion. The only prohibition in the Constitution is that no one church controls the state and dictates its own doctrines to be followed by every citizen as was the case in some of the Old World countries that our American ancestors came or even fled from.

The clear distinction between a U.S. president and a minister or priest is that the former while practicing his own Christian religion privately does not demand that the American people follow the particular beliefs of his or her own church, whereas a minister or priest by the very definition of the function is the theologian-in-chief of the members of his own church group who all believe the same doctrines. Romney, no doubt due to the theocratic influence of his Mormon Church, advertises himself as someone who has seen the light of the error of his former pro-choice belief, and is now espousing a correct pro-life doctrine! Romney must realize that his insistence on espousing a correct doctrine for himself as a self-imposed presidential qualification makes him a theologian and therefore a misfit as a future president. The majority of American people may not agree with his belief (and even if they do), what will he do with the rest of the Americans who are pro-choice? Since he will not be the supreme head of his church but of a state, as U.S. president, he cannot excommunicate any of them from membership in the body politic, for they have the right to be Americans! Neither can he treat them as second class citizens.

But, does Hillary qualify as a Christian woman leader of America at all? Is there not something in the Bible which says that "women are to keep quiet?" Yes, they are to "keep quiet *in church*" (emphasis supplied). That does not apply to a woman leader of society, like Hillary. The prohibition is against women becoming theologians within the church. Exceptional women leaders of society have always been allowed. During the period of the reign of Judges in the Old Testament, all the judges were men, but there was an exceptional woman with the name of Deborah who also became a judge (Jg. 5:1f). But that is in the old covenant, applicable to our Jewish brethren, you might object.

Where in the New Testament are women allowed to rule over men? It is not a direct, but only an implied proof: it has to do with a couple who were co-workers with Paul, initially mentioned by Luke in the order of the husband Aquila and his wife, Priscilla (Acts 18:1 KJV). But whenever their names appeared together afterwards, they were introduced by Paul not as (Mr.) Aquila and (Mrs.) Priscilla, but rather as "Priscilla and Aquila" (Acts 18: 18f). The woman had precedence over the man for some exceptional reason only known to Paul.

The test as to who would make the best president of our country is not the candidate's gender or his or her specific religious beliefs, but rather "whether he or she can do the most good for the most people." Hillary will show no favor to any type of Americans: Christian Protestants, Pentecostals, Catholics, or Orthodox; Evangelicals social conservatives or not; religious or non-religious, including those who belong to non-Christian religions; or even those who have no religion or atheists. As a Methodist layperson, Hillary will privately practice the doctrines of her church as led by her own Methodist minister. She allows room for flexibility as the future president of all Americans regardless of church, creed, or color. After all we are all Americans united in one country in spite of all our differences. Hillary's leadership exemplifies our country's motto: *E Pluribus, Unum* (Out of Many, One).

6

Presidential Candidates—Too Young at 42 & Too Old at 69?

◆

Hillary Is Slightly Older than Washington When He First Ran for President; McCain & Paul at 72, Nader at 74, & Gravel at 78 Are Out of the Running

The scholars Warren Mason, Kay Phillips, and Mostafa Rejai made the observation that just because almost all the presidents were between the ages of 45 and 65 when they were elected for the first time does not lead to any firm conclusion about any voting pattern, "except perhaps that the American electorate *does not believe that men beyond sixty-five* are presidential timber" (emphasis supplied).[126] Ninety per cent of all presidents ran for the office for the first time from the ages of 45 to 65.[127] Five per cent of them were above 65 years old—James Buchanan and Ronald Reagan—and 5% were 43 years of age—Theodore Roosevelt and John F. Kennedy—when they first served as president (*see* Table 6.0 & 6.1).

Table 6.0 Thirty-Eight Presidents Who Were 45 to 65 When They Were First Elected

Name	Age
1. George Washington	58
2. John Adams	61

3. Thomas Jefferson	57
4. James Madison	57
5. James Monroe	58
6. John Quincy Adams	57
7. Andrew Jackson	61
8. Martin Van Buren	54
9. William Henry Harrison	65
10. John Tyler	51
11. James Knox Polk	49
12. Zachary Taylor	64
13. Millard Fillmore	50
14. Franklin Pierce	48
16. Abraham Lincoln	52
17. Andrew Johnson	56
18. Ulysses S. Grant	46
19. Rutherford b. Hayes	54
20. James A. Garfield	49
21. Chester A. Arthur	51
22. Grover Cleveland	47
23. Benjamin Harrison	55
24. Grover Cleveland	55
25. William McKinley	54
27. William Howard Taft	51
28. Woodrow Wilson	56
29. Warren G. Harding	55
30. Calvin Coolidge	51
31. Herbert Hoover	54

32. Franklin Delano Roosevelt	51
33. Harry S. Truman	60
34. Dwight D. Eisenhower	62
36. Lyndon B. Johnson	55
37. Richard M. Nixon	56
38. Gerald Ford	61
39. Jimmy Carter	52
41. George H. W. Bush	64
42. William Jefferson Clinton	46
43. George W. Bush	54

Table 6.1 Two Who Were Below 45 When They Became President for the First Time

Name	Age
26. Theodore Roosevelt	43
35. John F. Kennedy	43

Table 6.2 Two Presidents Who Were Above 65 When They Were Elected for the First Time

Name	Age
15. James Buchanan	67
40. Ronald Reagan	68

How do the ages of the current crop of presidential candidates compare with the ages of previous winning presidents? First, let us take a look at the ages of 11

Democrats, 8 who have participated in debates, and 3 other possible last minute additions, Al Gore, Evan Bayh, and Wesley Clark.

Next, we will take a look at the ages of 14 Republicans, 10 participating in the debates, and 4 others who were mentioned as possibilities: Jim Gilmore, Condoleezza Rice, Newt Gingrich, and Jeb Bush.

Finally, we will look at the ages of 2 possible independent presidential candidates: Ralph Nader and Mike Bloomberg (*see* Table 6.3, 6.4, & 6.5).

Table 6.3 The Democratic Presidential Candidates' Ages as of Election Day, November 4, 2008

Name of Candidate	Age
1. Joe Biden	65
2. Hillary Clinton	59
3. Chris Dodd	63
4. John Edwards	54
5. Mike Gravel	78
6. Dennis Kucinich	60
7. Barack Obama	47
8. Bill Richardson	59
9. Al Gore	59
10. Evan Bayh	51
11. Wesley Clark	63

Table 6.4 The Republican Presidential Candidates' Ages as of Election Day, November 4, 2008

Name of Candidate	Age
1. Sam Brownback	50
2. Rudy Giuliani	63

3. Mike Huckabee	51
4. Duncan Hunter	59
5. John McCain	72
6. Ron Paul	72
7. Mitt Romney	60
8. Tom Tancredo	61
9. Tommy Thompson	65
10. Fred Thompson	64
11. Jim Gilmore	57
12. Condi Rice	52
13. Newt Gingrich	64
14. Jeb Bush	55

Table 6.5 The independent Presidential Candidates' Ages as of Election Day, November 4, 2008

Name of Candidate	Age
1. Ralph Nader	74
2. Mike Bloomberg	65

John McCain aged 72 is completely out of the running. This is not just a personal opinion. The real deciders on this matter of what is acceptable age for an American president have been the American voters. For the past 220 years, when they voted for 42 presidents, 100% of their choices were below 70 years of age when they ran for president for the first time.

When John McCain's campaign imploded in the middle of summer 2007, he blamed the top leadership of his staff for failing to raise the millions of dollars he expected. As a result the top 2 leaders of his presidential campaign, John Weaver and Terry Nelson resigned, followed by lower rank national staff, as well as regional and state campaign workers. The original budget was for $154 million which had to be reduced to $137 million, and because money was not coming as expected, it was further reduced by $100 million, to only $78 million. But, the campaign only raised $11 million in the second quarter, instead of the $45 million expected, and that only $2 million was left in the bank in June 2007. And because he made the wrong diagnosis as to what the cause of the problem was, he prescribed the wrong remedy. Because he was so insistent that he was right in blaming the top leadership of his campaign, he thought that the right solution would be to replace them with other presumably as good or even better and more qualified leaders than those who left it.

Unfortunately, the lack of financial backing that McCain expected from prospective contributors might not have anything to do at all with the fault of his campaign staff. It could have been due to his lack of an essential qualification for U.S. president. He must realize that the prospective contributors are not going to waste their money on what they perceive to be a losing candidate. McCain has been a losing candidate from the day he announced his presidential candidacy, because at 72 he is just too old!

Contrast the reluctance of financial backers to contribute to McCain's campaign with the eagerness of those who are behind the presidential candidacy of Hillary Clinton. According to the *USA Today*, "the presidential candidates receiving the most money from the 50 ZIP codes that are top sources of campaign contributions are Democrats (*see* Table 6.6):"[128]

Table 6.6 Top Contributors from January to June, 2007

Presidential Candidate	Amount Contributed (in Millions)
Hillary Rodham Clinton (D)	$12.9
Barack Obama (D)	$10.4
Rudy Giuliani (R)	$6.4
Mitt Romney (R)	$3.7

"Money follows winners," said Michael McDonald, a political scientist at George Mason University in Virginia. "People in the stock market are betting that Democrats are going to win the election." Even Terry Holt, George W.

Bush's GOP strategist in 2004, agrees that giving senators money is a "safe bet for donors ... because even if they don't win, they still will be in a position to influence legislation as a member of the United States Senate."[129]

The reason why Hillary's edge in fundraising is unequalled by any other presidential aspirant, Democrat or Republican, is "standing just beside her, Bill Clinton!" She is so confident that you, the American voter, will band together with others to give her the biggest possible financial support that you are capable of giving—including the few of you who have been blessed with extra resources to be able to share more generously—so that Hillary can communicate her message without worrying as to how she will pay (unlike some of her rivals) in this presidential campaign that may prove to be the longest ever in American history. In anticipation of your wholehearted backing, she also turned down the idea of matching funds which would have limited how much money she could raise, preferring to raise the money herself (or rather by Bill on her behalf.[130]

Some Contributions to Hillary in Selected States from Individuals from $200.00 & Up:

State	Number of Donors	Amount
• New York	6,444 donations	$5.63 million
• California	1,639 donations	$1.54 million
• DC	697 donations	$603,360
• Illinois	553 donations	$554,088
• New Jersey	526 donations	$543,305
• Texas	606 donations	$538,855

Total Amounts from Individuals to Hillary Each Year between 2001 through 2005:

Year	Amount
• 2001	$31,178,474
• 2001-2002	$1,094,192

- 2003-2004 $9,637,834

- 2005 $20,446,448

(1) McCain being too old is just one of several reasons why he is out of the running. If that were not enough, even if his age were younger than the historic minus 69-year-old uppermost limit imposed by the American voters in choosing 42 previous presidents in 220 years of our country's history, there are many other reasons why McCain would still not become a winner.

(2) McCain's additional failure is related to his prescribing the wrong solution for a wrong diagnosis: He has the tendency to be on the losing side of a major issue. When he ran against Bush for president, he was defeated because the voters thought his ideas for governing our country were not as good as Bush's. Now, that Bush has been shown to be governing the country not as good as we expected him to do, McCain sides with Bush!

(3) McCain was even invited by John Kerry to be his vice-presidential running mate in the 2004 presidential election against Bush and Cheney, but McCain did not accept. That ticket could have won, and we would not be in the mess that we are now. As a result, Kerry had to settle for an inexperienced John Edwards as his Democratic vice-presidential running mate, and the inevitable result was total defeat.

(4) While there is no upper limit for running for the presidency of the United States, it is understood that the president must be physically and mentally healthy. As for McCain's physical condition, although US Navy doctors declared him fit, after prolonged detention as a POW prisoner in North Vietnam, there is lingering doubt that he is healthy. You may wonder if his too frequent fits of anger are related to his aging years. Many times, in the midst of what to others are just ordinary conversations, he is driven to uncalled-for arguments, yelling, and the uttering of personal even sexual expletives!

(5) The *Los Angeles Times* on May 21, 2007 reported that "McCain loses temper again raising doubts about [his] fitness." They wrote about McCain's verbal exchange with his co-Republican Sen. John Cornyn who expressed that McCain was too busy with his presidential campaign to pay attention to the details of the immigration bill that was being taken up in the Senate prompting the former to say, "F ... you!"[131] No president in the history of our country was ever heard uttering the F ... word.[132]

Paul Levinson pointed out the irony that McCain used the F ... word at a time when he voted to increase fines for indecency over the broadcast airwaves, for infractions which include using language which is not as strong as McCain used. He even co-sponsored said Broadcast Decency Enforcement Act of 2005 which raised FCC fines from $32,500 to $325,000 for the use of "indecent language."![133]

(6) McCain was also one of the Keating Five U.S. senators who were involved in the scandal that had to do with the collapse of most Savings and Loan associations in the United States in the late 1980's. Lincoln Savings and Loan was insolvent due to some bad loans. In order to regain solvency, Lincoln sold investments in a real estate venture as a FDIC insured savings account. This caught the eye of federal regulators who were looking to shut it down. Charles H. Keating, on behalf of Lincoln Savings and Loan, contacted five U.S. senators to whom he made previous financial contributions to bail him out. Lincoln Savings and Loan happened to be a subsidiary of Charles H. Keating's American Continental Corporation. Between 1982 and 1987, McCain received approximately $112,000 in political contributions from Keating and his associates. In addition, McCain's wife and her father invested $359,100 in a Keating shopping center in 1986. Eventually, the real estate venture failed, making many elderly investors broke. Federal regulators ultimately filed a $1.1 billion civil racketeering and fraud suit against Keating, accusing him of siphoning Lincoln's deposits to his family and into political campaigns. In the end, none of the senators were indicted of any crime, but McCain received a rebuke from the Senate Ethics Committee for exercising "poor judgment" in interfering with the investigation of Lincoln Savings and Loan by federal regulators.[134]

(7) He co-authored the McCain-Feingold [-Fred Thompson] campaign reform bill that the Gun Owners of America (GOA) has criticized as being the "odious McCain-Feingold Incumbent Protection Act" that severely limits the rights of groups like the GOA to inform the public about the gun rights voting records of politicians already in office![135]

(8) There is the matter of McCain's having been divorced from his first wife. Forty out of 42 previous presidents were not divorced. Only 1 was divorced (Ronald Reagan) and 1 was unmarried (James Buchanan). Even if McCain were as young as or younger than Reagan when he ran for president the first time, McCain would still have between nothing to no more than 1 chance out of 42 to become America's future president. And he is no Reagan! This matter of divorce need not enter into the picture at all, since it is McCain's over-age at 72 that completely disqualifies him from being elected to the U.S. presidency.

(9) In any case, McCain may lack the necessary objectivity that is demanded of one who occupies the office of U.S. president. Mr. David Keene, chairman of

the American Conservative Union said that: "In McCain's world, there aren't legitimate differences of opinions.... There is his way and there is evil. That is how he approaches issues." [136]

(10) If he were elected president in 2008, our people will probably be wondering how long he will last in that most strenuous of all governmental jobs, the presidency of the most powerful country in the world! If anyone were to withdraw from running for president before it is too late, McCain must surely be the first one to do it.

A withdrawal is also appropriate for another Republican presidential candidate Texas Congressman Ron Paul who is 72 like McCain. Ralph Nader, a couple of years older at 74, must not consider joining the race, and even if he were much younger, he can never win as an independent presidential candidate anyway (*see* chapter 9 below). The oldest of all presidential candidates is Democratic ex-Senator of Alaska, Mike Gravel at 78! If McCain who started as the number 1 presidential front-runner of the Republican Party cannot win his party's nomination, let alone win the U.S. presidency, what makes Ron Paul, Ralph Nader, or Mike Gravel think that he can do better? We will discuss the case of Ralph Nader more extensively in chapter 7 below when we take up the impossibility of winning as an independent presidential candidate.

Even if Ron Paul were younger than 65—the maximum age at which 95% of American presidents were elected—his chance to win like McCain is practically nil. The fact that that he is a doctor of medicine is in itself extremely rare as a background of American presidents (only 1 president out of 42 was an MD). But, it is not his medical background that ultimately disqualifies Paul from becoming U.S. president. It is his being over-age at 72, just like his Republican colleague McCain.

As early as the middle of July 26, 2007, in its editorial, *USA Today* gave the opinion that the in-party debates among the Democratic and among the Republican presidential candidates respectively should be limited to those who have "a chance to win." "... As time passes by," the *USA Today* editorial continued, the idea looks more and more like a winner for voters.... Democrat Mike Gravel often registers 0% support—and still complains during debates that he is not given enough free air time. The Republican field of nine candidates includes six who have had about as much impact as the proverbial tree falling in a forest. Their combined support is in the single digits."[137]

Guess who strenuously objected to the idea of limiting the number of debaters? If you answered, "ex-Sen. Mike Gravel," you are absolutely right. He accuses two of the three Democratic front-runners, Hillary Clinton and John Edwards of trying to narrow the field of debaters that excludes him and 4 or 5 others from participating. He said that the following conversation took place during an NAACP forum in Detroit on July 12, 2007:

"**Edwards**: 'We should try to have a more serious, and a smaller group.'

Clinton: 'There was an attempt by our campaigns to do that, it got somehow detoured. We've gotta get back to it.... Our guys should talk'."[138]

Gravel said that because of this connivance, he was not initially invited to 3 other forums but that when he told their sponsors why it was unfair for him to be excluded, they changed their minds.

We think that it was not because of such tentative suggestion by ex-Sen. Edwards to Hillary to narrow the field of presidential debaters that had anything to do with the exclusion of Gravel by other sponsors of forums. Nor does it have anything to do with his having a learning disability being dyslexic, for he still managed to get a B.S. degree in general studies at Columbia University, NY. It is a matter of record that no president of the United States had ever been dyslexic or suffered any other similar disability. But, the number 1 reason for Gravel's disqualification for the U.S. presidency is that he is way, way too old! Of all the presidential hopefuls, Gravel has the least or bottom chance to win either the Democratic primary or the election on November 4, 2008. Past American voters had never voted for a president older than 68. Ronald Reagan ran for president for the first time when he was 68 and ran for a second term when he was 72 and ended his 2 terms when he was 76, 2 years short of Gravel's current age! The fact that Gravel gets 0% support in most polling by any organization is a clear indication that present-day American voters want to follow the previous pattern of not voting for presidential candidates who are older than 68!

When the U.S. Constitution was drafted by the fathers of our country, they had only in mind male candidates, for when they said "all men were created equal," they literally meant it to exclude women. After all, women along with slaves had no right to vote, let alone hold office, when our country's federal constitution was created. It was not till the 1920's that women finally were allowed to vote. Nevertheless, it was fortuitous that the minimum age for any man to run for president (or vice-president) is 35, for it was thought that a man at least needed to be that old before he can be considered a mature and experienced adult. At that age, a man will have completed his education, obtained a job, gotten married and taken care of his own family financially.

Thirty-five as a minimum age limit for women candidate is equally fine. We do not have to amend the U.S. Constitution to accommodate the needs of a woman presidential candidate. She will have completed her education, obtained a job, gotten married, and reared her children till they can take care of themselves. In reality all presidents were 43 years old and above when they were elected president for the first time.

Hillary, as a woman had to be as educated as her future husband, Bill, got married and fulfilled her role as a mother of her daughter, Chelsea (till she reached the age of maturity, completed her education, and even had a job on her own). Now, Hillary Clinton is only 59, or is slightly older than when George Washington was when he was elected president for the first time. It is only fitting that the first president ever and the first woman president of our country are about the same age when running for that office for the first time.

Many Historical Coincidences Make for Hillary's Destiny!

(1). If Walter Mondale won with Geraldine Ferraro in 1984, then as Vice-President the latter would have had the prior claim to succeed Mondale and therefore she would have run for president under the banner of the Democratic Party in 1992 instead of Bill Clinton.

(2). If Al Gore and Joe Lieberman had won as president and vice-president in 2000, and then they would most likely have won for re-election in 2004, and it would have been Lieberman who has a prior claim to run for president under the banner of the Democratic Party in 2008.

(3). If John Kerry and John Edwards had won as president and vice-president in 2004, then it would have been Vice-president Edwards who would have had a prior claim to run for re-lection (with President Kerry) under the banner of the Democratic Party in 2008, instead of just being a third ranked Democratic presidential candidate behind Hillary Clinton and Barack Obama according to most national polls this time.

(4). If even just one pair of Democratic candidates above had won, it would have pushed Hillary's age beyond 65, the maximum age that 95% of all previous presidents were elected!

7

Only Democrats & Republicans Can Win; Independents, Never

◆

Hillary Is Favored to Win; Independent Nader Will Spoil Her Opponents' Chances

There exists a well-known saying, "There is always a first time." To which do you apply this saying:

(1) To the fact that up to now no independent presidential candidate has ever won, but for some reason, an independent candidate will win in 2008? Or,

(2) To the fact that an independent presidential candidate, Ralph Nader, had spoiled Democrats Al Gore chance to win in 2000, but that he cannot spoil Hillary Clinton's presidential victory in 2008?

In the presidential election, only candidates of 2 political parties matter: the Democratic and the Republican. After the first president, George Washington who had no political party, there had always been 2 major parties although with different names, such as the Hamiltonian Federalists versus the Jeffersonian Democratic-Republicans (or anti-Federalists), followed by the Whigs versus the Democrats, and with the arrival of our 16th president, Abraham Lincoln, the Republican Party replaced the Whigs, resulting in our present Democratic versus Republican Parties.

There had been many independent or third-party presidential candidates, but there never was any independent or third-party candidate whoever won a presidential election. For all practical purposes independent and third-party candidates are only protest candidates. They think that both the 2 dominant parties are equally evil, and they want to point out said evils.

Politics, however, is not a matter of the contest between two evils, and the choice of the lesser evil. It is the art of compromise, true. But, it is a compromise of two goods, i.e., a matter of choosing the better of 2 political candidates in a 2-party system. Or, it is a matter of choosing the best of 3 or more good alternatives.

The independent or third-party candidate often rationalizes his entry as a presidential candidate that he is a better alternative as an opposition to the abuses of the party in power (i.e. the status quo). Since there is no way he can possibly win. The only result of his entry as an independent or third-party presidential candidate is to split the votes of the anti-status quo, thus resulting in the perpetuation of the said status quo. The end result is the choice of the less good between two major presidential candidates.

So, to vote for an independent or third-party candidate is the same as a vote to prevent change! For example, if you do not agree with the way George W. Bush is running the government, to vote for an independent candidate will be to split the votes against Bush's party and thus have the opposite effect of a vote against change, i.e., your vote will keep Bush's party in power!

Nothing illustrates this better than the career of Ralph Nader, the consumer advocate-turned politician. If you think with us that John McCain is out of the running because he is too old, then there is more reason not to vote for Nader, if he runs again as an independent candidate for president in 2008. Ninety-five per cent of all American presidents were under 65 years old when they ran for the office of president for the first time but Nader is almost a decade older than that, 74, or 2 years older than McCain at 72, and 1 year older than Ronald Reagan when he ran for re-election!

No independent or third-party candidate ever won in the presidential election for the last 220 years, so if Nader decides to run in 2008 it is not because he thinks he can win (which is impossible) but to serve as a spoiler i.e. to prevent Bush and company from being changed.

Independent candidate Nader's spoiler role worked quite well in 2000 when it was his votes subtracted from the votes of Al Gore that made George W. Bush win for the first time. Bush only won by 537 votes in Florida, but Nader got 97,000 votes some of which could have gone to Gore to make him win if Nader were not a presidential candidate. This fact was reported "in an episode of *The Simpsons* that aired after the 2000 presidential election in which [Nader] is portrayed as a clandestine member of the Springfield Republican Party and is thanked for all the fine work he has done for the Republicans."[139]

Important supporters of Ralph Nader, including former President Jimmy Carter who received a lot of advice from Nader in the Oval Office, urged him not to run in the 2004 presidential election for fear that he might help Bush get re-elected at the expense of John Kerry.

But Nader did not budge, saying that he was running against both the Republican and the Democratic presidential candidates for being both tools of "corrupt corporate business."

Ralph Nader's attempt at wrecking the presidential election against the Democrats might not be over yet. Early in February, 2007, he told Wolf Blitzer of CNN's Late Edition that he was contemplating another run for the presidency in 2008. In this interview, he did not even bother to pretend as previously that he is going to be an independent candidate to go against "corporate corruption of both the major parties." When he was asked to describe Hillary as a presidential candidate, he replied: "'Flatters, panders, coasting, front-runner, looking for a coronation … She has no political fortitude.' He says that his decision to run will be influenced, especially if the Democratic Party chooses Hillary Clinton."[140]

Nader does not yet even know who the opponent of Hillary will be, yet he already made up his mind to oppose her! Such a preconceived attitude is not presidential (and since he knows he cannot win as a third party candidate), he is showing his true color not as a truly independent presidential candidate running against 2 "corrupt-influenced parties" (as he calls it) but he is running only as an insidious spoiler against Democratic Hillary. If he were truly independent, how come he made up his mind that anybody, but Hillary can be the next president of the United States of America?

Can it be that much of Nader's anti-Hillary sexist attitude this time is due to a pre-conceived bias about women in general, and that was the reason why he remained single for all of 74 years (and still counting) of his life? His excuse for not getting married at all is that he did not like to be "an absentee father of his children." If so, why does he want to become a U.S. president of millions of American families who have children to be taken care of? Would it be okay for him to become U.S. president and be "an absentee father of millions of American children," but not "an absentee father of his own wife's children?"

Is Nader's real reason for wanting to run for president in 2008 simply a congenital hatred against anything and everything that has to do with women including the apple-eating wife of the first man Adam, Eve, and all women who are her descendants? Such inflexible attitude, which is worse than "the world of McCain" in which there is the right side, Nader's side, and everyone else's side is the wrong side is the clearest proof that Nader was not running for president in 2000 and 2004, and he will not be running for president in 2008, in order to win. His agenda is no more and no less than simply to spoil somebody else's chance to win, usually a candidate of the opposition whose votes will be split by his candidacy.

Ralph Nader Cannot Spoil Hillary's Victory

But, we have really bad news for Ralph Nader this time around. That is why we at Hillary's camp want to urge him to run! Why? It is because Nader's candidacy will benefit Hillary more than any of her Republican opponents. In 2008, regardless of the intention of Ralph Nader, his preconceived plan to wreck Hillary's chance at becoming the first woman president of the United States, the greatest country in the world, will *not* be successful. It is worth repeating, it will *not* be successful! The reasons are as follows:

(1) American voters have wised up to the real spoiler objective of Nader. They did not allow themselves to be hoodwinked in the 2004 election, so even if John Kerry lost to the incumbent George W. Bush, Nader cannot claim the credit of having elected the latter as he did in the 2000 election. "Some voters who preferred Ralph Nader's over John Kerry's positions voted for John Kerry to avoid splitting the vote against the incumbent, claiming to be choosing the 'lesser of two evils.' These voters used slogans such as, 'Anybody but Bush," and 'A Vote for Nader is a vote for Bush.' A group of people who supported Nader in 2000 released a statement entitled 'Vote to Stop Bush', urging support for Kerry/Edwards in swing states. Whether due to this campaign or other factors, the impact of Nader on the election's outcome ultimately proved inconsequential, as he received less than 1% of the national vote. In fact all of the independent candidates together polled fewer votes than Nader had in 2000."[141]

(2) In chapter 6 above, you read that Nader is 74 years old, 2 years older than McCain. If McCain is out of the running because of his age—Reagan, the oldest president ever, did run when he was only 68—how much more so is Nader doubly out of the running?

(3) In chapter 8 below, you will also read that Nader stayed single all his life. Even if he were younger, his being single will almost disqualify him, too, because there was only one unmarried president in American history, and that was James Buchanan. He turned out to be one of the 2 worst presidents that our country ever had! Only one president, Warren G. Harding, beat him to the bottom of the list of all the worst American presidents, according to the scholarly opinion of 3 different panels of historians (*see* Conclusion below).

(4) You just read at the beginning of this chapter that no independent candidate ever won from the beginning of our country's history 220 years ago, and after the election of 42 U.S. presidents.

(5) Ralph Nader's independent candidacy worked against the Democratic presidential nominee Al Gore in 2000 because all the candidates were males.

(6) In general, because American voters realize that the election of a woman president of the United States is long overdue, they will vote for Hillary in 2008 whether or not there is also a Nader or any other independent presidential candidate running.

(7) Nader's spoiler role will not work against Hillary because she is female. Most of the women who are for Hillary will still be for her. Most of the men who give Hillary only a slight lead will still be voting for her. It will be those men who have reservations about Hillary, but are angry at Bush's policies that will be split! Thus, a Nader independent candidacy will help Hillary win more than her white male opponent. That is so because Nader is also a white male candidate. If his name were Ralpha and female, she could be more effective in derailing Hillary's chance to become the first woman president of the United States ever, as it will split the female votes.

(8) Nader's spoiler role against Gore in 2000 was effective because the race was very close, especially in the battleground states, such as Florida.

(9) But, in 2008, the race will not be close anywhere, for Hillary is so far ahead of any white male opponent that the Republican Party can come up with, by as many as 135 electoral votes, or about 50% of the total national electoral votes needed to win at 270 (*see* chapter 10 below).

(10) If you object to McCain as lacking the flexibility of a future president, for very often a simple matter of disagreement drives him to fits of unexpected anger when contradicted by anyone, then you must be more wary of Nader becoming president because he has the same type of one-sidedness but is very calm about it as if everything is normal. McCain's fits of anger is possibly curable by attending anger-management classes, but Nader's pre-conceived idea, like the impossibility of his winning the presidency, is totally incurable. We are left with no other conclusion except to remind you that there is every good reason why the American electorate voted overwhelmingly at 95% for only presidential candidates below 65 years of age at least 43 times in the last 220 years, since those who are above that age, especially the ones who are about a decade older, are never presidential timbers!

It is even more problematic for Giuliani's successor as New York City mayor who had recently resigned from the Republican Party, Mike Bloomberg, to run as an independent presidential candidate in 2008. If he does, everything that disqualifies Giuliani from becoming president applies to him, and because he will be running as an independent everything that can be said against perennial independent presidential candidate Ralph Nader, who will find it impossible to win in the presidential election, can also be said against him.

The fact that Bloomberg only got divorced once, like Ronald Reagan, is an improvement on Giuliani who had divorced more than once. However, unlike Reagan, he did not remarry, so if he becomes president, he will reside in the White House as a bachelor. That only happened once before with the never-married James Buchanan in the 19th century. According to Fred Hochberg, dean of the Milano New School for Management and Urban Policy: "the nation had not elected an unmarried president since the 19th century, because voters tend to look for a parental figure in their executive leaders, there is an official residence, and we think about families living there."[142]

A Bloomberg independent candidacy will also be favorable to Hillary for the same reasons as the candidacy of Nader, because he is also a white male. Much more so, if Hillary's opponent will be Giuliani, for Bloomberg will most likely split Giuliani's potential voters, rather than Hillary's. According to Peter A. Brown of the Quinnipiac University Polling Institute, Bloomberg as an independent would take more votes from Giuliani if the latter were the Republican candidate rather than from Hillary. A similar scenario will take place with a different Republican opponent, because the votes of the male candidates will be split, not Hillary's, she being a female.

- Without Bloomberg in the Race: Hillary 44%, Giuliani 42%
- With Bloomberg in a 3-Way Race: Hillary 40%, Giuliani 35%, Bloomberg 10%.

The best strategy against the nuisance role of Ralph Nader or Mike Bloomberg or any other independent or third party candidate, is to simply ignore his presence, and concentrate on voting for one of the presidential candidates of the 2 major political parties, as they are the only ones who have a chance to win. In *the U.S. News & World Report*, it has been reported that since the end of the Second World War the Democrats and the Republicans held the U.S. presidency in alternating 2-terms, except in a couple of instances:

Truman, *Democrat* (the start of the alternating cycle)

Eisenhower, *Republican* (2)

Kennedy/Johnson, *Democrat* (2)

Nixon/Ford, *Republican* (2)

Carter, *Democrat* (1 exception)

Reagan/Bush, Sr., *Republican* (3 exception)

Clinton, *Democrat* (2)

Bush, Jr., *Republican* (2)

Projected Winner in 2008: Hillary Clinton (sure of 1 term, most likely 2), provided she gets nominated as the official candidate of the Democratic Party early in 2008. The reason why Bush, Sr. won in 1988 was because his term was really the extension of the popular Ronald Reagan 2-term presidency. It is a safe bet that the present 2-term presidency of the highly unpopular incumbent George W. Bush will not be extended into a third term by a candidate of his political party. A very clear indicator of this is the irrevocable decision of Vice-President Dick Cheney not to run in 2008 (the last time both the incumbent president and vice-president did not run was in 1928). Another very strong sign is the fact that Republican presidential candidates who are running realize the unpopularity of George W. Bush with approval ratings hovering below 30%, instead of defending are mostly attacking his policies. The Republican presidential candidates attack their party's president and his failed policies like Democrats.

Members of Congress have also been defecting from Bush's policy. These include Sen. John Warner of Virginia, Sen. Richard Lugar of Indiana, Sen. George Voinovich of Ohio, and Sen. Pete Domenici of New Mexico. There had been former GOP huge financial backers who also have shifted their support to Hillary, including hotelier Donald Trump, MTA Chairman Peter Kalikow, and New York City investment banker Jeffrey Volk.

The strongest reason why it is really the turn of the Democrats this time around is that the eventual candidate of the Republican Party in the 2008 presidential election will be a white man.

Catherine Brinkman, 28, of Foster City who heads the California Young Republicans admitted the widely-held perception that "we're still selling the same old white guys." [143] We already took up the arguments that at a time when Americans are ready to vote for a woman, the candidacy of a white man is old-fashioned and contrary to the trend (*see* chapter 1 above).

The worst sign of the outdated outlook of anyone of the Republican white male presidential prospects was their reluctance to participate in the CNN-You-Tube format of the debate originally scheduled for them on September 17, 2007 (excuses were made by both the 2 front-runners, Giuliani and Romney not to join). They are not as avant-garde as the Democrats who were so successful in first debating in this unique Internet-format on July 23, 2007. The Internet supporters of the Republican Party presidential prospects expressed their dissatisfaction. "The candidates," they wrote, "reinforced a notion already bedeviling their side: that Republicans don't 'get' the Web. While the Republicans have mastered talk radio, the Democrats have led in using the Web for fundraising, organizing and energizing the grassroots."[144] Andrew Sullivan, a conservative blogger, puts it this way: "The current old white men running for the GOP already seem from some other planet. Ducking YouTube after the Dems did so well will look like a party uncomfortable with the culture and uncomfortable with democracy."[145]

"Poll Shows GOP Losing Ground with Youth" was the headline of the *San Francisco*
Chronicle on August 27, 2007. It quoted the Washington firm of Greenberg Quinlan Rosner poll of 1,017 voters ages from 18 to 29 conducted on May 29-June 19, 2007: "The startling collapse of GOP support among young voters is reflect in the poll's findings that show two-thirds of young voters surveyed believe Democrats do a better job than Republicans of representing their views—even on issues Republicans once owned, such as terrorism and taxes."[146]

"String of Scandals Has Republicans Worried," is the headline of the *San Jose Mercury News* on August 29, 2007. "Scott Reed, a Republican strategist, was at a dinner in Philadelphia on Monday night when his cell phone and Internet pager began beeping like crazy. Only later did he learn why: His party was being rocked by a sex scandal involving a Republican U.S. senator—*again* (emphasized provided)." This latest sex scandal concerned Idaho Sen. Larry Craig, co-chair of the Mitt Romney campaign, who admitted committing "disorderly conduct" in a bathroom in an airport in Minneapolis, MN, but he later denied that he was a homosexual. Another senator, David Vitter, southern regional chair of Rudy Giuliani's campaign, got caught with his name in the D.C. Madam's rolodex. And the state representative who headed John McCain for president in Florida was charged with soliciting sex in a men's bathroom in a public park.[147]

Thus, candidates of both the Democratic and Republican parties can safely ignore any candidate who runs as an independent. Even without taking into account the unpopularity of the Republican leadership, the Democrats still have a great advantage in this election. If it is a general pattern of history that there is a

2-term rotation between the presidents of the 2 major parties—Democrats and Republicans—and since the incumbent George W. Bush is a Republican currently finishing his second term, any Democratic presidential candidate at this time will have a clear winning edge! If it is further true that the time has come to change the pattern of the last 220 years of only voting for a white male president, and elect a woman president in 2008 for the first time, then both historical trends converge on only one possible winner: President Hillary (Rodham Clinton)!

8

Forty Presidents Were Married; 1 Divorced Just Once, & 1 Single

◆

Hillary Has Bill; Giuliani & Gingrich, Too Many Exes, & Nader & Condi, Nobody

Of the 3 major types of marital relationships, Hillary's standing by her man, Bill, until death do them part agrees with 40 out of 42 U.S. presidents in the last 220 years. This type of relationship is best expressed by the Hillary Clinton presidential campaign official theme song which you had a hand in choosing through a YouTube Internet contest in June 2007: "You and I" sang by internationally famous Celine Dion who first received global recognition when she sang the background music of the Disney movie "Beauty and the Beast" followed by her singing the background music of the movie "Titanic:"[148]

YOU and I

(By Aldo Nova & Jacques Dubal)
(1). High above the mountains, far across the sea
I can hear your voice calling out to me
Brighter than the sun and darker than the night
I can see your love shining like a light
And on and on this earth spins like a carousel
If I could travel across the world
The secrets I would tell
(Chorus:) *You and I*

Were meant to fly
Higher than the clouds
We'll sail across the sky
So come with me
And you will feel
That we're soaring
That we're floating up so high
'Cause you and I were meant to fly.
(2) Sailing like a bird high on the wings of love
Take me higher than all the stars above
I'm burning, yearning
Gently turning round and round
I'm always rising up, I never
Want to come back down
(Chorus x2:) *You and I*
Were meant to fly
Higher than the clouds
We'll sail across the sky
So come with me
And you will feel
That we're soaring
That we're floating up so high
'Cause you and I were meant to fly.

The theme song is intended for Hillary to sing to each of you individually. Imagine yourself as the person alone that she is singing, too. Then, imagine what the words say about "you and I" (you and Hillary) as the lyrics tell you to fly with her above the skies because both of you are like birds who "were meant to fly." That is what true love means for the song was originally a love lyric after all, like the love that Hillary has for Bill and vice-versa. Now that it has become Hillary's a campaign theme song, "You and I" has become a heartfelt friendship song as well.

And how friendly is Hillary as a person? Former New York Sen. Alfonse D'Amato and ex-New York City Mayor Ed Koch, after an experience of having dinner with her at the Four Seasons in mid-town Manhattan, both said that patrons flocked to the Senator and former First Lady like long lost friends seeing each other again. "My God, it was incredible, like the whole place came over to see her and pay their respect—and she knew everybody by their first name," D'Amato told the New York Post. "She walks into a place, she is the buzz—they come over like bees to honey," added Koch.

Here is a similar story that shows the friendly side of "the real Hillary" in the words of Peter Feddo, host of *votehillary.org*: "Last summer, I went to a party she was giving at her house—hidden away off Massachusetts Avenue, a stone's throw from the British embassy—and took the opportunity to introduce her to a teen-age boy who I knew was going to intern for her later in the summer. She gave the kid about five seconds of her time, beaming at him before moving on to the next hand to shake.

Probably six weeks later, having not so much as eyes on her since, the boy was walking down a Senate corridor when Hillary approached in the opposite direction. Meeting his eyes, she greeted him without hesitation: 'Good to see you again, Pete.' Then, three weeks after that, the same kid and zillions of other Hillary interns gathered in a small, overheated office to have their photographs taken with the senator. Suddenly, overcome by the heat, the boy collapsed almost literally into her arms. He came round a couple of seconds later, lying on his back and seeing the face of (possibly) America's 44th president peering anxiously down at him, proffering her bottle of water. 'She was really kind, sort of motherly,' he told me later."[149]

Of the 42 presidents, 40 were never-divorced married men: 32 of whom married single women, 3 married widows, 3 re-married after the death of their first spouse, and 2 married divorced women. Only 1 president was divorced once, Ronald Reagan, and his second wife was his First Lady, Nancy Reagan nee Davis (when he was married to his first wife, actress Jane Wyman, he was not yet president). And only 1 U.S. president was never married, that is, James Buchanan (*see* Table 8.0).

Table 8.0 Presidents Who Were Married and Not Divorced (40)

Married Single Women (32)	*Spouse:*	*First Lady:*
1. John Adams	Abigail Smith	Abigail

2. James Monroe	Elizabeth Kortwright	Elizabeth/Eliza Hay (daughter, sub)
3. John Quincy Adams	Louisa Catherine Johnson	Louisa
4. Martin van Buren	Hannah Hoes	Angelica Singleton (daughter-in-law)
5. William Henry Harrison	Anna Symmes	Jane Irwin Harrison (daughter-in-law)
6. James Knox Polk	Sarah Childress	Sarah
7. Zachary Taylor	Margaret Mackall Smith	Mary Elizabeth Taylor Bliss (daughter)
8. Millard Fillmore	Abigail Powers	Mary Abigail Fillmore (daughter)
9. Franklin Pierce	Jane Means Appleton	Jane
10. Abraham Lincoln	Mary Todd	Mary
11. Andrew Johnson	Eliza McCardle	Martha Johnson Patterson (daughter)
12. Ulysses S. Grant	Julia Dent	Julia
13. Rutherford B. Hayes	Lucy Ware Webb	Lucy
14. James A, Garfield	Lucretia Rudolph	Lucretia
15. Chester A. Arthur	Ellen Lewis Herndon	Mary Arthur McElroy (sister)
16. Grover Cleveland	Frances Folsom	Rose Cleveland (sister)/Frances
17. Benjamin Harrison	Caroline Lavinia Scott	Caroline/Mary McKee (daughter)
18. William McKinley	Ida Saxton	Ida

19. William Howard Taft	Helen Herron	Helen/Helen Manning (daughter,sub)
20. Calvin Coolidge	Grace Anna Goodhue	Grace
21. Herbert Hoover	Lou Henry	Lou
22. Franklin D. Roosevelt	Anna Eleanor Roosevelt	Anna Eleanor
23. Harry S. Truman	Elizabeth "Bess" Wallace	Elizabeth "Bess"
24. Dwight D. Eisenhower	Mary "Mamie" Geneva Doud	Mary "Mamie"
25. John F. Kennedy	Jacqueline "Jackie" Bouvier	Jackeline "Jackie"
26. Lyndon B. Johnson	Claudia "Lady Bird" Taylor	Claudia "Lady Bird"
27. Richard M. Nixon	Thelma "Patricia" Ryan	Thelma "Patricia"
28. Gerald Ford	Elizabeth "Betty" Warren	Elizabeth "Betty"
29. Jimmy Carter	Rosalynn Smith	Rosalynn
30. George W. H. Bush	Barbara Pierce	Barbara
31.William Jefferson Clinton	Hillary Rodham	Hillary/Chelsea (daughter, sub)
32. George W. Bush	Laura Welch	Laura
Married Widows (3)	*Spouse:*	*First Lady:*
33. George Washington	Martha Dandrige Custis	Martha
34. Thomas Jefferson	Martha Wayles Skelton	Dolley Payne Todd (friend)
35. James Madison	Dolley Payne Todd	Dolley
Married Divorced Women (2)	*Spouse:*	*First Lady:*
36. Andrew Jackson	Rachel Donelson Robards	Emily Donelson Jackson (niece)

	(Died prior to presidency)	Sarah Yorke Jackson (daughter-in-law)
37. Warren G. Harding	Florence Kling de Wolfe	Florence
Re-married after First Spouse Died (3)	*Spouses:*	*First Lady:*
38. John Tyler	(1) Letitia Christian	Priscilla Cooper (daughter-in-law)
	(2) Julia Gardiner	Julia
39. Theodore Roosevelt	(1) Alice Hathaway Lee	(Not yet elected president)
	(2) Edith Kermit Carow	Edith
40. Woodrow Wilson	(1) Ellen Louise Axson	Margaret Wilson (daughter)
	(2) Edith Bolling Galt	Helen Woodrow Bones (cousin)

Table 8.1 Divorced & Remarried (1)	*Spouses:*	*First Lady:*
41. Ronald Reagan	(1) Jane Wyman	(Not yet elected president)
	(2) Nancy Davis	Nancy

Table 8.2 Remained Single (1)	*Spouse:*	*First Lady:*
42. James Buchanan	(None)	Harriet Rebecca Lane (niece)

Who among the 42 previous American presidents is Hillary most like? If your answer is Bill Clinton, you are absolutely right. And for the following reasons:

(1) They were previously listed together as Bill Clinton (president) and Hillary Rodham Clinton (spouse) {*see* number 31 in Table 8.0}. After you will have made your choice come the presidential election of November 4, 2008, hopefully they will be listed together again, but in reverse sequence, Hillary Rodham Clinton (president) and Bill Clinton (spouse).

(2) How did it all begin? Bill Clinton met Hillary for the first time in the Yale Law library, New Haven, CT. They were both studying. As Hillary recalled later, "there was this handsome young man who kept staring at me across an almost empty library room." She walked towards him and extended her right hand, and continued: "As long as we are here together, we might as well get acquainted. My name is Hillary Rodham from Illinois. What's yours?" Bill was so taken aback by Hillary's direct (aggressive?) approach that he dropped his book, and wanted to know more about her. The rest is herstory!

(3) Bill Clinton dated Hillary for a few months. He wanted to be certain that she was willing to go back home with him to Arkansas to fulfill his dream of entering politics. He did not like to let her commit to a situation that might stifle her own dream of a different future career. Hillary assured him that her only dream is what every American woman dreams after she has finished her studies, which is to get married to the man she loves, settle down, and raise a child or two. And she does not mind going to Arkansas with Bill, because a woman's place is beside her loving husband, wherever that may be.

(4) So, Bill proposed to marry Hillary. She accepted. And they got married in 1975 in Fayetteville, Arkansas. And Chelsea was born in 1980. It was also clear from the start that Hillary, like Bill, is a "baby boomer" and that motherhood was not the only thing she was destined to do. She did not spend all that time, money, and energy to study in Wellesley College and Yale Law School just "to bake cookies and do the baby's diapers." As a woman, she had to do those too, but they are not the "be-all and end-all of her entire existence." And as a married woman, she made a vow to love her husband "until death do us part," that she would carefully choose work that will keep her beside him and complement rather than compete with his dream of rendering public service all through life.

(5) Bill became governor of Arkansas for 12 years (1979-1981 & 1983-1993). Hillary became First Lady of Arkansas during those 12 years that her husband was governor.

(6) Bill became president of the United States for 2 4-year terms (1993-2001). Hillary became First Lady of the United States for 8 years when her husband was U.S. president. And they could have "lived happily ever after" in retirement. If their story ended right there, it would still be one of the greatest love stories of all

time! But, the story continues. They had arrived only at the half-way point of their lives of service "for God, for country, and for Yale." Now, it was Hillary's turn.

(7) Hillary became junior senator of New York. Bill followed her to New York and he established his presidential library in Arkansas and his non-profit foundation.

(8) Hillary ran for re-election as U.S. Senator from New York with an almost 70% of the votes cast in 2006; Bill continued to run his non-profit foundation.

"Reflecting on all my experiences since law school," Hillary reminisces, "it's hard for me to imagine any other path. I have been blessed with so many opportunities: being part of the newly created Children's Defense Fund, becoming a staff attorney in Congress and partner at a law firm, serving our nation as First Lady and serving New York in the United States Senate. And, of course, I met my husband when we were both students at Yale Law School."

"But the truth is," she continues, "my decision to attend law school was by no means assured. I felt pulled in million different directions. My graduating class at Wellesley was the class of 1969, a time of great change and anguish for America. My time as an undergraduate coincided with years of cultural tumult, controversy, and tragedy, including the escalation of the Vietnam War, the withdrawal of President Johnson from the presidential race and the assassinations of Martin Luther King, Jr. and Robert Kennedy."

(9) Now, it is Hillary turn to run for president in 2007. Bill stands by her woman. We agree with Joe Trippi's view that Hillary has all what it takes to win as America's first woman president in 2008: "the ability to raise the money; a political team that is among the best, if not the best, in the party; a strong base of support; and an uncanny ability to avoid political mistakes. And I don't care what anyone says—her husband is one of two rock stars in the Democratic Party and a huge asset."[150]

Hillary insists that she is the strongest Democratic presidential candidate. "I know what Gingrich (R, GA) tells people privately; I know what Karl Rove (Bush adviser) tells people privately, [and] I know what Tom Delay (R, TX) tell people privately," she says. "I'm the one person they are most afraid of. Bill and I have beaten them before and we will again." Astonishingly, Tom DeLay does not hesitate to make his assessment of Hillary's prospects publicly (see Conclusion below).

Bill will become the first First Gentleman of the United States. Chelsea will be the first First Child to repeat (she was already that with her father; she will be that again when her mother becomes president!)

(10) Hillary will take care of the needs of millions of families in this great country, and the needs of families in other "villages" in the world. It will be Bill's turn to stay in the background as First Gentleman, as Hillary did as First Lady when Bill was president. \

Between Reagan and Buchanan, the 2 oldest presidents, the former was one of the best, but the latter was one of the worst. It was the former who was partly responsible for ending the Cold War between our country and the U.S.S.R. (the nucleus of which has become Russia). The American electorate favored presidents who married and remained married to the same spouse. An exception was made of Ronald Reagan as having been divorced once because they had seen that he was repentant, and he also had a positive relationship with his first wife, actress Jane Wyman. Reagan learned how to handle his relationship with his second wife, Nancy, from any mistake that he might have made in his first marriage.

It was the never-married James Buchanan who had no experience with inter-personal relationships that marriage entailed that just happened not to know how to handle the slavery question and it was during his administration that the American civil war began. During his term as president, he also mishandled the country's relation to the Church of Jesus Christ of Latter-day Saints under the leadership of Brigham Young which partly contributed to the massacre of over a hundred passengers of a train wagon. Sally Denton reports that "Emigrating from Arkansas to California in September, 1857, a train of wagons had the misfortune to pass through the Utah Territory during a time of violence and heightened tension between the territorial government (under Brigham Young) and the United States government (under President Buchanan, who was determined to replace Young). The result was the massacre of around 140 men, women, and children—many being killed only after surrendering on the promise of safe conduct."[151]

Buchanan did not develop the necessary flexibility that love fosters but only the strong one-sidedness that hate engenders, just like Ralph Nader (the latter's failed story you already encountered in chapter 7 above). Their solution to family life was to avoid marriage, which was a negative solution of avoidance.

Buchanan, lacking experience in problem-solving in his own family, he was equally inexperienced in handling the problem of unifying our country. The earliest 7 southern states that seceded from the United States blamed Buchanan for his failure to accommodate their rights. In the ranking of presidents that had been done three times in 1948, 1962, and 1984 by historians, Buchanan was consistently listed the third from the bottom of the list. But, since William Harrison listed at next to the bottom never had a chance to serve as president having died of pneumonia just after his inauguration, Buchanan was really next to the bottom occupied by Warren G. Harding (but *see* table 8.3 that makes James Buchanan the worst president of all).[152]

But, according to the *U.S. News & World Report*, President James Buchanan was re-evaluated by 4 polls of modern-day Americans in February 2007 and they averaged out to his occupying the bottom position or the worst American president we have ever had (*see* the following Table 8.3).

Table 8.3 Buchanan Is the Worst President according to U.S. News & World Report (2/26/07)

1. James Buchanan

2. Warren G. Harding

3. Andrew Johnson

4. Franklin Pierce

5. Millard Fillmore

6. John Tyler

7. Ulysses Grant

8. William Harrison

9. Herbert Hoover & Richard Nixon (tied)

10. Zachary Taylor

The American electorate voted for Buchanan as the first and last bachelor president ever. It has learned its bitter lesson in entrusting the affairs of our nation (of million families) in the hands of one who refused to know how to handle the affairs of his family by avoiding having one.

It is highly unlikely that the American electorate will depart from this lesson when faced with the prospect of voting for an unmarried presidential candidate like Condi Rice, as proposed by Dick Morris and Eileen McGann in their book, *Condi vs. Hillary*. Foremost in their minds will be to worry whether she will be another Buchanan. She has not demonstrated that she can solve her own family problems, because she does not have one of her own. The major reason for George W. Bush's unpopularity is his failure in the field of foreign relations. Since the architect of America's foreign policy is Secretary of State Condi Rice, she has to bear the biggest blame for failing to advise her Commander-in-Chief how to be a winner in her area of expertise.

The American electorate generally favors a presidential candidate who has a normal family life. The American electorate frowns upon presidential aspirants with known problems with the opposite sex. The American electorate expects presidents to be role models of family behavior and relationships. No president was ever divorced more than once and remarried twice or more. No one who divorced 2 previous spouses ever tried to run for president, i.e., none until now. The general perception is that if a man (or woman) cannot even demonstrate skill in solving his or her personal family problems, how can we expect him or her to solve the problems of the nation that is composed of millions of families, as well as the problems of relating to the families of other "villages" in the world?

Condi Rice with Ralph Nader and Rudy Giuliani with Newt Gingrich illustrate two different flawed ways of solving one's family relationships. The Nader and Condi way is not to trust anyone of the opposite sex to be your spouse. That is slightly better—though still bad—than the Giuliani and Gingrich way, i.e. after failing to stay married to your first spouse, try again with a second spouse, and when that also fails, then try yet again with a third spouse.

The unacceptability of Rudy Giuliani as president was already exhaustively dealt with previously (*see* chapter 4 above). Newt Gingrich has had as bad, if not more, of marital problems as Giuliani. He even had to admit to the evangelical leader James Dobson in a radio interview of *Focus on the Family*: "There are things in my own life that I have turned to God and have gotten on my knees and prayed about and sought God's forgiveness."[153]

Tony Center, his Democratic opponent, in the Congressional race in Georgia in 1992, ran an ad that claimed Gingrich had "delivered divorce papers to his wife the day after her cancer operation." That was not strictly true, but his friends disclosed that he discussed divorce terms with his wife while visiting her in the hospital, as if this was any less reprehensible. And even worse, in March 2007, he admitted that while a House Speaker, he had an affair with his present wife—when she was a Congressional staffer—while spearheading the move to impeach Bill Clinton for his involvement with a White House intern.[154]

The best type of family relationship is the Hillary Clinton way which is in sync with 95% of all presidents in American history, that is, marry once and stand by your spouse no matter what! True, she has had serious problems with her husband as pointed out by Carl Bernstein in *A Woman in Charge: the Life of Hillary Rodham Clinton* in June 2007. Who does not? No person or family is perfect. How she went about to solve her problems with flying colors is a great example for the rest of us. It is a clear indication of her great skill in solving the most difficult of family problems which can be brought to bear on any problem that faces our nation of millions of families and even families of other "villages" in the world.

Michael Barone writing in *U.S. News & World Report* agrees with Bernstein that we saw Hillary "endure humiliations—the collapse of her healthcare plan, the revelations of her husband's infidelities—that would make most of us want to crawl in a hole. Yet she persevered, concentrating on her work and winning office in the most raucous political environment in America.... You can't deny that she's shown perseverance and grace under pressure—a good quality for any president."[155]

Even before Hillary met Bill, she never thought of being single all her life. The Condi solution was never in her mind. And when she met Bill, she was certain she was the man of her prayers and dreams. Considering the whole picture, she made up her mind that Bill was the man she wanted to be the father of her child (or children) and to spend her whole life time with. As a devoted Methodist Christian woman, her husband, children, and family came first. A career was also important, but it would never have priority over love and marriage.

Some of her female ancestors stayed with their husbands, no matter how difficult their lives might have been, because they had no other means of support besides their husbands both for themselves and their children. Not so Hillary, because she was as highly educated as her husband and could easily take care of her own financial needs and her child, Chelsea when she was young. Some of her friends advised her to divorce Bill as others did their own husbands. But, she refused to follow their advice. She decided to stand by her man, not because she needed his financial support, and not even because it might jeopardize her chance at being a future president herself (Reagan, after all, managed to become president in spite of having been divorced once).

If Hillary has stayed with her man only because of her political ambition, then the moment she has become president, would she dump him? If that has been her plan, why then is there so much talk about what sort of a responsibility she will assign to her husband as the first First Gentleman in her future administration? "Oh, no, she won't divorce him, if she wants to get re-elected," someone might add. That is rather the height of skepticism about Hillary which is totally uncalled for.

There is only one reason why Hillary is standing by her husband: she truly loves him. She loved him the day she first met him at the Yale Law School library. She loved him through the years when other women wanted him for themselves. And she still loves him now. We have no doubt that she will keep on loving him in the years to come, and that she will fulfill her marital vow to him "until death do [them] part!"

We applaud her for her love. That is the kind of person we want in the White House again as president and not just First Lady. She is someone who does not easily give up. She has not given up on her own husband and family. She will not easily give up on our nation of millions of families. Nay, she will not give up on the families and women and children of the other "villages" in the world. She is a role model of modern American womanhood, the kind of woman all parents want their daughter to emulate when they grow up! After all, she is someone who was reared by her parents "androgynously, i.e. to grow up to be able to do whatever any man can do, although a woman!"

"Three for 1 Price:" President Hillary, 1ˢᵗ Gentleman Bill, & 1ˢᵗ Lady Chelsea?

When Bill Clinton was a candidate for President in the 1990's, it was billed as "2 for 1 price:" President Bill and First Lady Hillary. In a Gallup Poll, a sampling of Americans were asked if they thought Bill would have a role to play in Hillary's administration, 70% answered that he will be most helpful to his wife and that he will use his influence. And the poll also indicated that 75% believed that he will have more clout than previous presidents' spouses.

This time when you elect Hillary for president in her own right, will you get "3 for 1 price:" President Hillary, First Gentleman Bill, and a new First Lady Chelsea? At first, it did not seem to make sense that Bill insisted on the use of the word "price," but now it does. In his case when he ran for the presidency in 1992 and 1996, it was indeed, "2 for 1 price!" You see, only he received a salary as president, but his First Lady Hillary was the extra bonus America got, *gratis et amore*, for her services. And when she did not do very well in pushing through a comprehensive health care plan in Congress for her husband, some of her critics got really mad: "For that she does not deserve to be elected president, etc., etc." But, what do you really expect for something that is done for free? You must not expect too much; it did not cost you anything! You must be grateful someone cared enough to try to work for your welfare. That it did not work out was not entirely her fault. She can try again when she is president, this time through her *paid* husband perhaps (emphasis supplied)?

The titles of Bill as the First Gentleman and of Chelsea as the First Child (a second time) are definite, although the nature of their future roles will have to be defined. When Bill was asked about what he thought will be his future role when Hillary becomes president, he said that the question should be directed to her. Hillary on a number of occasions, in answer to reporters' questions, said that Bill's role in her administration would be that of a roving American ambassador.

Why is Bill not happy simply as the First Gentleman in Hillary's administration? Why should he have another designation like an ambassador? Well, for the simple reason that an ambassador gets paid for his work, but a First Lady (or First Gentleman) does not. Who says so? First Ladies have not been paid because the salary of their husbands-presidents traditionally included their board and lodging (the White House). But, since Hillary is not a man, but a woman, presumably her salary as future president will be less than Bill did because she is not a man. In that case her salary will not include the support of her spouse although lodging in the White House is included.

Therefore, as First Gentleman, Bill should be given his own pay (that way he will not have to do anything else but just perform the role of the First Gentleman). That is not fair, someone might object. No First Lady of 42 previous presidents in 220 years of American history ever received a salary.

Just because it was not fair for 220 years, it does not mean that the practice has to be continued forever. We are living in a new age of equality. At this time when we will have our first woman president, let us do away with the unpaid position of a First Lady (or First Gentleman) beginning with Bill. Unpaid First Ladies are 200+ years outmoded—only good for a period of time when a woman had to be fully supported financially by her man—and she had a full-time unpaid work at home to take care of her husband and had to give birth to dozens of children and nurture them. The division of labor was neat and clear: when a man worked as a cook (well, chef) in a restaurant, he had to be paid, because he had a family to support. When a woman cooked at home, she did not have to be paid, because her husband was already supporting her and the children with the money he was earning as a cook (well, chef) in a restaurant!

Can you really expect Bill as First Gentleman to play the role of a host in the White House? Why not? Hillary did it for him for 8 years, and now that it is Hillary who (hopefully) will be president, the least Bill can do is to perform what Hillary used to do during his presidency. Hillary, on behalf of her precedent-setting government, should offer a decent salary to his position as First Gentleman.

If that offer is not accepted by Bill, because he prefers to occupy some other position that is a decision he has to make. We live in a free country, so free that we can even elect a woman president for the first time after 200+ years of waiting! In that event, the position *with pay* of First Lady should be offered to Chelsea (emphasis supplied). It should never be an automatic thing, just because she hopefully will be the First Child (the second time around). She should be given a chance to decide, with the help of her boy-friend, Marc Mezvinsky. This is where the idea of fairness and gender-equity comes into the picture appropriately: why should Chelsea give up her highly paid position in industry in order to accept an unpaid position of First Lady? If the position of First Lady will be offered to Chelsea when Hillary becomes president in 2009, there is a lot of historical precedent for it.

There had been at least 15 women who served as First Ladies of the United States who were not spouses of the presidents, but close relatives or friends. Even Buchanan who had no spouse had to have a surrogate First Lady perform that important task. There were presidents whose spouses died before they started to serve or before their term of service ended. There was a president who got married in the White House, and so he had another First Lady before his future wife arrived. Still some presidents whose spouses preferred not to perform the role of First Lady at all. They considered being a First Lady as a thankless job. Do you blame them?

James Buchanan, the only unmarried president, had to depend on her 27-year-old orphaned niece, Harriet Lane, to become First Lady during his term (1857-1861). Buchanan was the guardian of Harriet, and he provided for her education and political exposure when he served as a congressman as well as when he was a foreign minister. After the White House, Harriet went on to marry a banker, had 3 sons, and spent the rest of her life in charitable work.

Thomas Jefferson was a bachelor when he was elected the third American president in 1800, as his wife herself formerly a widow, Martha Wayles Skelton Jefferson died while giving birth to their sixth child, Lucy Elizabeth, in 1782. She was the first wife who died before her husband Thomas Jefferson was elected the 3rd U.S. president (1801-1809). Although the fourth president James Madison did not succeed Jefferson till the end of his second term in 1809, James's wife—also a widow who had no children of her own—Dolley Payne Todd Madison doubled up as a hostess or Acting First Lady during the 2-terms of Thomas Jefferson starting in 1801. When Jefferson was succeeded by James Madison, she continued serving as First Lady during the 2-terms of her husband (1809-1817).

The second wife who died before her husband, Andrew Jackson was elected the 7th president (1829-37) was Rachel Donaldson Robards Jackson. She died of a heart-attack soon after her husband was elected in 1828. The major cause of her death was possibly the merciless attacks of the press during the election campaign that accused her of committing adultery, because her divorce from her first husband was not yet final when she married Jackson. The women who became First Ladies during Jackson's 2-terms were: Emily Donelson Jackson, his niece, and Sarah Yorke Jackson, his daughter-in-law.

The third wife who died 17 years prior to her husband Martin van Buren's election as the 8th president (1837-41) was Hannah Hoes van Buren. Angelica Singleton van Buren, his daughter-in-law, acted as First Lady.

The fourth wife who died before the election of her husband Chester A. Arthur as the 21st president (1881-85) was Ellen Lewis Herndon Arthur. Mary Arthur McElroy, the sister of the president, served as First Lady.

The first wife who was too ill to discharge the duties of a First Lady for Zachary Taylor, the 12th president (1849-50), was Margaret Mackall Smith Taylor. Mary Elizabeth Taylor Bliss, her daughter, performed the duties of First Lady instead.

The second wife who was incapacitated by illness, i.e. a broken ankle, from serving as First Lady for Millard Fillmore, the 13th president (1850-53), was Abigail Powers Fillmore. Her daughter, Mary Abigail Fillmore, took over her place.

The third wife who was too sick to serve as First Lady of Andrew Johnson, the 17th president (1865-69), was Eliza McCardle Johnson. The tasks of a First Lady devolved on her daughter, Martha Johnson Patterson.

The only wife who got married in the White House was Frances Folsom, wife of Grover Cleveland, and was First Lady during her husband's first term as the 22nd president (1885-1889). When her husband lost to Benjamin Harrison in 1888, Mrs. Harrison told the caretakers of the White House not to move any of the furniture because she said, "I'm coming back in 4 years." She did when Grover Cleveland beat Harrison in 1892 to become the 24th president (1893-97).

Before Mrs. Frances Cleveland arrived in the White House, Grover's sister Rose was First Lady.

There was only one president who died of pneumonia one month after he was inaugurated, before his wife, Anna Symmes Harrison, could join him at the White House, William Henry Harrison, the 9th president (1841). She remained in Indiana to settle some personal matters before she would go to Washington. She was not on time to see him alive. Fortunately, William Harrison was accompanied by his son and his wife, Mr. and Mrs. William Harrison, Jr. It was the wife of junior, Jane Irwin Harrison who served as First Lady for one month in lieu of her mother-in-law.

The first First Lady who died before the end of her husband John Tyler's term (1841-45) the 10th president was his first wife, Letitia Christian. The job of First Lady was discharged by Priscilla Cooper, a daughter-in-law, until the arrival of the second Mrs. John Tyler, Julia Gardiner who became First Lady in her own right.

The second First Lady who died before the end of her husband Benjamin Harrison's term (1889-93) as the 23rd president was Caroline Lavinia Scott Harrison. During the last months of her father's presidency, Mary Harrison McKee, her daughter functioned as First Lady.

The third First Lady who died during the first term of her husband was Ellen Axson Wilson, first wife of Woodrow Wilson, 28th president (1913-21). She died in 1914. For one year, Margaret Wilson, his daughter served as First Lady, until the second Mrs. Wilson, Edith Bolling Galt Wilson arrived in 1915. The latter sometimes delegated the work of a hostess to Helen Woodrow Bones, her cousin, especially from 1919 to 1921 when the president suffered a stroke and was partly paralyzed. Some of Wilson's enemies called her "the first female president," for she ran the government on her husband's behalf, rather than surrender the powers of the presidency to the vice-president, Thomas Riley Marshall.

There were 3 other First Ladies who enlisted the help of other female relatives to host occasionally at the White House when they were unable to do so. Elizabeth Kortright Monroe, First Lady of James Monroe, the 5th president (1817-25), used to delegate the responsibility of hosting at the White House to her daughter, Eliza Monroe Hay.

Helen Herron Taft, spouse of William H. Taft, the 27th president (1909-1913), often requested her daughter, Helen Taft Manning, to take her place as White House hostess.

Finally, Hillary Clinton upon her election as New York's junior senator had to report to her constituency early in January 2001. She asked her daughter, Chelsea, to cover for her as hostess at the White House for one whole month till her husband, Bill, could finish his presidential term (1993-2001).

If Hillary wins as president and she decides to choose Chelsea as the First Lady during her administration, and the latter accepts, it will be most natural. Chelsea will only be following in the footsteps of her mother. Her being the First Child twice over when she returns to Washington with her victorious mom will only strengthen her resolve to pursue a career in public service.

That was not always what Chelsea had in mind. At first, she thought she would pursue medicine, and it would have taken her many years of study and away from her parents for a long time. After she graduated from Stanford University with honors in June 2001, she went to Oxford University to follow in the footsteps of her father, Bill who was a Rhodes scholar there as a young man.

Then something happened that dramatically determined the direction of Chelsea's plans for the future: the terrorist attacks on 9/11/01 just a few days before she left for Oxford University. She and her American colleagues had to wrestle with what best they could do to help their country, just like his dad and his contemporaries tried to grapple 3 decades earlier with problems connected with the Vietnam War. What went on in Chelsea's mind can be seen from an article she wrote a few months later for *Talk magazine*: "For most Americans I know, 'serving' in the broadest sense seems like the only thing to do…. Is banking really important right now?" Her words are so reminiscent of Hillary, who, when she was at a similar cross-road in life, as her campaign keeps reminding us, "chose children's advocacy over corporate work after law school."[156]

In the meantime, Chelsea has been pitching in for both her parents, especially in fund-raising for her Mom's election campaign as well as for her dad's non-profit foundation, and she has been very successful in raising millions of dollars for both. Her mom has been quoted as saying that her "two most important advisers" are Bill and Chelsea. She had rendered effective assistance to both her parents, in spite of the fact that she had only done them on part-time bases. Chelsea still works for a firm, Avenue Capital Group, a hedge fund (the second company she has served after starting as an employee of McKinsey Consulting Firm right after college graduation). She plans to keep working until either duty or love or both leads her somewhere else.

9

Twenty-Six Presidents Were Lawyers; 4 Of Last 6, Yalies

◆

Yale Alumna Hillary Has the Best Chance to Be the 27th Lawyer-President; Thompson's Actor & Condi's Professor = 1 Apiece

In 3 separate surveys of opinions of American historians, conducted in 1948, 1962, and 1982, the ten greatest American presidents with slight variations in their order are the following:

1. Abraham Lincoln

2. George Washington

3. Franklin D. Roosevelt

4. Woodrow Wilson

5. Thomas Jefferson

6. Andrew Jackson

7. Theodore Roosevelt

8. Grover Cleveland

9. John Adams

10. James Polk

How many of them were lawyers? If you said, all of them, except George Washington, who was a soldier and a planter, you are correct.

Majority of American presidents were professionals prior to becoming U.S. president. There were 26 lawyers, so that when Hillary gets elected, she will be the 27th lawyer. And the favorite educational channel through which most presidents graduated from were Ivy-League colleges. There were 16 presidents who went to Ivy-League and Colonial colleges, including Bill Clinton who went to Yale Law School where he met his spouse and hopefully America's next president, Hillary Clinton nee Rodham.

The second most popular method of professional training was by apprenticeship to another professional, including a practicing lawyer. There were also 16 presidents who had attended 16 individual non-Ivy League colleges scattered throughout the country. Three presidents went to armed forces academies (2 in West Point and 1 in Annapolis). There were 5 presidents who only had up to a high school formal education or less, and 2 who had no formal education at all: Zachary Taylor, and Andrew Johnson (*see* Table 9.0, 9.1, 9.2, 9.3, 9.4, & 9.5).

Table 9.0 Favorite Alma Maters of American Presidents

Ivy-League & Colonial Colleges	16
Other Colleges 1 each	16
Military & Naval Academies	3
High School Formal Education or Less	5
No Formal Education	2
Total	42

Table 9.1 Presidents Who Graduated from Ivy-League & Colonial Colleges (16)

1. John Adams	Harvard, MA
2. Thomas Jefferson	William & Mary, VA
3. James Madison	Princeton, NJ

4. James Monroe	William & Mary, VA
5. John Quincy Adams	Harvard, MA
6. John Tyler	William & Mary, VA
7. Rutherford B. Hayes	Harvard, MA
8. Theodore Roosevelt	Harvard, MA
9. William Howard Taft	Yale, CT
10. Woodrow Wilson	Princeton, NJ
11. Franklin Delano Roosevelt	Harvard, MA
12. John F. Kennedy	Harvard, MA
13. Gerald Ford	Yale, CT
14. H.W. Bush	Yale, CT
15. William Jefferson Clinton	Yale, CT
16. George W. Bush	Yale, CT & Harvard, MA

Table 9.2 Presidents Who Went to Other Colleges (16)

1. Martin van Buren	Kinderhook Academy, NY
2. William Henry Harrison	Hampden-Sydney, VA
3. James Knox Polk	North Carolina, NC
4. Franklin Pierce	Bowdoin, NH
5. James Buchanan	Dickinson, PA
6. James Garfield	Williams, OH
7. Chester Arthur	Union, NY
8. Benjamin Harrison	Miami, OH
9. James McKinley	Allegheny, PA
10. Warren Harding	Ohio Central, OH
11. Calvin Coolidge	Amherst, MA

12. Herbert Hoover	Stanford, CA
13. Harry S. Truman	University of Missouri, KA
14. Lyndon B. Johnson	Southwest Texas, TX
15. Richard Nixon	Whittier, CA
16. Ronald Reagan	Eureka, IL

Table 9.3 Presidents Who Graduated from Armed Forces Academies (3)

1. Ulysses S. Grant	West Point, NY
2. Dwight D. Eisenhower	West Point, NY
3. Jimmy Carter	Annapolis, MD

Table 9.4 Presidents Who Had High School Formal Education or Less (5)

1. George Washington
2. Andrew Jackson
3. Millard Fillmore
4. Abraham Lincoln
5. Grover Cleveland

Table 9.5 Presidents with No Formal Education (2)

1. Zachary Taylor
2. Andrew Johnson

Among Ivy-League colleges, Harvard is first with 7 alumni presidents, and Yale is 2nd with 5. The election of Hillary Clinton as our next president will give Yale 6 alumni-presidents, just 1 shy of first-place Harvard. That is the more likely scenario, for as you will see in this chapter below, in the past 30 years Yale graduates predominated in both the number of elected presidents and in those who ran for president and vice-president. Except for the incumbent president, George W. Bush who is both a Yale and a Harvard alumnus, the last time we had a "pure" Harvard alumnus preside over our country as president was John F. Kennedy in 1960.

Table 9.6 Presidential Career Background

Previous Lawyers	26
Previous Armed Forces Officers	8
Others	8
Total	42

Table 9.7 Presidents Who Were Previous Lawyers (26)

1. John Adams

2. Thomas Jefferson

3. James Madison

4. James Monroe

5. John Quincy Adams

6. Andrew Jackson

7. Martin van Buren

8. John Tyler

9. James Knox Polk

10. Millard Fillmore

11. Franklin Pierce

12. James Buchanan

13. Abraham Lincoln

14. Rutherford B. Hayes

15. Chester Arthur

16. Grover Cleveland

17. Benjamin Harrison

18. James McKinley

19. Theodore Roosevelt

20. William Howard Taft

21. Woodrow Wilson

22. Calvin Coolidge

23. Franklin Delano Roosevelt

24. Richard Nixon

25. Gerald Ford

26. William Jefferson Clinton

Table 9.8 Presidents Who Were Previous Armed Forces Officers (8)

1. George Washington	Landowner to Military Career
2. William Henry Harrison	Medicine to Military Career
3. Zachary Taylor	Military Career

4. Ulysses S. Grant   Military Career

5. Dwight D. Eisenhower   Military Career

6. John F. Kennedy   Naval Career

7. Jimmy Carter   Naval Career

8. George H.W. Bush   Air Force Career

Table 9.9 Presidents Who Had Other Previous Occupations (8)

1. James Garfield   Professor (Classics)

2. Lyndon B. Johnson   Teacher

3. Andrew Johnson   Tailor

4. Warren Harding   Newspaper Publisher

5. Herbert Hoover   Engineer

6. Harry S. Truman   Farmer/Haberdasher

7. Ronald Reagan   Actor

8. George W. Bush   Businessman

Although Fred Thompson is a lawyer and had served as a U.S. senator from Tennessee, taking over Al Gore, Jr.'s former seat, he treated those as merely temporary assignments. His favorite occupation is that of an actor, which he at first had a chance to do while still a senator. Eventually, he gave up his senate post to pursue full-time acting and instead of actually practicing law he acts on T.V. and in films in the roles of lawyers.

Now some interested people, who are not enthusiastic about other announced candidates for president in the Republican Party, are urging Thompson to be the savior of his party by running for president just like Ronald Reagan—the only previous actor among our 42 presidents.

These Thompson-for-president recruiters are in for a total disappointment. The two are really totally different, for several reasons:

(1) Reagan won as president, not because he was a previous actor, but because he was a good governor of California. Reagan's position as a governor is the second most popular steppingstone to the presidency (only overshadowed by the position of a vice-president). Thompson, like his counterpart in the Democratic Party John Edwards, had only limited legislative and no executive, national security, or diplomatic experience. Thompson as a one-term senator, by not remaining in the U.S. senate has lost what would have been a third-priority ranking in being promoted to the presidency. He spent 8 years in the U.S. senate, but his legislative record was rather slim. A former adviser said of him: "While the Senate is filled with ambitious men who aren't in a rush to get home at night, Senator Thompson kept a lean formal schedule. Did the bare minimum to get by and then hightailed [it] to the Prime Rib or Capital Grille."[157]

(2) Their character traits are far apart. Reagan was genial, but Thompson's manner can be brusque and his most natural expression is a scowl. Reagan was serious-minded, hard-working, and highly motivated. Thompson is undisciplined, resisting demanding schedules, and easy-going. His former football coach in Lawrenceburg, TN, told the *Nashville Tennessean*: "He was smart, but he was lazy. He probably could have been a straight-A student if he'd applied himself."[158]

(3) Reagan had always the electoral-votes rich (the biggest in the country) California as his home base. Reagan also had Illinois, where he was born, as his second home base. Thompson, because he discontinued representing Tennessee as senator when he decided to return to full-time acting, just like Al Gore whose senate seat he took over, might find himself without a home base, not even Tennessee.

(4) Reagan also served as president of the Screen Actors' Guild, which gave him more executive experience in the private sector. Thompson did not have any executive experience in the private arena, to compensate for his lack of executive experience in government.

(5) Reagan became an actor, but it was just a steppingstone to a full-time career in politics. Thompson is a first rate performer, whose first love is being an actor, and who had previously showed preference for the latter profession to the extent of resigning his senate seat to devote full-time to acting.

(6) Reagan did not have a sideline as a lobbyist for corporations. Fred Thompson did. His rich corporate clients include Equitas Ltd., deposed Haitian ruler Jean-Bertrand Aristide, Teamsters Central States Pension Fund, U.S. Cablesystems, American Business Coalition, Westinghouse, and the Free Choice group. With such a track record, do you think Thompson will ever work fully for the

benefit of all Americans? If he becomes president, you might wonder if he will make decisions that are favorable to his corporate friends, at your expense. Ralph Nader, if you are looking for someone who is so identified with "corporate interests" more than anyone else with presidential aspirations, Fred Thompson is your right target man!

(7) Reagan before becoming president was so determined that politics was the real calling of his life, so that in spite of 2 previous failed attempts to be nominated for president in the Republican ticket, he persisted until his time came on the third try in 1980. Thompson does not have Reagan's determination to succeed in politics. It has taken him so long to decide and even longer to form an exploratory presidential committee, and when he finally formed one, he still kept on postponing his decision. He cannot seem to make up his mind as to whether he wants to be a full-time politician or a full-time actor.

(8) Reagan was once divorced and he successfully handled its problems because the reason was uncontroversial: the refusal of his first wife, actress Jayne Wyman, to be the spouse of a politician. Because of his deep commitment to politics, and he must have wished his marital partner would share his commitment. When Jayne Wyman was not willing to share his real passion in life, he had to sacrifice his marriage for it, with another hope that someone else more amenable to his political career would come along. He had children with Jayne, as well as with the "someone else" Nancy Reagan, who became First Lady. Thompson divorced his first wife partly because they should not have married in the first place. He was forced to marry his teenage girl friend in high school because she became pregnant. They had 2 adult sons. Now, Thompson and his new wife Jeri Kehn Thompson have 2 very young children—3-year-old daughter, Hayden, and 9-month-old son, Samuel, who sometimes get in the way of his campaigning. Being divorced is a rare case for American presidents. Apart from the once-divorced Ronald Reagan, and James Buchanan who remained single, all the others were married and stayed married.

(9) Reagan's second wife, Nancy Davis Reagan, his First Lady stayed in the background and did stand by her man. *Newsweek* reported that some close to the Tennesseean "question whether moving into the White House is truly Thompson's life ambition—or more the dream of his second wife, Jeri, a former GOP operative who is his unofficial campaign manager and top adviser."[159] Jeri Thompson has become so involved in running his presidential exploratory committee that some important staff members, like his campaign-manager-in-waiting Tom Collamore, decided to quit in July 2007. He was followed by the communications-director-in-waiting Linda Rozett the next month, and citing the same

reason. To complicate the matter, Thompson said that there was nothing that his wife did that he did not authorize. Worse than John McCain's, it looks like Thompson's presidential campaign has already imploded even before it had officially started![160]

(10) Reagan was highly endorsed by Dr. James Dobson of the radio program, *Focus on the Family.* Thompson was not endorsed by Dobson. Not only that, he also expressed his doubt that Thompson was a Christian. George Will of *Newsweek* had an even stronger negative on Thompson being referred to as another Reagan. He said that what is Reagnesque about Thompson is "99% charm, and 1% substance." Bill O'Reilly in a recent episode of *the Factor* on television also said that Thompson's "rise in the polls was simply due to his acting and his TV stint in Law & Order."[161] Michelle Cottle, in the *New Republic*, echoed similar sentiments: "In Thompson's presence (live or on screen), one is viscerally, intimately reassured that he can handle any crisis that arises, be it a renegade Russian sub or a botched rape case." But she wondered, was he really "enough of a man for his fight," or just someone who meandered through life, creating the illusion of a masculine mystique?[162]

The person that could duplicate Reagan's background is current Governor Arnold Schwarzenegger of California:

(1) Schwarzenegger left acting, because he was not frankly very good at it, as Reagan was not. Schwarzenegger never won an Oscar, just as Reagan did not. Thus, politics as a career is a better alternative for him like Reagan.

(2) Schwarzenegger and Reagan married women who had extremely strong attitudes towards politics. Schwarzenegger married Maria Shriver, a Kennedy Democrat, and converted her to the Republican Party; Reagan had to divorce Jane Wyman because she did not want to have anything to do with politics. Reagan's second wife, Nancy Davis, who became his First Lady, was as supportive of her husband, as Maria Shriver was of hers.

(3) Schwarzenegger had some military background, so did Reagan.

(4) Schwarzenegger is a Republican as Reagan was.

(5) As governor, Schwarzenegger had successfully worked with a Democratic-controlled legislature, as Reagan did.

There is only one problem with Schwarzenegger: he cannot run for president because he was born in a foreign country, Austria. Even if Sen. Orrin Hatch's proposal for amending the U.S. Constitution to allow Schwarzenegger to run will be approved by Congress and 2/3 of the states, it will not be on time for him to run in the 2008 presidential election! That was why some Las Vegas odds makers put his chance at getting nominated as a presidential candidate in this election at the long shot odds of 1 out of 105.

By way of contrast the odds in favor of Hillary, according to our favorite odds maker Danny Sheridan is 3 to 1. That is a great advantage compared to her potential opponents: John McCain at 6 to 1 and Rudy Giuliani at 7 to 1. It was also Sheridan who predicted that the underdog Bill Clinton would win the Democratic nomination in 1991! The *New York Times* had also indirectly revealed on whom it was gambling to win when it appointed a full-time reporter, Anne Kornblut, to do nothing but to keep track of Hillary's activities while she was running for re-election in New York for her U.S. Senate seat, and "for anything else that follows after."

Just like Condi, Thompson should decline the draft-Thompson-for president in 2008. Only war heroes get drafted to run for president, not civilians such as a professor in the case of Condi or an actor as in the case of Thompson. Just as Vice-President Dick Cheney did earlier in a Sherman-like manner, he should also say: "If nominated for president, I will not accept. If I am elected, I will not serve." There is no doubt in our mind that Thompson would rather act at being president, rather than being president.

Many prominent Hollywood actors and other leaders of the movie industry were supporters of Ronald Reagan when he ran for president for 2 terms. Most of the big names that support the presidential candidate in this election does not have the name of Fred Thompson, but rather of Hillary Clinton: Steven Spielberg, Susan Sarandon, Jodie Foster, Jennifer Lopez, Tom Hanks, Robin Williams, Robert de Niro, Owen Wilson, Rita Wilson, Tony Bennett, J.J. Abrams, Tobey Maguire, Brian Grazer, will.i.am, Eric Dane, Rebecca Gayheart, Alex Avant, Quincy Jones, Rupert Murdock, Ari Emanuel, Peter Chernin, Haim Saban, Casey Wasserman, Noah Mamet, Chad Griffin, Bruce Cohen, Roland Emmerich, Greg Berlanti, and others.

The odds in favor Condi winning if she were a candidate, like Fred Thompson, is also 1 out of 42. There was only one professor among all presidents. That was President James Garfield. He was professor of Classics, not Political Science, Condi's specialty. For some reason the American electorate did not consider experience in college teaching as a strong background in preparation for the presidency.

It is also very strange that there was only one school teacher among all previous presidents, and that was Lyndon Johnson. That is so in spite of the fact U.S. presidents and teachers have many qualities in common, according to Susan H. Fuhrman, president of the Teachers College, Columbia University. "Each job requires answering to a large, varied and vocal constituency. You must think on your feet while working in consultation with others. You must function as a role model.... Presidents and teachers must be receptive to new information while gathering evidence to make decisions based on facts rather than opinions.

For both presidents and teachers, challenges are constantly repeated. Negotiations ... are carried on over extended periods, and today's failure could set the table for tomorrow's breakthrough. That's where *the human capacity to connect* remains so vital (emphasis supplied).[163]

That did not prevent Richard Norton Smith, director of several presidential libraries (Lincoln, Hoover, Eisenhower, Ford, and Reagan) from fantasizing that several presidents could have been successful high school teachers in these subject fields:[164]

- George Washington   Geography

- James Madison   World History

- Theodore Roosevelt   Gym teacher

- James Garfield   English teacher

- Warren Harding   Newspaper adviser

- Woodrow Wilson   Speech teacher

- John Quincy Adams   Foreign Language teacher

- Gerald Ford   Football coach

- Jimmy Carter   Science teacher

- Franklin D. Roosevelt   American History

- John F. Kennedy   Debate coach

- Bill Clinton   Band director

Who is missing from the list? A Social Studies teacher is missing. Is this because the most qualified president to teach it has not yet been elected—Hillary Clinton, whom you will help elect on November 4, 2008?

Fantasizing aside, the favorite profession of previous presidents is that of a lawyer. Why are lawyers favored to occupy the office of president? It is because political leadership is part of their preparation. Law has private and public divisions. In the private section, lawyers also specialize, criminal and civil being the largest divisions. There are subdivisions of both, such as commercial law, real estate law, international law, political law, and so on. Since the government is divided into 3 branches: good lawyers are considered the most qualified to fill top positions in them. Law-trained legislators make the laws. Presidents implement the law that legislators make. Judges and justices, also law-trained, interpret the law to be sure they conform to the U.S. Constitution, the fundamental law of our land.

TV debates have become the staple of presidential contests since 1960. Debates happen to be the forte of lawyers. Presidential candidates who are lawyers have an advantage. They are generally flexible or in Professor Robert Kegan's words "complex thinkers."[165] One of the best complex thinkers was our "greatest American president" Abraham Lincoln who received nationwide recognition initially because of a debate. John F. Kennedy, though not a lawyer by occupation, was Harvard-trained, certainly won the first formal TV presidential debates against Richard Nixon in 1960. Hillary has the best combination of being a lawyer, Ivy-League training in forensics (being able to think fast on one's feet), and adequate experience to know what to say.

Hillary Is an Alumna of 2 Top Public Service Colleges: Wellesley & Yale

One of the best arguments in favor of Hillary as your best choice for president in 2008 is that her career is that of a lawyer which is in sync with no less than 26 of the 42 presidents who were elected in the last 220 years. When elected with your indispensable votes on November 4, 2008, she will be the 27th lawyer-president. Her being a graduate of Yale University makes her in sync also with the favorite academic background of all 42 presidents, that is, one of the Ivy-League and colonial colleges. As 16 of the 42 previous presidents had that type of background, she will be the 17th Ivy League graduate when she will hopefully join their ranks as the first woman president in January 2009.

There is something quite unique about Hillary having graduated from Yale University. The *Boston Globe* wrote that "if there's one school that can lay claim to educating the nation's top national leaders over the past three decades, it's Yale."[166] "Yale alumni have been represented on the Democratic or Republican ticket in every U.S. Presidential election since 1972. Yale-educated presidents since the end of the Vietnam War include Gerald Ford, George H.W. Bush, Bill Clinton and George W. Bush, and major party nominees during this period include John Kerry (2004), Joseph Lieberman (Vice President, 2000), and Sargent Shriver (Vice President, 1972). Other Yale alumni who made serious bids for the Presidency during this period include Howard Dean (2004), Gary Hart (1984 and 1988), Paul Tsongas (1992) and Jerry Brown (1976, 1980, 1992).

Yale ... alumna Hillary Rodham Clinton is considered a front runner for the 2008 Democratic Presidential nomination."[167]

What is the reason why Yale has been so prolific in providing the top leadership of our country in the last 3 decades, and not before? It has to do with the university's traditional motto: "For God, for Country and for Yale." That motto has not changed, but its meaning has. The turning point was the Vietnam War. In previous years, when Yalies talked of "For God, for Country and for Yale," it meant serving our country in defense of freedom and democracy, and they were among the top leaders in the military. Following the Vietnam War, due to the leadership exerted by Yale Chaplain William Sloane Coffin, the university shifted its focus from simply training our country's highest military officers to preparing our national leaders for broader public service.

Hillary Clinton went to study at the Yale Law School which has been ranked as the number 1 school of law in America for many years, including the present one. Only 2 other previous presidents graduated from Yale Law School: Gerald Ford and Bill Clinton. (Both Bushes, George Sr. and Jr., finished undergraduate studies at Yale. William H. Taft had done undergraduate studies at Yale, but he took his law degree from Cincinnati Law School in Ohio).

---

*We agree with Peter Feddo that "It may be easy to forget, considering all that came after, but [**Hillary**] **was famous before anyone heard of Bill Clinton** (emphasis supplied). Back in 1969 at Wellesley College, years before she met her future husband, Rodham was the first student to deliver a commencement address at the school, and it caused a ruckus. Rodham, who spoke of 'liberation enabling each of us to fulfill our capacity,' wound up on the front page of the* Boston Globe *and on the pages of* Life *and was heralded as a voice of her generation."[168]*

10

Electoral College Favors Multiple Home-States

◆

Hillary Has 7; Everyone Else, Only 1 or None!

If you were a horse racer, and you are told at the outset that one of your opponents will start at 135 yards or half-way to the finish line at 270 yards, but the rest of the racers will start at the starting line or 0 yard, will you still continue to race anyway? Or, will you do what every normal thinking person will do, protest the unfairness, and if you do not succeed in your complaint, quit this particular race and save your energy for another day when you have an even chance to win?

This presidential contest is like that type of a one-sided horse race with Hillary starting at about half of the length of the course, but her opponents are mostly starting at or near the beginning of the line. But, everybody seems to be quite happy with the lop-sided arrangement. Of course, there were a few who had the sense to quit the race before hand, and in so doing stand a good chance of being chosen as a vice-presidential running mate by the eventual presidential nominee of his or her political party.

Now, how exactly did Hillary plan that she will have this winning edge? Based on the Electoral College voting system, we discern the development of 4 major strategies that Hillary has been pursuing.

First Strategy: *Have multiple home-state*s. The more a presidential candidate can claim as his or home state, the better is his or her chance to win. This is not a strategy that just developed overnight or even during the beginning of this particular presidential election. That is why, Geraldine Ferraro said, Hillary "has been preparing for the U.S. presidency for a long time." Just how long is a "long time?" How about a whole lifetime? In her lifetime, Hillary managed to combine at least 7 purple states as her own home bases. These states are "purple," as in the tallest purple-headed mountain of Everest, because they are neither blue-leaning for Democrats nor red-leaning for Republicans, but a combination of those 2 colors of the states that Hillary has exclusively dominated.

1. *Illinois is her mother state.* She had to be born somewhere in one of the 50 states (51, if Washington, D.C. is counted separately) of the United States. If she had been born in a foreign country, like Arnold Schwarzenegger, well she would not even qualify to run for president. Her state of birth is Illinois in mid-West America.

Still, Hillary could have chosen a different career. Her childhood dream was not always to be involved in public service. "I wanted desperately to be an Olympic athlete," she confessed. "I tried everything. I ran every race, and if I was really lucky I finished second to last.... I couldn't jump, I couldn't run, I couldn't swim." After determining that she could not be an athlete, she thought she could become an astronaut, "So I wrote NASA and said, 'How do I sign up to be an astronaut?' And they wrote back politely and said, 'We don't take girls'."

Hillary's folks and 2 brothers are still actively working and serving people in the state of Illinois. By election time on November 4, 2008, only one candidate from Illinois will represent the Democratic Party. The other Democratic candidate who was born in Hawaii but had gone on to work and get married in Illinois, Barack Obama, and now represents that state in the U.S. Senate would either have eliminated Hillary, or *more likely* would have been eliminated by Hillary in the national Democratic convention toward the end of summer 2008. When Hillary will have become the Democratic nominee, the opposition which Obama would be giving her on the way to the Democratic national convention, will no longer be there.

Hillary has 2 main political committees—HILLPAC and Friends of Hillary—that share offices in the same building at K Street in Washington, D.C., manned and *wo*manned by Illinois old-time friends John Gans and Patty Solis Doyle respectively. Mr. Costello, a political leader from Southern Illinois, extended an open invitation to Hillary to return to that region at any time in the future, even to ride in a similar bus that she rode during the Bill Clinton-Al Gore campaign in the early 1990's.

As per a poll in July, 2007, by the *American Research Group*, in the state of Illinois, Hillary and Obama are virtually tied with Obama getting 36% and Hillary 33% of the votes among Democrats sampled, followed far behind by Edwards at 7%, and Richardson at 4%, with 12% undecided.

2. *Massachusetts is her state of undergraduate study.* Hillary could have studied in Chicago, for that city is one of the centers of learning. Most undergraduate

students would probably choose to study near home. But, that would have meant spending 4 years of formative time in the same state you have been born in. It does not increase the number of your home states. If Hillary was not a brilliant high school student, then she might as well forget about going to Wellesley College in Wellesley, Massachusetts. Wellesley College just happens to be number 1, or the Harvard, of the 6 top women's colleges in America. After graduation, Hillary had gone back to her alma mater to speak to the student body several times.

3. *Connecticut is her state of professional study.* If Hillary did not do well as an undergraduate in Wellesley, then she would have had to compromise and study law where the requirements for entrance are not too strict. But, because she did extremely well in her undergraduate studies both in academics and co-curricular activities, she was readily admitted to the premier school of law in America, Yale Law School, in New Haven, Connecticut.

It comes as no surprise that both Massachusetts and Connecticut, far eastern New England states, are also in favor of Hillary as per an *American Research Group* poll:

- Massachusetts   Hillary Clinton 36%, John Kerry 10%, Al Gore 7%, John Edwards 4%

- Connecticut   Hillary Clinton 38%, Al Gore 4%, John Kerry 4%, John Edwards 3%.

4. *Arkansas is her state-in-law.* She could have married her childhood boy friend in the state of Illinois, or one of her boy friends in Boston, Massachusetts. Anyone of them could not have contributed to her widening base of future political support. If she did not go to Yale Law School, she would not have met Bill Clinton from Hope, Arkansas. Bill could have come from a northern state, but he came from Arkansas, a Dixie state that was in the other side of the Civil War. And he had presidential ambition! Hillary could have done to Bill what Jane Wyman did, that is, to refuse to live with her husband, Ronald Reagan, because she did not want to have anything to do with his going into politics. Hillary could also have had her own legal career, independent of Bill. Instead, she followed her heart's desire to be with Bill, wherever he wanted to live and to serve. She was willing to subordinate her ambition for that of her husband. When she was told that her continuing to use her maiden name while married to Bill was one of the reasons why her husband lost a state election, she changed her family name from Rodham to Clinton immediately! When Bill became Governor of Arkansas for 4 terms, she became his state's First Lady.

Hillary is not an Arkansan like her wildly popular husband, Bill Clinton, and she has not visited the state since they left in 1992. But she has a 20-year record of public service in Arkansas and political ties that will make her a good bet to win both the primary and the electoral votes of that state. "She's certainly the clear favorite to win [Arkansas]," said political scientist at Hendrix College, Jay Barth, who also sits on the state Democratic Party's executive committee.[169] Since Bill is one of the most popular Southerners in history, it should benefit Hillary being his wife. Obviously, Hillary will use Bill more to help her campaign throughout the rest of Dixieland: Louisiana, Alabama, Georgia, Tennessee, Kentucky, North and South Carolina, Virginia, West Virginia, Oklahoma, and even Texas.

Arkansans prefer Hillary to their own former governor, Republican Mike Huckabee. Compared to Mike Huckabee, Hillary has a definite advantage. In a poll between the 2 conducted by *the Arkansas Times*, the results were:

- Sen. Clinton   52%
- Gov. Huckabee   43%

The majority of Arkansas voters in this poll think Hillary is qualified to be president; only 39% say the same about Huckabee.

5. *Washington, D.C., became her home city as a former First Lady.* From 1993 to 2001, Bill Clinton served as U.S. President, and Hillary lived with him in the White House as his First Lady for 8 years. Their daughter, Chelsea, also lived with them as the First Child. So, Hillary has acquired a home base in the eastern or Atlantic Seaboard. Quite apart from the White House, Bill and Hillary have, in fact, their own private home in D.C. Because of a large African American presence in our country's capital, Democratic presidential candidates had always won it since it started as a separate Electoral College voting unit in 1964.

6. *New York is the state of her identity.* She is the junior Democratic senator from New York, serving with her senior co-Senator Chuck Schumer who has indicated his whole-hearted support for her presidential run. She was Sen. Patrick Moynihan's choice to take his place. This was not unprecedented: Robert Kennedy formerly of Boston, Massachusetts, also became a senator from New York in the late 1960's.

It was not too long ago when it was said "Hillary can't win." That was when she ran in New York for the U.S. Senate in 2000 for the first time. Well, she won by a margin of 12%. "Hillary can't win" is being repeated in connection with the current presidential contest. Hillary's advisers who also helped her husband's successful 2-term presidential bid are confident that if Hillary runs for president, she will win, too. "Why? First, because strength matters…. The latest *[Washington] Post-ABC News* poll shows that 68% of Americans describe Hillary as a strong leader. That comes after years of her being in the national crossfire. People know that Hillary has strong convictions, even if they don't always agree with her. They also know that she is tough enough to handle the viciousness of a national campaign and the challenges of the presidency itself."[170]

Hillary got re-elected as New York senator in 2006 by a very big margin, i.e. 67% of the votes. That included the support of 62% of independents and even 40% of Republicans. Even before she won re-election, New York voters already indicated by several polls that they would support her, if she were to run for U.S. president in 2008!

Early in 2007, Hillary declared that she is the best candidate for the job. "It'll be a great contest with a lot of talented people and I'm very confident," she declared. "I'm in, and I'm in to win and that's what I intend to do." Geraldine Ferraro, who lost the vice-presidency with Walter Mondale in 1984, was among the first to congratulate Hillary on her decision to run for president. "In 22 years, a lot had happened," Ferraro told the *New York Daily News*. "She has all the attributes that it takes to be a president, and she'll be a good one. Sen. Clinton (*D*, N.Y.) is battle-hardened after 8 years as First Lady and 6 more as a popular senator—which makes her far better equipped to handle the spotlight than Ferraro ever was, the former Queens congresswoman said.

As soon as she announced her intention to run for the U.S. presidency, the *New York Daily News* had a poll of voters in New York, and it showed that 43% would choose Clinton; 24% would choose Obama, and 33% were either undecided or would vote for another candidate. Hillary did even better among registered Democrats, beating Obama, 49% to 23%.

Because New York is Hillary's main home-state, former mayor Rudy Giuliani cannot claim it as his own home-state, too. An exclusive *NY1* poll has made this very clear. Both of them will beat their competition in their respective Democratic and Republican primaries. But, in a general election, if both of them will be the candidates head-to-head, Clinton will beat Giuliani by 14 percentage points, i.e. 53 to 39!

Well, Hillary has 6 states under her belt, so to speak. Where is the 7th one? This is where Chelsea comes in to give a helping hand.

7. *California is her daughter state.* When Chelsea decided to do her undergraduate study, she could have gone to one of the Ivy League colleges in which she was already accepted, but she decided to go to Stanford University all the way

to the Far Western Pacific seaboard, Palo Alto, California. To all Stanford alumni and alumnae: Remember that when you vote for Hillary on November 4, 2008, you are not only voting for her as U.S. president and not only for Bill Clinton as First Gentleman, but also for your co-alumna Chelsea Clinton as First Child and potential First Lady!

By not going to an Ivy-League university in the East, did Chelsea sacrifice too much just so that she could help her mom's political dream? The answer is, definitely, "No." For, she went to Stanford University in Palo Alto, CA, which is as good as any Ivy-League university. Some even refer to Stanford as the Harvard of the West.

The source of this information is the Rev. Dr. Robert S. Schuller, pastor of the Crystal Cathedral in Anaheim, CA. He said that "the parents of Leland Stanford, after whom that famous university was named, went to the president of Harvard University in Cambridge, MA, to offer to put up a building on campus to honor their son, who was one of their alumni. Harvard's president refused by saying, 'If every Harvard graduate will be honored with a building on campus, there will not be enough room to please everybody who wants to do the same.' Mr. and Mrs. Stanford were quite disappointed. 'Before we leave,' Mrs. Stanford asked the president, 'how much is the cost of erecting a building?' 'At least $50,000.00,' he replied. Mrs. Stanford whispered to her husband, 'Is that all? Let's go back to California and honor our son with a whole university!' And that was how Stanford University began," Dr. Schuller concluded.

Stanford University has always had an Ivy-League type of standard from the beginning of its existence. Furthermore, it is also only 1 of 2 California colleges that produced a U.S. president, Herbert Hoover, who graduated from the College of Engineering. (The other college was Whittier College, Richard Nixon's alma mater).

Hillary received the endorsement of all the major political leaders of California, capped by its most popular and beloved Senator Dianne Feinstein who referred to her senatorial colleague from New York as having "the experience, the heart and the strength to be a great American president.... We need a president who can restore America's international understanding while addressing crucial issues at home, who can rebuild confidence in government and demand accountability." "She is a woman of strength and compassion who has a powerful voice," Feinstein said, and adding, "She has been deeply impressed with how Hillary has handled herself in the Senate."[171]

In California, "Hillary is clearly the front-runner ... and she has the most formidable team imaginable, starting with her husband. They have been through national wars before and know the landscape," says Michael Semler, Professor of Politics at California State, Sacramento. "Everyone else is in the catch-up mode—including Obama. He can't wait for Hillary to trip," he continued, "He has to generate some love ... and I don't know where he's going to get it."[172]

In California where a Field Poll was taken in August, 2007 showed that Hillary was ahead of her nearest competitor, Obama, by 30 points. "That surprised me," said political analyst Sherry Bebitch Jeffe from the University of Southern California. "I assumed Clinton would come in first, but I did not assume it would be a 30-point spread."[173]

"Clinton Soars in California" reports the *San Jose Mercury News* on Aug. 17, 2007 and "Clinton Leaving Obama in the Dust in Latest State Poll," is the title of the *San Francisco Chronicle* report on the same day. Both newspapers were enthusiastically informing their readers about the result of a Field Poll conducted from Aug. 3-12, 2007, in the state of California. The poll "found 49% support Clinton, followed by Obama at 19%, and former North Carolina Sen. John Edwards with 10%. That's a shift from the Field Poll in March [2007], when Clinton held a 41%-28% lead over Obama, and Edwards had the backing of 13% of the voters.... Clinton's strengths in California include a crushing 4-1 lead among Latino voters, a more than 2-1 lead among women and African American voters, and at least a 2-1 lead in every geographic region in the state, the poll showed. She is also the overwhelming favorite in all age groups and ethnic groups and at every education level."[174]

If Hillary were to be matched up with any of the front runners in the Republican Party, Rudolph Giuliani, John McCain, Fred Thompson, or Mitt Romney, in the middle of September 2007, according to a *SurveyUSA* poll in the state of California, she will not only beat any of them by 9 points as did John Kerry over George W. Bush in 2004, but "she would destroy her GOP rivals by twice that."[175]

Hillary will have to do a difficult juggling act to follow the traditional geographical balance when choosing a vice-presidential running mate. Fortunately, Bill Clinton was the first one that broke that tradition by choosing Al Gore, a fellow-Southerner from Tennessee to run with him in 1992.

If Hillary starts as a senator from New York, an eastern state, she needs a vice-president from the west. That is already balanced by California in the far west. If she starts from Arkansas in the South, she needs a vice-president from the north. But, she already has Illinois to balance Arkansas, and vice-versa. If she needs eastern states to balance her being from the middle-west and south, then she needs a vice-president from the far northeast. But, she already has both Massachusetts and Connecticut from New England. And having Washington, D.C., as her home base, she needs a vice-president that represents the rest of the country. Any state will serve the purpose, including Hawaii in the middle of the Pacific Ocean or Alaska near the North Pole!

Instead of a geographical balance, the most important thing for Hillary is a gender balance. To have a woman or a minority vice-presidential running mate is out of the question.

That would send the wrong message. Hillary is not running as a fringe "angry at the establishment"-type of politician like Ralph Nader. She is running as a middle-of-the-road presidential candidate representing mainstream America. Her vice-presidential running mate must have these 4 qualifications: (1) he must be white, (2) he must be male, (3) he must *not* come from one of Hillary's 7 purple states, and (4) he must come from a battleground state.

Based on the 2000 federal census, the summary of electors as of the 2004 presidential elections will remain the same for 2008 (see Table 10.0).[176]

Table 10.0 Distribution of 2008 Electoral Votes

State	Allocated Electoral Votes
(1). Alabama	9
(2). Alaska	3
(3). Arizona	10
(4). Arkansas	6
(5). California	55
(6). Colorado	9
(7). Connecticut	7
(8). Delaware	3
(9). Florida	27
(10). Georgia	15
(11). Hawaii	4
(12). Idaho	4
(13). Illinois	21

(14). Indiana	11
(15). Iowa	7
(16). Kansas	6
(17). Kentucky	8
(18). Louisiana	9
(19). Maine	4
(20). Maryland	10
(21). Massachusetts	12
(22). Michigan	17
(23). Minnesota	10
(24). Mississippi	6
(25). Missouri	11
(26). Montana	3
(27). Nebraska	5
(28). Nevada	5
(29). New Hampshire	4
(30). New Jersey	15
(31). New Mexico	5
(32). New York	31
(33). North Carolina	15
(34). North Dakota	3
(35). Ohio	20
(36). Oklahoma	7
(37). Oregon	7
(38). Pennsylvania	21
(39). Rhode Island	4
(40). South Carolina	8

(41). South Dakota	3
(42). Tennessee	11
(43). Texas	34
(44). Utah	5
(45). Vermont	3
(46). Virginia	13
(47) Washington	11
(51). Washington, D.C.	3
(48). West Virginia	5
(49). Wisconsin	10
(50). Wyoming	3
Total	538 (270 of which will win).

Table 10.1 Projected Starting Electoral Votes for Hillary in 2008

State	Electoral Vote
Arkansas	6
California	55
Connecticut	7
Illinois	21
Massachusetts	12
New York	31
Washington D.C.	3
Total	135 = 50% of winning total at 270

The starting total number of electoral votes from Hillary's 7 home states is 135 or exactly 50% of the total magic winning number of 270. Each of her potential Republican opponents has a total of no more than 34 electoral votes or even as low as zero (*compare* Table 10.1 and 10.2).

Table 10.2 Hillary's Starting Electoral Votes vs. Potential Opponents'

Name of Opponent	Home State Source	Electoral Vote	Hillary's Starting Edge
Rudy Giuliani	New York	0	135
Mitt Romney	Utah	5	130
John McCain	Arizona	10	125
Sam Brownback	Kansas	6	129
Mike Huckabee	Arkansas	0	135
Duncan Hunter	California	0	135
Ron Paul	Texas	34	101
Condi Rice	Alabama	9	126
Tom Tancredo	Colorado	9	126
Fred Thompson	Tennessee	11	124
Newt Gingrich	Georgia	15	120

No professional jockey at Belmont or elsewhere would be in his right mind to try to run a race in which one of his competitors is already half-way to the finish line. But, that is exactly what is happening in the presidential race of 2008. Let us a assume that the finish line of the race-track is at 270 yards to win, and the starting line for those who have no home states is at zero. That would be the cases of Giuliani, Huckabee, and Hunter who are all starting at zero, right at the beginning of the starting line because their states are in conflict with one of the 7 states that Hillary has preempted. By the time Giuliani, Huckabee, or Hunter reaches the middle point of the race-track, i.e., 135 yards, Hillary is already at the 270 yards finish line!

Hillary's closest Republican presidential opponent would be Ron Paul of Texas who has 34 electoral votes. The race is a bit closer, if you consider a 101-yard difference closer than a 135-yard difference. Still, the end result is the same:

by the time Paul reaches 169 yards, Hillary is already at the 270 yards finish line. But, there is a strange twist to this imaginary race. In actual race horse-racing, there might be something that a contestant might do that could disqualify him (or her) from winning. In the case of Ron Paul, he is as old as John McCain at 72, and as far as American voters are concerned only those who are 68 years old and under are qualified to win (*see* chapter 6 above on presidential ages).

The rest of the field, including McCain, Romney, Brownback, Tancredo, Gingrich, Thompson, Rice, or any other Republican presidential aspirant, will not lose as bad as Giuliani, Huckabee, or Hunter. But, still they will be unable to beat Hillary!

There have been presidential prospects who realized that it was useless to oppose Hillary and therefore either withdrew or did not announce their candidacy at all, including John Kerry, Al Gore, Joe Lieberman, Tom Vilsack, General Wesley Clark of the Democratic and Dick Cheney, Tommy Thompson, Chuck Hagel, George Allen, Rick Santorum, Jeb Bush, Colin Powell, and Condi Rice of the Republican Parties respectively.

Do you not think that the Electoral College voting system on which Hillary's 4-fold strategy is based needs reforming? You may be among those who say, "Yes." One way to go would be to have a uniform proportional distribution of electors based on the congressional winners within each state, as is now done in 2 states: Maine and Nebraska.

But, the attempt at proportional representation only in a single state like California, a blue-leaning state, but not Texas, a red-leaning state, can only be unfair to one political party, that is, the Democratic Party. For, Republicans can get a slice of California's 55-winner-take-all electoral votes, if this initiative will pass in June 2008, but Democrats will not have a similar chance to get a portion of Texas's electoral votes or anywhere else.

The *San Francisco Chronicle* and the *New York Times* in their editorials on August 20, 2007 and August 22, 2007 respectively both had expressed opposition to the California initiative proposed for June 2008 as a one-sided ploy to favor the Republicans. They correctly pointed out that far from being a real reform proposal this initiative is "an elaborate trick posing as reform [that] twists the nation's system of electing presidents to give one party an unfair advantage."[177]

A better method of achieving fairness in reform is to abolish the Electoral College in all states completely. It would be more democratic to have every single vote count nationwide rather than state by state as it is now. That way, it will guarantee that the candidate who gets the majority of all the votes becomes president, and not otherwise. Accordingly, a counter-initiative to the foregoing is also being presented at the same time as the "unfair" one in June 2008. The latter proposes that the Electoral College be abolished and in its place the entire country should adopt a uniform one-person-one-vote system.

The reform of the Electoral College voting system may have to wait till the 2012 election, if at all. The over-all reform of the Electoral College will be more favorable to the Democratic Party, since there are more registered Democrats nationally. In both the 1876 and the 2000 presidential elections, Democrats Samuel J. Tilden and Al Gore won the over-all popular vote, but Republicans Rutherford B. Hayes and George W. Bush who won the electoral votes became presidents respectively. Thus, it is in the best interest of the Republican Party to stick with the Electoral College.

How Hillary Can Get 135 More Electoral Votes to Win

Second Strategy: The states that can give Hillary the additional 135 electoral votes to win are those that voted Democratic both in 2000 and 2004 in spite of the fact that both Al Gore and John Kerry lost to the incumbent Republican George W. Bush. These are the so-called blue-leaning states that will most often vote for a Democratic presidential candidate (*see* Table 10.3).

Table 10.3 Blue-Leaning States (Favoring Democratic Candidates)

State	Electoral Votes
(1). Delaware	3
(2). Hawaii	4
(3). Idaho	4
(4). Iowa	7
(5). Kansas	6
(6). Maine	4
(7). Maryland	10
(8). Michigan	17
(9). Minnesota	10

(10). Nebraska	5
(11). New Hampshire	4
(12). New Jersey	15
(13). New Mexico	5
(14). North Dakota	3
(15). Oregon	7
(16). Rhode Island	4
(17). South Dakota	3
(18). Vermont	3
(19). Washington	11
(20). Wisconsin	10
Total	135 + 135 (from 7 home states) = 270 to win!

Tom Vilsack, former governor of Iowa decided to withdraw his own presidential bid announced in November 2006 three months later in February 2007. Then, examining the remaining Democratic candidates numbering at least 8 others, he decided to endorse Hillary as the best presidential candidate in 2008: "At this critical time, Hillary Clinton has the experience, strength and vision our country needs to get us back on track and moving in the right direction," he said. "There is no candidate who will create a stronger and better America than Hillary Clinton." Vilsack has now become one of Hillary's prominent members of her campaign staff.

You might wonder what kind of help former Vilsack's endorsement of Hillary might give to her presidential campaign. The answer is "quite a lot in Iowa." "Vilsack" might not be a household name anywhere else in the United States, but in Iowa he has strong support. One of Vilsack's strongest backers, Gordon Fisher, a one-time chairman of the state's Democratic Party, said "if the governor's organization gets behind Mrs. Clinton, her ground operation will see an instantaneous boost."[178]

Jim Splaine, veteran Congressman from New Hampshire, recognized that Hillary was a presidential timber even before she became Bill Clinton's First Lady: "When I first met this incredible woman in Portsmouth in 1991, after she spoke I told her SHE should be the candidate for president. It was not an intentional slight at her husband. But after hearing her speak and answer a barrage of questions, it was clear to me that she was in her league. She laughed at my comment. I don't think she will next time we meet. No, Hillary isn't perfect. But she is a perfect fit for what we need in 2008: someone who can lead us on important issues like health care, national security, and economic stability."[179]

Two weeks after leaping into the presidential race, Hillary finds herself securely at the top in all early primary/caucus states of Iowa, South Carolina, and New Hampshire, as reflected by a poll conducted by the *American Research Group*, as reported by the *New York Daily News*:

- Iowa   Clinton 31%, Edwards 20%, Vilsack 17%, Obama 10%

- South Carolina   Clinton 34%, Edwards 31%, Obama 10%

- New Hampshire   Clinton 27%, Obama 21%, Edwards 18%.

Maine and Vermont are also for Hillary in 2008 according to the same *American Research Group* poll:

- Maine   Clinton 36%, Edwards 6%, Gore 5%, Kerry 5%, Undeclared/Others 37%

- Vermont   Clinton 34%, Gore 6%, Kerry 4%, Edwards 3%, Undeclared/Others 36%

As per *Delaware Online*, while Joe Biden (*D*, DE) might be campaigning busily in Iowa and New Hampshire, Hillary Clinton might end up depriving him of his home state, because she is ahead of him by double digits there according to a local university poll. Hillary was favored by 34% out of 346 registered Delaware voters.

Michigan also favors Hillary, according to a poll conducted by the *Detroit Free Press*/Local 4 Union, with nearly a 30-point lead over her closest rival, Obama.

Hillary also leads in a Washington state conducted by *Strategic Vision*:

- Hillary Clinton   39%

- Al Gore   18%

- John Edwards   9%
- Undeclared/Others   20%

Obama's presidential campaign might have missed out of millions of dollars by failing to return the calls of financial high rollers in New Jersey. Having waited for more than a month for a reply from Obama's people, and failing to receive one, they shifted their financial support to Hillary's campaign. "The gaffe highlights Clinton's organizational advantage over her chief rival for the Democratic nomination. It shows how Obama's focus on the Internet and running an outsider's campaign may undermine his ability to cultivate traditional political allies."[180]

Third Strategy: All that Hillary has to do in order to be a sure winner is choose one of the battleground states from which to pick her vice-presidential running mate. They are battleground states because they do *not* always vote in favor of one major party's presidential candidate election after election. Therefore, if a vice-presidential running mate from one of those battleground states can turn the neutral color of that state to blue, then the winner of the ball game will definitely be the Hillary Clinton-headed team. It would be a mistake for Hillary to choose her vice-presidential team mate from a red-leaning state, as John Kerry did in 2004 when he picked John Edwards from South Carolina to run with him. The battleground states voted for Bill Clinton in the 1990's but for George W. Bush in 2000 and 2004 (*see* Table 10.4).

Table 10.4 Battleground States (Favoring neither Democratic nor Republican Candidates)

States:	Electoral Votes:
(1). Arizona	10
(2). Colorado	9
(3). Florida	27
(4). Indiana	11
(5). Missouri	11
(6). Montana	3

(7). Nevada	5
(8). Ohio	20
(9). Pennsylvania	21
(10). Wyoming	3
Total	120

When James Carville, a well-known Democratic political consultant, was asked as to whether Hillary could win any southern state if she were the Democratic nominee, his surprise answer was, "She has the best chance to win Florida." Without a doubt, Florida has always been a battleground state that does not vote for one major party's presidential candidate every election time; the other southern states are mostly red or Republican-leaning states.

Under normal circumstances, we would have agreed with James Carville considering he has such an impeccable credential as an unwavering Clinton loyalist dating from the time of Bill and Hillary in Arkansas dating as far back as 25 years ago. But, these are supernormal—*not* abnormal—times when for the first time in 220 years of American history we have 3 candidates who are not both white and male (Hillary who is not male, Obama who is not white, and Richardson who is Hispanic) that demand exceptional prognostications. So since nobody can really see what will happen in the future, we can only hazard a guess—a most enlightened guess based on incontrovertible evidences that are easily available—that Hillary will not only have the best chance of winning Pennsylvania (which will be enough to catapult her and her vice-presidential running mate directly into the Oval Office), but also Florida (which Al Gore & Joseph Lieberman lost despite their winning majority of the country's total popular votes in 2000), and as well as Ohio (which John Kerry & John Edwards also lost in 2004). Now, for the evidences:

In a *Quinnipiac University* poll, Democrats in the battleground state of Pennsylvania have given Hillary a 30-point lead over Obama:

- Hillary Clinton   42%, Al Gore 13%, Barack Obama 12%, and John Edwards 8%.

A similar early poll of Florida Democratic voters, Hillary was the overwhelming choice:

- Clinton   44%
- Kerry   10%
- Edwards   17%
- Undeclared/Others   29%

Hillary has a potent secret weapon in Ohio against her opponents in the person of the incumbent first-term Democratic Gov. Ted Strickland who won in 2006 with more than just the blessings of the junior senator from New York.

Democrat Hillary Clinton appears to be pulling away from her rivals in Ohio—both Democrats and Republicans—in a *Quinnipiac University* Poll on the 2008 presidential race released on September 6, 2007. Overall, the poll showed Democrats holding the upper hand against Republicans in all but one of 12 possible general election matchups, a sign that right now Ohio appears to be continuing a Democratic trend that started with major victories last year. "Ohio is very blue these days," said Peter A. Brown, assistant director of the Quinnipiac University Polling Institute. These are the results of the *Quinnipiac University* poll (09/06/07):

In the race for the Democratic nomination:

- Hillary Clinton   44%, Barack Obama 15%, John Edwards, and 11%, Al Gore, 8%.

In a race against Republicans:

- Hillary Clinton   47%   vs.   Rudolph Giuliani   40%
- Hillary Clinton   46%   vs.   John McCain   41%
- Hillary Clinton   49%   vs.   Fred Thompson   37%
- Hillary Clinton   50%   vs.   Mitt Romney   37%

Hillary would have wanted the 2008 Democratic national convention to be held in New York, but New York City mayor Michael Bloomberg was not willing to contribute to the financing of it. Denver, Colorado won the bid to host it. It will be a blessing-in-disguise for Hillary. Holding the Democratic convention in New York will not add to Hillary's winning column, for the electoral votes of

New York are already fully in the bag for her! But holding the convention in Denver could add Colorado's battle-ground electoral votes to Hillary's total!

The next 2 states, though comparatively smaller in population and consequently smaller in their number of electoral votes, are nevertheless symbolically important: (1) Nevada, the gambling capital of the world, whose odd makers have been predicting a Hillary Clinton presidential victory right from the beginning, along with the impossible (1 out of 105) odds of Arnold Schwarzenegger's winning it, and (2) Missouri, the "show-me" state, resident of Americans who are as skeptical as anyone can be, yet apparently not as skeptical when it comes to voting for a woman like Hillary.

The winner of the Nevada Democratic caucus will succeed because of "the campaign's organizational strength, its ranks of energetic foot soldiers and its knowledge of Nevada." Judged by those measurements, Hillary has an early lead: "In less than a month, she has assembled an organization that is unparalleled in its mix of institutional knowledge, national experience and local leadership."[181]

Robert Fowler, pastor of the Victory Missionary Baptist Church in Las Vegas, NV, and 1 of 34 religious, leaders, educators, activists and business people that constitute the Nevada African American Leadership Council, said: "I believe [Hillary] has a strong awareness of what's happening in Nevada and the ability to make some central change for us here in Nevada."

An early poll taken by the *Review Journal* shows that Nevada Democrats overwhelming prefer Hillary as their party's presidential nominee:

- Hillary Clinton   37%, John Edwards 13%, Barack Obama 12%.

In a poll on August 6, 2007, of Missouri Democrats conducted by the *American Research Group,* Hillary was also in the clear lead.

- Hillary Clinton   40%, John Edwards 22%, Barack Obama 15%, Undeclared/Others 12%.

Fourth Strategy: Hillary is even doing very well in traditionally red-leaning states. Her strategy there appears to be to depend mainly on strong local state support both finance-and leadership-wise (*see* Table 10.5).

Table 10.5 Red-Leaning States (Favoring Republicans)

States:	Electoral Votes:
(1). Alabama	9
(2). Alaska	3
(3). Georgia	15
(4). Kentucky	8
(5). Louisiana	9
(6). Mississippi	6
(7). North Carolina	15
(8). Oklahoma	7
(9). South Carolina	8
(10). Tennessee	11
(11). Texas	34
(12). Utah	5
(13). Virginia	13
(14). West Virginia	5
Total	148

Nine of Clinton's 20 most lucrative fund-raising states went to President Bush in the 2004 election, according to the review of federal records by *PoliticalMoney-Line*, a fund-raising watchdog group. This group found that Bush's own home-state of Texas, the reddest of the red, is among the most fertile source of Clinton's funds. She has gobbled up from there, $760,000 since 2005, almost as much as the $780,000 she got from true-blue Massachusetts.

In a poll of Texas Democrats early in March, 2007, taken by the *American Research Group*, Hillary came out slightly ahead of Obama:

- Hillary Clinton   34%
- Barack Obama   32%
- John Edwards   11%
- Undeclared/Others   10%

In the first poll of the preferences of voters among Democrats in Georgia, home of former Republican Speaker of the U.S. House of Representatives, Newt Gingrich, the results were:

- Hillary Clinton   27%
- Barack Obama   20%
- John Edwards   15%
- Undeclared/Others   27%

The *Civitas Institute* poll conducted by Tel Opinion Research on June 14, 2007 reported that among North Carolina Democrats, John Edwards who used to be that state's U.S. Senator, was slightly in the lead with 25%, but Hillary Clinton was nipping at his heels with 20%. The ratings improved for Hillary in August, 2007: Edwards was at 34% and Hillary at 31%, which is statistically within the margin of error and therefore a tie. But, North Carolina is a red-leaning state that had always voted Republican except only when Democratic Jimmy Carter, former governor of neighboring Georgia won it in the 1970's. Edwards won North Carolina's primary against John Kerry prior to the 2004 presidential election, but in the presidential election itself, the John Kerry-John Edwards Democratic ticket lost by a wide margin to the incumbent George W. Bush-Dick Cheney Republican ticket (*see* Chapter 2 above). This time, Republicans are stunned to learn in the same *Civitas Institute* poll that Rudy Giuliani and Fred Thompson are running neck to neck with 24% each while John McCain is lingering behind with 16%.

In Hillary's first visit to Columbia, South Carolina, to speak at the John Hurst Adams Gymnatorium of Allen University, it was a standing room only crowd with so many lining up early one block down Pine Street to have the first chance to get in. It was estimated that no less than 3, 200 people were in attendance, and some people had to be seated in an adjoining overflow room.

Both Hillary and Bill Clinton were among the guests at the 42nd anniversary of the civil rights march across a bridge in Selma, Alabama, that helped end segregation in the south. She spoke in an African American church, with Bill in the audience. They also attended meetings among Democrats in Montgomery, Alabama's capital.

The result of a poll on August 2, 2007, among Alabama Democrats conducted by the *American Research Group* was overwhelmingly in Hillary's favor:

- Hillary Clinton   38%
- John Edwards   19%
- Barack Obama   17%
- Undeclared/Others   16%

If you happen to be a Democrat but you live in a red state, what is the best thing you can do to support Hillary? You can still vote for her in the primary to make sure she becomes the nominee of your party. But, when the election comes, and you are sure that the Republican candidate will win your state's electoral votes, you can still vote for the Democratic nominee (hopefully Hillary). There is something else you can do to make yourself a *sure winner* with Hillary, that is, send to her campaign office the biggest cash contribution you can possibly afford. That is exactly what Meg Avereti, a Democrat residing in the red state of Utah, had done!

A very significant move that Hillary made was to transfer the site of her national campaign headquarters from K Street, Washington, D.C., to the state of Virginia. Just as the location of the national Democratic convention in Colorado is better than in New York, the latter being Hillary's main home state, so is Virginia preferable to Washington, D.C., since the latter is not only one of Hillary's 7 home-states, it had always voted Democrat since it had the right to have its share of the electoral votes in the 1960's. It could be the factor that will make Virginia turn from red to blue.

Hillary also has mounted the most aggressive super delegates, winning endorsements from 37 so far including 3 senate colleagues and the governors of Maryland, New Jersey and New York. She even deputized several House members as "whips" to woo uncommitted colleagues including Ohio Rep. Stephanie Tubbs-Jones, Florida Rep. Debbie Wasserman-Schultz, and New York Reps. Nita Lowey and Joseph Crowley. No other presidential candidate, Democrat or Republican, can match her tremendous success here, too.

How can you tell that Hillary's 4-fold strategy is working? The best way is to check the latest *national* polls. The following 2 sets of poll results were obtained by asking 600 Democratic and 600 Republican prospective voters respectively during the second week of September 2007, when Fred Thompson had just officially declared as a Republican presidential candidate, by the *American Research Group*. For comparative purposes, we provide here this poll's results for the Republicans first, and then followed by the Democrats.

In the Republican side, Rudy Giuliani and Fred Thompson are tied for the lead. Fred Thompson leads among men, and Giuliani leads among women followed by John McCain.

National Primary

Republicans	Rep.	Ind.	Men	Women
	(88%)	*(12%)*	*(52%)*	*(48%)*
• Rudy Giuliani	22%	38%	17%	31%
• John McCain	14%	16%	7%	22%
• Fred Thompson	23%	25%	37%	7%
• Undeclared/Others	15%	16%	17%	16%

On the Democratic side, Hillary Clinton continues to lead over her opponents. She has a 2-to-1 lead over Barack Obama among women.

National Primary

Democrats	Dem.	Ind.	Men	Women
	(88%)	*(12%)*	*(46%)*	*(54%)*
• Hillary Clinton	40%	33%	35%	43%
• John Edwards	15%	17%	19%	11%
• Barack Obama	19%	34%	20%	21%
• Undeclared/Others	12%	14%	15%	13%

The *Associated Press/Ipsos* poll conducted in the second week of September 2007, tells exactly the same Hillary Clinton success story. "The poll shows that Sen. Hillary Clinton of New York has a clear, across-the-board lead in the Democratic primary campaign over Sen. Barack Obama of Illinois, 34% to 20%, roughly the *same margin she has enjoyed for months"* (emphasis supplied).[182]

Nationwide, as of the middle of September, 2007, the *USA Today*/Gallup Poll found that "on the Democratic side, New York Sen. Hillary Clinton continues to lead the field, at 45%, over Illinois Sen. Barack Obama, at 24%. Former North Carolina Sen. John Edwards is third at 16%, up 3% since August. In a head-to-head race, Democrats favor Clinton over Obama by 31 points, 63%-32%, *the biggest margin to date"* (emphasis supplied).[183]

Conclusion

An independent opinion survey conducted in April 2007 sought the responses of potential voters on two questions: (1). "Who is your favorite among previous American presidents?" (2). "Who among the present presidential candidates closely resembles your previous favorite?"

The top 3 answers to the first question were: Franklin D. Roosevelt, Ronald Reagan, and John F. Kennedy. There were only 2 top answers to the second question and both are Democrats: Hillary Clinton for those who chose Roosevelt and Reagan as their favorites, and a distant third, Barack Obama for those who chose Kennedy.

You already had a chance to compare Barack Obama with John F. Kennedy in chapter 3 above and noted that in many respects, there are no real similarities between them. You also had an opportunity to compare Fred Thompson with Ronald Reagan in chapter 9 and, as in the case of Obama and Kennedy there are no close correspondences between them.

Hillary claims that she is "the real JFK of 2008." How does she justify it? This is what she told the New Hampshire Democrats' 100 Club Fund-raisers about Kennedy: "He was smart, he was dynamic, he was inspiring and he was Catholic. A lot of people back then [1960] said, 'America will never elect a Catholic as president.' But those who gathered here almost half a century ago knew better," she continued. "They believed America was bigger than that and Americans would give Sen. John F. Kennedy a fair shake, and the rest, as they say, is history."[184] Just as the majority of American voters did not heed those who objected to Kennedy, because of his non-Protestant religion, so should you *not* when others oppose Hillary's becoming the first female Commander-in-Chief of our country's armed forces, just because she is not a he.

It does not make much sense for any white male politician (including those who are only 50% Caucasian) to try to swim against a really strong tide of change. If he does and he succeeds, he will forever be negatively branded as the ungentlemanly one who blocked the first woman candidate from becoming America's president. But, if he loses he will be remembered as a total failure, for he cannot even defeat a woman!

"Sometimes the Best Man for the Job is a Woman!"

Hillary's video presented during the CNN/You-Tube Democratic Presidential debate on Monday, July 23, 2007 has summarized her appeal for your votes, "Sometimes the best man for the job is a woman!" That is a fitting summary of Hillary's presidential prospects in 2008. And we would add, "Sometimes the wrong thing to do is to choose a man for president just because he is not a woman.

To summarize the 10 best reasons to support and vote for Hillary Clinton on November 4, 2008, we can do no better than reproduce here the ones given by Hillary Clinton for President:

1. *To end the war in Iraq.*

2. *To achieve universal, affordable healthcare.*

3. *To create good jobs for middle-class Americans with the right investments in modern infrastructure and in new clean, energy-efficient technologies that reduce our dependence on foreign oil and combat global warming.*

4. *To provide world-class education, from universal pre-kindergarten to affordable college for all.*

5. *To promote 21st century scientific innovation, including stem cell research.*

6. *To return to fiscal responsibility, move back toward a balanced budget, and safeguard Social Security and Medicare for future generations.*

7. *To restore competence and end cronyism in government, with a president who cares about and works for Americans who have been invisible to this administration.*

8. *To combat terrorism, strengthen our military, and care for our veterans.*

9. *To restore America's standing in the world and repair our alliances.*

10. *To build a more tolerant, united America, working to achieve big goals again, with a president who's ready for change and ready to lead from day one.* [185]

Hillary is more qualified than any other American woman to run for president, true. And in her own words, she is also "the most qualified person to hit the ground running." In advertising the book *Her Way: The Hopes and Ambitions of Hillary Rodham Clinton* authored by Jeff Gerth and Don Van Natta, Jr., *the New York Times* headlined the page this way: "The Truth about the Most Important Woman in America."[186] Apparently, Gerth and Van Natta do not think that "the most important woman in America" and "the world's most famous woman" is good enough to be president of the United States, the greatest country in the world. If so, what kind of woman are we supposed to wait for who can qualify to be an American president?

How many of the previous 42 presidents of our country could remotely qualify as the most important man in America in his time? There were very few, if at all. Some of them won as "dark horse" candidates. A "dark horse" was so-called because he was chosen as a compromise between 2 equally strong candidates who were unwilling to give in to the other. Thus, many presidents were mediocre. As per the 3 lists of the most important presidents in history rated by American historians, only about 10 were great and near great. The rest were average, below average, and even 2 or 3 failures (*see* Table 11.1; 11.2, & 11.3).

Table 11.1 1948 Poll conducted by Arthur M. Schlesinger of 55 historians, published in *Life Magazine* on November 1, 1948

Great

1. Abraham Lincoln

2. George Washington

3. Franklin D. Roosevelt

4. Woodrow Wilson

5. Thomas Jefferson

6. Andrew Jackson

Near Great

7. Theodore Roosevelt

8. Grover Cleveland

9. John Adams

10. James K. Polk

Average

11. John Quincy Adams

12. James Monroe

13. Rutherford B. Hayes

14. James Madison

15. Martin Van Buren

16. William Howard Taft

17. Chester A. Arthur

18. William McKinley

19. Andrew Johnson

20. Herbert Hoover

21. Benjamin Harrison

Below Average

22. John Tyler

23. Calvin Coolidge

24. Millard Fillmore

25. Zachary Taylor

26. James Buchanan

27. Franklin Pierce

Failure

28. Ulysses Grant

29. Warren G. Harding

Table 11.2 **1962 Poll conducted by Arthur M. Schlesinger of 75 historians, published in *The New York Times* magazine on July 29, 1962**

Great

1. Abraham Lincoln

2. George Washington

3. Franklin D. Roosevelt

4. Woodrow Wilson

5. Thomas Jefferson

Near Great

6. Andrew Jackson

7. Theodore Roosevelt

8. James K. Polk

9. Harry Truman

10. John Adams

11. Grover Cleveland

Average

12. James Madison

13. John Quincy Adams

14. Rutherford B. Hayes

15. William McKinley

16. William Howard Taft

17. Martin Van Buren

18. James Monroe

19. Herbert Hoover

20. Benjamin Harrison

21. Chester Arthur

22. Dwight D. Eisenhower

23. Andrew Johnson

Below Average

24. Zachary Taylor

25. John Tyler

26. Millard Fillmore

27. Calvin Coolidge

28. Franklin Pierce

29. James Buchanan

Failure

30. Ulysses Grant

31. Warren G. Harding

Table 11.3 1982 Poll conducted by Chicago Tribune of 49 historians, published in the *Chicago Tribune* magazine on January 10, 1982

1. Abraham Lincoln

2. Franklin D. Roosevelt

3. George Washington

4. Theodore Roosevelt

5. Thomas Jefferson

6. Andrew Jackson

7. Woodrow Wilson

8. Harry Truman

9. Dwight Eisenhower

10. William McKinley

11. James Polk

12. Lyndon Johnson

13. Grover Cleveland

14. John Kennedy (tie)

14. John Adams (tie)

16. James Monroe

17. James Madison

18. Martin Van Buren

19. John Quincy Adams

20. William Taft

21. Herbert Hoover

22. Rutherford Hayes

23. Gerald Ford

24. Chester Arthur

25. Benjamin Harrison

26. Jimmy Carter

27. Calvin Coolidge

28. Zachary Taylor

29. John Tyler

30. Ulysses Grant

31. Millard Fillmore

32. Andrew Johnson

33. James Garfield

34. Richard Nixon

35. Franklin Pierce

36. James Buchanan

37. Warren Harding

38. William Harrison

Has Hillary, with the aid of her husband Bill, orchestrated all the events that will lead to her presidential victory in 2008, as declared by Jeff Gerth and Don Van Natta in their book, *Her Way?* Granting but not admitting that Hillary is manipulating events, it would be to underestimate the intelligence of the American people to be thought of as being that easy to influence. Quite the contrary, it is Gerth and Van Natta who are trying to manipulate history by their claim that through their thorough investigative methods they found "the truth about the most important woman in America" in our time, when in fact what they are presenting are quite false. All that they are attempting to do is to derail the legitimate aspiration of Hillary to be the first woman president of America, the greatest country in the world!

This is not the first time that Gerth tried to claim by using the same investigative methods to have discovered "the truth." Early in the 1990's he informed the American people that the Clintons were connected with an alleged "Whitewater scandal" in Arkansas to derail the presidential aspiration of Bill Clinton, the most important man in America in his time. The American people still voted for Bill Clinton as president. They did not believe Gerth, for none of his allegations turned out to square with the actual facts. Why should our American people believe Gerth and company to be telling us the real truth now?

History cannot be totally controlled. Only the opportunities that it presents can be taken advantaged of by the wise and honest ones. Most of history is his-story (man's story), rather than her-story (woman's story). It is not easy to succeed in a high political office. For women, to pursue a high public position is doubly hard. You can ask Nancy Pelosi how difficult it was for her to become the 60th House Speaker after 218 years of American political history.

Thanks to the foresight of Hillary's parents, Mr. Hugh E. Rodham, Sr. and Mrs. Dorothy Emma Howell-Rodham, in naming their daughter the way they did because they wanted her to fulfill her role in history as if it were herstory! Like other dedicated American parents, they had hoped and prayed that their first-born female child, Hillary Rodham (now Mrs. Bill Clinton), and their two younger male children, Hugh E. Rodham, Jr. and Anthony Rodham will all be successful adults. They did not know how all their children's future careers will exactly turn out. As Christian devoted parents, their prayers and dreams for all their children turned out quite well. Hugh, Jr. and Anthony have become quite productive as a lawyer and a businessman respectively. They would have been equally happy if Hillary turned out to be an Olympic athlete as she originally dreamed as a child, or when that did not work out, if she turned out to be an astronaut (*see* detail of story in chapter 10 above). But, Hillary's God-given destiny took her to a different path, and her parents must be pleasantly surprised that she has come a long way in becoming a first rate American politician, like any man, though a woman!

"No Republican Male Candidate Can Beat Hillary!"

Dick Morris and Eileen McGann in the oft-cited *Condi vs. Hillary* made an observation that must be absolutely right since they are making it as Republicans: "No male Republican candidate can beat Hillary. Only Condi can."[187] Tom Delay (R, TX), former Republican Majority Leader of the U.S. House of Representatives even went farther than that when he said, "[Hillary] will win the Democratic primary and she will be our next president."

If Condi runs, it is quite doubtful if even she can defeat Hillary. But, when Condi was asked in Palo Alto, California in June 2007, she answered that she had no plan to run for president. After her term as Secretary of State, she said that her preference will be to return to her former job as Provost of Stanford University. First Lady Laura Bush confirmed this fact as early as May 2007 when she said: "Condi is my favorite candidate for president in 2008." "But," she continued, "I don't think she is going to run because she is single."

If the only person who can beat Hillary is another woman, Condi, but then she decides not to run: Well, Giuliani, McCain, Romney, Thompson, and other male Republican candidates, why waste your time, energy, and money to proceed with a surely failing endeavor? The best thing you can do is: Avoid losing to Hillary; join her! This kind of perfect consensus only happened once in American history, when our forbears elected George Washington as our first president in 1788. It is fitting that this unanimous choice of Hillary Clinton as president be repeated in 2008—220 years later—because we are electing a woman president for the first time!

END

Endnotes

[1]. Carl Bernstein's *A Woman in Charge: the Life of Hillary Rodham Clinton* was published by Knopf Publishing Group, a division of Random House, Inc. in 2007. Jeff Gerth and Don van Natta's *HER WAY: the Hopes and Ambitions of Hillary Rodham Clinton* was published by Little, Brown & Co. in 2007. Peggy Noonan's *The Case against Hillary Clinton* was published by Regan Books in 2000. Susan Estrich's *The Case for Hillary Clinton* was also published by Regan Books in 2005.

[2]. According to Sarah E. Igo in "Pollsters Painting America by Numbers," *San Jose Mercury News,* page 1P, the public by and large does not challenge the data obtained by polling. This is a dangerous trend, for polling is not a perfect instrument of arriving at the truth. For example, in the 1948 presidential election, some newspapers based on last minute polling projected Truman's opponent, "Dewey Wins!" instead of Truman.

[3]. 25th Anniversary *USA Today*, "A World under Their Influence," September 4, 2007, p. 10B.

[4]. Published by Praeger Publishers in Westport, CT Other earlier scholarly books include J.H. Silbey et al, *The History of American Electoral Behavior* (1978); E. H. Rosenbloom, *A History of Presidential Elections* (3rd ed. 1970), and J. M. Clubb, ed., *Electoral Change and Stability in American Political History* (1971)

[5]. *The Lubbock Advance Journal* is published in Lubbock, Texas.

[6]. Susan Page, "Clinton Gets Close-Up Glimpse of Nurses's Life," *USA Today*, August 14, 2007, p. 4.

[7]. *Reuters*, as reported in http://www.votehillary.org/CMS/InThe-News?page=44

[8]. Emily T. Douglas, *Remember the Ladies*, (New York, NY: G.P. Putnam Sons, 1966), 150f.

[9]. Barbara A. Wilson, Captain, USAF (Ret), *Women's Military History* http://www.undelete.org/military.html.

[10]. The astronauts are listed at http://womenshistory.about.com/library/pic/bl_p_astronauts_women.htm, and the armed forces officers are listed at http://userpages.aug.com/captbarb/stars.html.

[11]. The following also served in the military at sometime in their lives: James Monroe, Franklin Pierce, Abraham Lincoln, James Garfield, Benjamin Harrison, William McKinlery, John Kennedy, Gerald Ford, Jimmy Carter, and George H.W. Bush.

[12]. As reported by Noor Khan, in Kandahar, Afghanistan, on January 5, 2006, *the Associated Press*.

[13]. Matt Rosenberg writes in *Your Guide to Geography* that there are exactly 192 U.N.-member countries, plus the Vatican a non-U.N. member, adding to a total of 193 countries in the world. http://geography.about.com/od/countryinformation/a/capitals.htm

[14]. ZPC Collections, Roberto Ortiz de Zarate, 1996-2005, *Women World Leaders 1945-2005*
http://www.terra.es./personal2/monolith/00women.htm

[15]. "Cherie Blair Pleased with Clinton Bid," from News.Com.Au

[16]. ZPC Collections, Roberto de Zarate, 1996-2005, *Women World Leaders, 1945-2005*

[17]. ZPC Collections, Roberto de Zarate, 1996-2005, *Women World Leaders, 1945-2005*

[18]. Incidentally, our suggestion for a change of name of the Manila International Airport in honor of President Cora Aquino's husband, Ninoy Aquino, Jr. was implemented by her. Our further suggestion to change the colonial name of the Philippines to a more nationalistic one was not. Neither was it done by the incum-

bent Philippine President Gloria M. Arroyo when the latter sugges-tion was repeated to her by us.

[19]. David E. Drew & Hedley Burell, "Will Another White Male Become Elected President in 2008?" in the January 5, 2007 edition of Commentary Opinion of *the Christian Science Monitor,* csmoni-tor.com http://www.csmonitor.com/2007/0105/p09s01-coop.html

[20]. Wikipedia, http://en.wikipedia.org/wiki/Speaker_of_the_United_States_House_of_Representatives, & Center for Women in Politics, http://www.cawp.rutgers.edu/Facts3.html

[21]. "Speaker of the United States House of Representatives" http://en.wikipedia.or/wiki/Speaker_of_the_United_States_House_of_Representatives

[22]. Nancy Pelosi on her inauguration as first woman Speaker of the U.S. House of Representatives on January 4, 2007

[23]. Janet L. Holmgreen, "Right Woman, Right Time: President Hill-ary Clinton," San Jose Mercury News, Sept. 17, 2007, p. 11A.

[24]. Geraldine Ferraro, "What We Learned the Hard Way," *Time Magazine*, January 1, 2007, p. 40.

[25]. Geraldine Ferraro, *idem*

[26]. A Sherman (esque) statement is American political jargon for a clear and direct statement by a political candidate for an office that they will never run for election to that office. The term derives from the Sherman pledge, a remark made by American Civil War General William Tecumseh Sherman when he was being consid-ered as a possible Republican candidate for the presidential election of 1884. He declined, saying "If drafted, I will not run; if nomi-nated, I will not accept; if elected, I will not serve." (http://en.wiki-pedia.org/wiki/Shermanesque_statement).

[27]. As reported on February 13, 2006 by CNN: http://www.cnn.com/2006/POLITICS/02/12/cheney/

[28]. It is 30+ vice-presidents because a few presidents had a different running mate in their second term.

[29]. Only President Franklin D. Roosevelt served more than 2 terms. Before him, all presidents, following the tradition established by the first President George Washington served no more than 2 terms. After the death of Franklin D. Roosevelt, the U.S. Constitution was amended to allow only a 2-consecuttive 4-year term for American presidents.

[30]. Amanda Ripley & Karen Tumulty, "America's 5 Best Governors," Time Magazine, Nov. 13, 2005: http://www.time.com/time/magazine/article/0,9171,1129494,00.html.

[31]. Mark Warner announced that he "wants real life, not the oval office." http://www.cnn.com/2006/POLITICS/10/12/warner.pres./index/html

[32]. Joe Johns, http://www.cnn.com/interactive/allpolitics/0407/gallery.edwards.analysis/content.4.html.

[33]. "John Edwards Stumbles Again" posted by Scott at http://www.aolelectionsblog.com/2007/06/01/john-edwards-stumbles-again/

[34]. Jonathan Darman, "The Down and Out Tour," *Newsweek,* July 30, 2007, p. 34.

[35]. *USA Today* editorial, May 30, 2007, p. 12A

[36]. Karen Tumulty, "The Real Running Mates," *Time*, Sept. 24, 2007, p. 40.

[37]. Patrick Healy & Robin Toner, "Wary Clinton Lays Out Health Plan," San Francisco Chronicle, Sept. 18, 2007.

[38]. Hillary Clinton's book, *It Takes a Village*, was pubslished by Simon and Schuster in 1997.

[39]. Jane Gross, "A Grass-Roots Effort to Grow Old at Home," the *New York Times*, August 14, 2007, p. A1.

[40]. Leslie Wayne, "Clinton Rejects Rival's Attacks on Luncheon" in the *New York Times*, September 19, 2007, p. A16.

[41]. Published by Regan Books in 2005

[42]. American President.org: http://www.americanpresident.org/ history/johnadams/firstlady/printable.html.

[43]. Byron York, "Hillary Clinton, Executive?" in the *National Review* as reprinted in the *U.S.A. Today,* July 11, 2007, p. 13A.

[44]. Wikipedia, http://en.wikipedia.org/wiki/Edith_Bolling_Wilson.

[45]. "I'm Battle-Hardened," in Harry Smith's CBS News Early Show interview as reported in http://www.votehillary.org/CMS/ InTheNews?page=46

[46]. *Idem*

[47]. Joe Klein, "Hillary's Quandary," *the Time Magazine*, May 21, 2007, p. 31.

[48]. Richard Borreca, "Inuoye Believes Obama Is Too Early," *Honolulu Start Bulletin,* http://www.freerepublic.com/focus/f-news/ 1754450/posts

[49]. http://en.wikipedia.org/wiki/Women_in_the_United_States-Senate

[50]. "The First American" is the title of a biography of Benjamin Franklin by H.W. Brands of Texas A&M University in Bryan, TX.

[51]. Bill Clinton, *My Life* (New York, NY: Alfred A. Knof 2004), p. 870; On statistics about how many people climbed Mt. Everest, see Nepal Vista, http://www.nepalvista.com/travel/efacts.html. See also Mount Everest from Wikipedia, http://en.wikipedia.org/wiki/ Mount_Everest

[52]. Quoted from Peter Feddo, http://www.votehillary.org/CMS/ InTheNews?page=121

[53]. Paul Bedard, "Washington Whispers," *U.S. News & World Report*, Marchy 5, 2007, p. 16.

[54]. Liz Szabo, "FDA Should Aggressively Regulate Tobacco, Panel Says," *USA Today*, May 25-28, 2007, p. 1A.

[55]. *The New York Times* editorial, May 25, 2007, p. A24.

[56]. *U.S.A. Today*, July 9, 2007, p. 10A.

[57]. *U.S.A. Today* May 9, 2007, p. 1.

[58]. *U.S.A. Today* May 9, 2007, p. 1. and *U.S.A. Today* editorial on September 12, 2007, p. 10A.

[59]. Madeline Vann, "Smokers More Likely to Develop Dementia," *Health Today* in http://body.aol.com/condition-center/smoking-cessation/news/article/_a/smokers-more-like…

[60]. Delivered on the steps of the Capitol Building in Washington D.C., on August 28, 1963

[61]. Jesse L. Jackson, "What We Learned the Hard Way," *Time Magazine*, Jan. 1, 2007, p. 40.

[62]. Jeff Zeleny, ""2 Competitors, Once Collegial, Now Seem Cool," *USA Today*, p. A15.

[63]. Maria L. La Ganga, "Michelle Obama Works on Balancing Act," *Los Angeles Times*, reprinted in the *San Francisco Chronicle*, Aug. 23, 2007, p. A4

[64]. *Idem*

[65]. *Idem*

[66]. Michele Obama was quoted in *U.S. News & World Report*, August 27, 2007, p.20.

[67]. *Biography* http://www.biography.com/search/article.do?id=9362930&page=print.

[68]. Rohan Sullivan, "Obama Infuriates Pakistanis," *Associated Press*, as repeated in the *San Francisco Chronicle*, Aug. 4, 2007, p. A4.

[69]. Susan Page, "GOP Hopefuls Set Selves Apart from Bush in Iowa Clash," *USA Today*, August 6, p. 4A.

[70]. Jesse J. Holland, "Democratic Hopefuls Woo Union Activists," *Associated Press,* reprinted in the *San Francisco Chronicle*, August 8, 2007, p. A13.

[71]. Gloria Borger a commentary on Politics, "On the Outside Track," *US News & World Report*, September 17, 2007, p. 40.

[72]. John Kass, "Obama Fuzzy on Fence that Tony Built," November 2, 2006, http://www.chicagotribune.com/news/politics/chi-0611020249nov02,0,6206196.column

[73]. Chris Fusco and Tim Novak of the *Chicago Sun-Times* quoted in Wizbangblog, http://politics/wizbangblog.com/2007/06/18/obama-lied-the-dream-died.php

[74]. Leslie Fulbright, "Obama's Candidacy Sparks Debates on Race" the headline of *the San Francisco Chronicle* (San Francisco, CA), February 19, 2007, p. A1.

[75]. As reported in http://www.votehillary.org/CMS/InTheNews?page=132.

[76]. Orlando Patterson, "the New Black Nativism," Time Magazine, February 19, 2007, p. 40.

[77]. DeWayne Wickham, "Clinton's Connection with Blacks Is Good Starting Point," *USA Today*, Aug. 14, 2007, p.11A.

[78]. An opinion expressed by Dick Morris and Eileen McGann in *Condi vs. Hillary.*

[79]. Washington Post-ABC poll, May 29 to June 1, 2007, reported by Anne E. Korblut and Matthew Mosk, "Revisiting the Gender Gap," in the *Washington Post National Weekly*, June 18-24, 2007, p. 17.

[80]. Susan Page, "More Democrats Favor Clinton over Obama, Poll Finds," *USA Today*, August 7, 2007, p. 5A.

[81]. Katharine Q. Seelye, "Obama and Clinton Find Pluses in Polls," *New York Times*, Aug. 16, 2007, p. A15.

[82]. Thomas Lifson, "Obama Campaign Retreats in the Face of Gaffes," *American Thinker*, Aug. 20, 2007, http://www.american-thinker.com/blog/2007/08/obama_campaign_regrouping_in_t.html

[83]. Quoted from Peter Feddo, http://www.votehillary.org/CMS/InTheNews?page=102

[84]. Susan Page, "As States Play 'Me First,' Primaries Fall into Chaos," headline story in the *USA Today*, p. 2A.

[85]. *Democratic Underground.Com*, September 16, 2007 headline, http://www.democrsaticunderground.com/discuss/duboard.php?az=view_all&address=334x...

[86]. Marian L. Smith, "American Names/Declaring Independence" Immigration and Naturalization Service, http://149.101.23.2/graphics/anoutus/history/articles/NameEssay.html

[87]. Noted by Peter Feddo in http://www.votehillary.org/CMS/InThe-News?page=104

[88]. Wikipedia, "Rudy Giuliani," http://en-wikipedia.org/wiki/Rudy_Giuliani

[89]. Jonathan Darman, "Rudy: 'Swift Boat-able' on 9/11?" in *Newsweek*, July 2/July 9, 2007, p. 45.

[90]. Liz Halloran, "Giuliani's Law and Order Armor," referring to Wayne Barrett and Dan Collins's *Grand Illusion*, in the *U.S. News & World Report*, p. 23.

[91]. Martha T. Moore, "Giuliani's Role in '01 Gives Him Slight Edge," *USA Today*, September 11, 2007, p. 2A.

[92]. Libby Quaid, "Under Fire, Giuliani Says He Misspoke," *Associated Press*, http://news.aol.com/elections/story/_a/under-fire-giuliani-says-he-misspoke/20070810195...

[93]. Russ Buettner, ""For Giuliani, Ground Zero as Linchpin and Thorn," the New York Times, Aug. 17, 2007, p. A1.

[94]. *Idem*

[95]. *Idem*

[96]. *Idem*

[97]. Huma Zaidi in More Oh-Eight, http://firstread.msnbc.msn.com/archive/2007/03/09/85835.aspx

[98]. *Idem*

[99]. Richard Cohen, "Giuliani Shows How to Keep Religion Out of Politics," *San Jose Mercury News,* Aug. 14, 2007, p. 13A.

[100]. Alec Macgillis, "Bloomberg's presence casts harsh light on Giuliani," as reprinted in *the Argus* (Fremont, California), July 8, 2007, p. 14.

[101]. David E. Drew & Hedley Burrell, *loc. cit.*

[102]. Modified from http://www.adherents.com/adh_presidents.html

[103]. BIOLA Connections, "What Should Christians Know about 'Evangelicals & Catholics Together'?" summer 2007, p. 07.

[104]. *Associated Press*, reporting from Geneva, Switzerland, reprinted in the *New York Times*, Aug. 16, 2007, p. A5.

[105]. *Orlando Sentinel,* 9 July 2005.

[106]. Mark I. Pinsky, "Who Speaks for America's Evangelicals?" *USA Today,* Aug. 6, 2007, p. 13A.

[107]. Religious Tolerance, "Theological Criticism of the Mormon Movement," http://www.religioustolerance.org/lds_crit.htm

[108]. Sally Denton, "Romney's Cross to Bear" http://www.latimes.com/news/opinion/la-op-denton10jun10,0,975063.story?coll=la-opin-ion....

[109]. Religious Tolerance, "Theological Criticism of the Mormon Movement," http://www.religioustolerance.org/lds_crit.htm

[110]. *Idem*

[111]. *Idem*

[112]. *Idem*

[113]. Religious Tolerance, "Theological Criticism of the Mormons, *loc. cit.*

[114]. Todd Compton's publisher's introduction to his book, *In Sacred Loneliness: The Plural Wives of Joseph Smith,* http://www.lds-mormon.com/isl.shtml

[115]. Religious Tolerance "Fundamentalist Church of Jesus Christ of Latter Day Saints," http://www.religioustolerance.org/flds.htm

[116]. Religious Tolerance "Theological Criticism of the Mormons," *loc. cit.*

[117]. Quoted by Michael Kinsley in his commentary, "God as Their Running Mate," *Time,* September 17, 2007, p. 27.

[118]. Reported by Patrick Healey & Michael Luo, "Edwards, Clinton and Obama Describe Journeys of Faith," in *The New York Times,* June 5, 2007, p. A20.

[119]. D.G., "Dems Get Religion," *U.S. News & World Report,* March 5, 2007, p. 31.

[120]. *Idem*

[121]. Susannah Meadows, "Hillary's Religious Roots," *Newsweek,* Feb. 12. 2007.

[122]. Nancy Gibbs and Michael Duffy, "The Pastor in Chief," *Time,* Aug. 20, 2007, p. 45.

[123]. *Ibid,* pp. 46-47.

[124]. Wikipedia, "Billy Graham," http://en.wikipwdia.org/wiki/Billy_Graham

[125]. Nancy Gibbs & Mciahel Duffy, *op. cit.,* p. 44.

[126]. Mason, Phillips, & Rejai, *Demythologizing an Elite: Amewrican Presidents in Emperical, Comparative, and Historical Perspective*, p. 11.

[127]. Mason, William, et al, *idem*

[128]. Fredereka Schouten, "Biggest Donor Areas Go for DEMS," *USA Today*, headline, Aug. 16, 2007.

[129]. Fredreka Schouten, "Top Giving Industries Get Behind Dem Candidates," USA Today, August 27, 2007, p. 2A.

[130]. Quoted from Peter Feddo in http://www.votehillary.org/CMS/InTheNews?=123.

[131]. Ralph Vartabedian & Michael Finnegan, "McCain Loses Temper Again; Raising Doubts about Fitness" in *the Los Angeles Times*, May 21, 2007

[132]. *Idem*

[133]. "John McCain," Wikipedia, http://en.wikipedia.org/wiki/John_McCain.

[134]. *Idem*

[135]. *Idem*

[136]. Ralph Vartabedian & Michael Finnegan, "McCain Loses Temper Again; Raising Doubts about Fitness" in *the Los Angeles Times*, May 21, 2007

[137]. *USA Today* editorial, "Every Candidate in Every Debate? Fair but a Mistake," p. 12A.

[138]. *Idem*

[139]. http://en.wikipedia.org/wiki/Ralph_Nader, p. 5.

[140]. *Idem*

[141]. "United States Presidential Election 2004," Wikipedia, http://en.wikipedia.org/wiki/U.S,_presidential_election,_2004

[142]. Dianne Cardwell, *New York Times*, reprinted in *the Mercury News* (San Jose, CA), June 24, 2007, p. 7A.

[143]. Carla Marinucci, "Poll Shows GOP Losing…," San Francisco Chronicle, August 27, 2007, p. A9.

[144]. Katherine Q. Seelye, "Critics say GOP doesn't 'get' Internet, *"New York Times*, reprinted in the *San Jose Mercury News*, August 2, 2007, p. 6A.

[145]. Theatlantic.com, *idem*

[146]. Carla Marinucci, "Poll Shows GOP Losing…," op. cit., p. A1.

[147]. Sheryl Gay Stolberg "Craig Just the Latest Plitician to Embarrass the GOP," *New York Times* quoted in the *San Francisco Chronicle*, August 29, 2007, p. A4 & Gail Collins, "Men's Room Chronicles," *New York Times*, August 30, 2007, p. A23.

[148]. "You and I" was co-written by Aldo Nova & Jacques Dubal.

[149]. Peter Feddo in http://votehillary.org/CMS/InTheNews?page=5.

[150]. "Joe Trippi on Front-runner: Hillary Clinton," as reported in Peter Feddo, http://www.votehillary.org/CMS/InTheNews?page =66

[151]. Sally Denton, "American Massacre: The Tragedy at Mountain Meadows, September 11, 1857," http://ateism.about.com/library/books/full/aafprAmMassacre.htm?p=1.

[152]. http://bessel.org/presfmy.htm

[153]. Wikipedia, "Newt Gingrich," http://en.wikipedia.org/wiki/Newt_Gingrich

[154]. *Idem*

[155]. Michael Barone in "the National Interest," *U.S. News & World Report*, September 11, 2006, p. 48.

[156]. Jodi Kantor, "Chelsea Clinton, Primed for a Second Stint as First Daughter," headline of the *New York Times*, July 31, 2007 p. A1.

[157]. Mark Halperin, "A New Role for Fred Thompson," *Time*, May 24, 2007.

[158]. *Idem*

[159]. Quoted by Maureen Dowd, "Old-School Masculinity Fails to Make Up for Inane Logic," *San Jose Mercury News*, September 11, 2007, p. 13.

[160]. *The Associated Press*, quoted in the *San Francisco Chronicle*, Aug. 28, 2007, p. A4

[161]. *Yankee in Gator Country*, "Answering misguided criticism from the Right about Fred Thompson," http://yankeegator.wordpress.com/2007/06/17/answering-misguided-criticism-from-the-rig...

[162]. Quoted by Maureen Dowd, "Old-School Masculinity Fails to Make Up for Inane Logic," *San Jose Mercury News*, September 11, 2007, loc. cit.

[163]. Richard Norton Smith, "A Lesson in Leadership, USA Weekend, the Mercury News, September 7-9, 2007, p. 6-7.

[164]. *Idem*

[165]. Claus Otto Scharmer, "Conversation with Robert Kegan," http://www.dialogonleadership.org/Kegan-1999.html

[166]. *Boston Globe* quoted in Wikipedia, "Yale University," http://en.wikipedia.org/wiki/Yale_University

[167]. *Idem*

[168]. Quoted from Peter Feddo, http://www.votehillary.org/CMS/InTheNews?page=91

[169]. "Announcement Generates Excitement in Arkansas," *the Arkansas Morning News* as reported in http://www.votehillary.org/CMS/InTheNews?page=46

[170]. Quoted from Peter Feddo, http://www.votehillary.org/CMS/InTheNews?page=103.

[171]. Staff Reports, *The Oakland Tribune*, "Feinstein Backs Clinton, Praises Strength, Heart," July 26, 2007, p. 9

[172]. Carla Marinucci, "Obama Courts Californians," *San Francisco Chronicle*, September 8, 2007, p. B6.

[173]. Julia Prudis Sulek, "Clinton, Obama Battle for Califronians' Support," *The Argus* (Fremont, CA), September 8, 2007, p. 9.

[174]. Carla Marinucci, "Clinton Leaving Obama in the Dust...," *San Francisco Chronicle,* Aug. 17, 2007, p. A4.

[175]. Quoted from Peter Feddo in http://votehillary.org/CMS/InThe-News?page=1.

[176]. NARA/Federal Register/U.S. Electoral College, "Distribution of 2004 and 2008 Electoral Votes," http://www.archives.gov/federal-register/electoral-college/2008/allocation.html

[177]. *The New York Times* editorial, Aug. 22, 2007, p. A22

[178]. From the *New York Sun,* as reported in http://www.votehillary.org/CMS/InTheNews?page=26

[179]. Rep. Jim Splaine, NHInsider.com as reported in http://www.votehillary.org/CMS/InTheNews?page=61

[180]. From *the Hill* as reported in http://www.votehillary.org/CMS/InTheNews?page=28.

[181]. The *Las Vegas Sun* as reported in http://www.votehillary.org/CMS/InTheNews?page=26.

[182]. The *Associated Press* as reported in the *San Francisco Chronicle,* Sept. 15, 2007, p. A4.

[183]. Susan Page, "Republicans Happier with Choices; Thompson Gets Slight Uptick," *USA Today*, September 10, 2007, p.6A.

[184]. *The New York Post* as reported in http://www.votehillary.org/CMS/InTheNews?page=29

[185]. To contribute and get involved in Hillary's presidential campaign, you are cordially invited to visit her website: http://www.hillaryclinton.com.

[186]. *The New York Times,* June7, 2007, p. A16

[187]. An opinion expressed by Dick Morris and Eileen McGann in *Condi vs. Hillary.*

Afterword™

The Next B.E.S.T.™ (Basic Expositions-on-Selected Topics) to be published through *iUniverse* due before July 4, 2008 by Benjamin Franklin Camins will be:

HILLARY
BEST BLENDS EXPERIENCE & CHANGE

Illustrated by 101 Lyrical Poems on Lifelong Love,
Forever Friendships & Deathless Dreams

978-0-595-47453-0
0-595-47453-5